Pyramids of Sacrifice

PYRAMIDS
OF
SACRIFICE

POLITICAL ETHICS

AND

SOCIAL CHANGE

❦❧❦❧❦❧❦

PETER L. BERGER

Basic Books, Inc., Publishers

NEW YORK

Library of Congress Cataloging in Publication Data

Berger, Peter L (date)
  Pyramids of sacrifice: political ethics and social
change.

    Includes bibliographical references.
    1.   Underdeveloped areas—Economic policy.
2.   Underdeveloped areas—Social conditions.
3.   Political ethics.   4.   Right and left (Political
science)   I.   Title.
✓ HC59.7.B38864   309.2′3′091724   74-78304
    ISBN 0-465-06778-6

Contents

CONTENTS

Preface

THIS BOOK deals with two topics, which are intertwined throughout. One is Third World development. The other is political ethics as applied to social change. It seems to me that these two topics belong together. No humanly acceptable discussion of the anguishing problems of the world's poverty can avoid ethical considerations. And no political ethics worthy of the name can avoid the centrally important case of the Third World. It follows from these assumptions that this book is not primarily a scholarly work in the sense of "value-free science." It tries to bring together scientific analysis and ethical concern, with a full awareness of the risks of such a conjunction (one of the risks, needless to say, is being dismissed as a bleeding-heart idealist by one's scientific colleagues). It also follows that the book is addressed to a rather mixed audience —those concerned with development and social change, those concerned with the relation of social-scientific analysis to policy, and finally those with an interest in raising ethical questions in the political arena. In other words, I hope that this book has something to say to the professionals in the areas of development and "policy research," but I'm also anxious to address myself to that larger audience that (perhaps optimistically) has been called the "moral constituency" in this country.

At least this side of pure mathematics (and, for all I know, even in that realm), most books are rooted in biography. But the biographical background is not always relevant to the understanding of a book. In this instance it might help to explain briefly how I came to have these particular interests.

I became interested in the problems of Third World development by way of concern with American policies in Indochina. In 1968 I was invited to serve as a "consultant" to the steering committee of Clergy and Laymen Concerned about Vietnam (which was then a pretty straightforward opponent of the war; soon after, it became a sort of religious chaplaincy to the New Left). As I recall, I wasn't much consulted, which was just as well, since I would have had little to contribute. However, as a result I did become interested in American policies in Latin America, which then looked as a plausible site for future Vietnam-like interventions. In pursuance of this interest I traveled in the Caribbean, Venezuela, and Mexico in 1969, and I started a lot of reading in the field. In the summer of 1969 I was invited by Ivan Illich to teach a course at the Centro Intercultural de Documentación in Cuernavaca. It was during that summer, in long conversations with Illich and others of the varied group typically assembled at his unconventional think tank, that I came to see a connection between my new political interests and my previous scholarly work, especially in the so-called sociology of knowledge. Beginning then, and continuing still, the problems of Third World development moved into the center of my professional work as a sociologist. In consequence, I have become involved in a variety of professional activities linked to this interest, with further travel in Latin America and in Africa serving to convince myself (if not necessarily others) that I was serious about all this.

The most important scholarly fruit of these endeavors was another book, *The Homeless Mind—Modernization and Consciousness*, written together with Brigitte Berger and Hansfried Kellner (New York: Random House, 1973). We tried in that book to formulate a theory of modern consciousness on the basis of a specific approach in the sociology of knowledge. This was, in principle, an exercise in "value-free science," although we appended a postscript entitled "Political Possibilities." My dissatisfaction with this very limited political statement led to the decision to write the present book. I should emphasize that the two books are quite independent of each other, and that the coauthors of the earlier book are in no way responsible for what I say in the present one.

It would be impossible to acknowledge my indebtedness to all those with whom I have talked about these matters over the last five years. Brigitte Berger's comments and contributions have been invaluable. Conversations as well as collaboration with Hansfried Kellner and Richard Neuhaus have been helpful to me. I shall always be grateful to Ivan Illich for mediating to me what Alfred Schutz has so aptly called an *"aha* experience" in my thinking about development. The Vienna Institute for Development and its director, Arne Haselbach, had enough confidence in me to entrust me with the coordination of the project "Alternatives in Development," as a result of which I have been able to discuss a variety of matters with a distinguished international group of scholars in this area. I have particularly profited from my discussions with Warren Ilchman, Yehuda Landau, Rodolfo Stavenhagen, Hanns-Albert Steger, and Ivan Varga. I would also like to thank Shmuel Eisenstadt, Joseph Kahl, and Paul Leser for criticisms and encouragement. Any outsider venturing into the field of development must worry especially about the economists, high priests of a particularly intimidating esoteric lore. For this reason I want to make grateful mention of Paul Streeten, who, by the way he received me at the 1973 meetings in Oxford of the Society for International Development, helped to relieve my anxieties on this score. Students at several institutions were probably the major victims of my efforts to acquire clarity in this area. They were not all silent victims, and I'm particularly grateful to those who quarreled with me in endless seminar discussions—those "on the left" above all. Last but by no means least, I want to thank Erwin Glikes, of Basic Books, who believed in this book from its inception.

As might be expected from what I said at the outset, the argument of the book may seem circuitous at times. I have therefore thought it useful to summarize the main thrust of the argument in twenty-five theses that follow immediately. No Lutheran delusions of grandeur should be read into this. The footnotes are sparser than one would expect in a strictly scholarly book. I have, in the main, inserted footnotes as a help to the reader who wants to familiarize himself further with the relevant literature.

TWENTY-FIVE THESES

1. *The world today is divided into ideological camps. The adherents of each tell us with great assurance where we're at and what we should do about it. We should not believe any of them.*

2. Underlying the major ideological models for social change (including Third World development) are two powerful myths —the myth of growth and the myth of revolution. *Both* myths must be debunked.

3. Such debunking is not an end in itself. Rather, it opens up new avenues of understanding and policy. This is particularly important for an assessment of capitalist and socialist models for social change.

4. *Capitalist ideology, as based on the myth of growth, must be debunked.*

5. Capitalist development imposes severe human costs. In many Third World countries these costs are prohibitive.

6. The major achievements of capitalism have been unprecedented productivity and institutions favoring individual freedom. Case by case, these achievements must be weighed against the costs.

7. In many Third World countries the assessment is likely to lead to noncapitalist policies. Such policies are *not* plausible in the West.

8. *Socialist ideology, as based on the myth of revolution, must be debunked.*

9. Socialist revolutions have imposed severe human costs. An assessment of the achievements of socialism (such as a more egalitarian distribution of the good things of life) must weigh these costs, case by case.

10. *The critics of capitalism are right when they reject policies that accept hunger today while promising affluence tomorrow (and they are right when they question the promise). The critics of socialism are right when they reject policies that accept terror today on the promise of a humane order tomorrow (and, again, when they question whether such a tomorrow is believable).*

11. We must seek solutions to our problems that accept *neither* hunger *nor* terror. The quest for such solutions will benefit from a sovereign disregard of current ideological definitions of the situation. In other words: We should start taking a very fresh look at many of the problems that plague the world today.

12. *Policies for social change are typically made by cliques of politicians and intellectuals with claims to superior insights. These claims are typically spurious.*

13. It is, in principle, impossible to "raise the consciousness" of anyone, because all of us are stumbling around on the same level of consciousness—a pretty dim level.

14. Every human being knows his own world better than any outsider (including the expert who makes policy).

15. *Those who are the objects of policy should have the opportunity to participate not only in specific decisions but in the definitions of the situation on which these decisions are based. This may be called* cognitive participation.

16. Most political decisions must be made on the basis of inadequate knowledge (*postulate of ignorance*). To understand this is to become very gingerly toward policy options that exact high human costs.

17. The most pressing human costs are in terms of physical deprivation and suffering. The most pressing moral imperative in policy making is a *calculus of pain.*

18. Brazil and China are commonly perceived as opposite poles among development models—as, respectively, the biggest capitalist and socialist experiments in the Third World—and thus as decisive alternatives for the future. Yet in one morally crucial respect the two belong in the *same* category: *Both* models are based on the willingness to sacrifice at least one generation for the putative goals of the experiment. *Both* sets of sacrifice are justified by theories. The theories are delusional and the sacrifices are indefensible. Rejection of *both* the Brazilian *and* the Chinese models is the starting point for any morally acceptable development policy.

19. Human beings have the right to live in a meaningful world. An assessment of the costs of policy must also include a *calculus of meaning.*

20. *Modernity exacts a high price on the level of meaning. Those who are unwilling to pay this price must be taken with utmost seriousness, and* not *be dismissed as "backward" or "irrational."*

21. *The viability of modern societies, be it in the West or in the Third World, will largely hinge on their capacity to create*

institutional arrangements that take account of the counter-modernizing resistances.

22. A key area for such institutional innovation will be in the creation of *intermediate structures*—intermediate, that is, between the modern state and the undifferentiated mass of uprooted individuals typical of modern societies. This policy imperative cuts across the capitalist/socialist dichotomy.

23. Americans have long understood themselves as having a mission to save the world. The fact that this self-understanding has become shaky is much to be welcomed. There are many moral problems in the relation of America to the rest of the world, but none of these adds up to some overriding national mission.

24. America can be most significant for the rest of the world *by being itself.* Among other things, this means that America, the most modernized large-scale society, can be a vast laboratory for innovative experiments to solve the dilemmas of modernity.

25. *We need a new method to deal with questions of political ethics and social change (including those of development policy). This will require bringing together two attitudes that are usually separate—the attitudes of "hard-nosed" analysis and of the utopian imagination. What this book is finally all about is just this—some first steps toward a* hard-nosed utopianism.

Pyramids of Sacrifice

PRELUDE

THE GREAT PYRAMID AT CHOLULA

CHOLULA is a small town in the Mexican state of Puebla. It is the site of the archaeological excavation of one of the largest pyramids in Mesoamerica. What was once the great pyramid is today a fair-sized mountain, covered with trees and shrubs, topped by a rather undistinguished church. The excavation has laid free parts of the old structures, and some of the archaeological work now takes place under the open sky. The archaeologists have also dug deep tunnels into the mountainside. Gradually, the artificial mountain is being hollowed out by these tunnels, pushing further and deeper into the buried pyramid.

Before the Spanish conquest Cholula was called Cholollan. For many centuries it was one of the most important cult centers of central Mexico, to which pilgrims came from far away. It retained its status as a place of pilgrimage over a period spanning successive cultures and empires. This is not unusual. All over Mesoamerica it was common for each new wave of conquerors to erect their sanctuaries over the ruins of the sanctuaries they destroyed, so that the religious geography of this region has a strange stability if compared with the political, economic, and cultural geographies. The Spaniards continued this pattern. Unlike other Mesoamerican cult centers, however, the great pyramid at Cholula was built not at once, but

3

level by level, over a period of centuries. Each new occupant of the site did not just build sanctuaries on top of sanctuaries, but new levels of one, ever-more gigantic structure.

Cholula has been continuously settled at least from the beginnings of the Teotihuacan period, that is, from the third century A.D. It was an important town during the time when the empire of Teotihuacan dominated most of the region. In the ninth century the Olmecs came from the south, conquered central Mexico, and made Cholula the center of their state. Later, the Toltecs came from the north and conquered the area. It was they who brought with them the cult of Quetzalcoatl, the god of the feathered serpent, probably the most bloodthirsty deity in the history of human religions. The Aztecs too maintained Cholula as a holy city and place of pilgrimage. At the time of the Spanish conquest Cholula was said to have contained four hundred temples, grouped majestically around the great pyramid.

Cortés, faithful to the role of Quetzalcoatl *redivivus* in which the Aztecs first cast him, staged one of his bloodiest massacres in Cholula, where he stopped briefly on his march up to the Valley of Mexico. After that, when their rule was firmly established, the Spaniards destroyed all the temples and buried the great pyramid under a mountain of dirt. They not only built a church on top of the artificial mountain thus created, but also an estimated three hundred churches all around it, possibly making Cholula the most churched town in all of Christendom. If one stands on the mountain today, one can still see many of these churches, forming a huge ring circling the site of the pyramid, to make sure that the old gods would never again emerge from their tomb. In this the Spaniards were successful. But they wanted not only to bury the old gods, but to obliterate their memory, and in this too, remarkably, the Spaniards succeeded. Excavation of the great pyramid began only a few decades ago, when some pre-Columbian artifacts were discovered by accident in the course of repairs undertaken on the foundations of the church on top of the mountain. Until then, it appears, no one remembered what was hidden under that mountain.

Most of the churches are in ruins now, some just fallen into disuse, some burned down during the Mexican Revolution. But only a slight expansion in the notion of mythology is needed to see that

4

the cultic continuity has, after all, remained unbroken. The mountain that contains the pyramid is now in the custody of the National Institute of Archaeology and History, an agency of the Mexican government. And right next to it rises the new campus of the University of the Americas, a monument to modernity erected by *yanqui* missionary zeal.

There are scholarly debates as to the degree to which the ancient civilizations of Mexico can be called theocracies. In any case, there is no doubt that there existed close relations between priests and warriors, between those who constructed the theories and those who built the empires. The history that we know of is, almost exclusively, the record of what these two groups thought and did. What about all the others—the peasants? We can only surmise what *they* thought about the pyramid. We do know that it was they who built it. They carried the stones, they piled them one on top of the other, they sweated in the hot sun. If they were unlucky, they ended up as victims on the sacrificial platform. And they were silent.

The great pyramid at Cholula provides a vision of a succession of theoretical schemes, each embodied in stone and superimposed upon successive generations of silent peasants. To see Cholula is to understand the relation among theory, sweat, and blood. For the pyramid was not designed for aesthetic purposes, as an exercise of *art pour l'art*. The meaning of the pyramid was provided by its sacrificial platform, the theory behind which was cogent and implacable: If the gods were not regularly fed with human blood, the universe would fall apart. The Aztecs distinguished themselves by realizing that theory with extreme consistency. They ravaged the region under their domination in quest of victims, recruiting them through conquest, by way of tribute, and in the ceremonial combat of the "wars of the flowers." It is estimated that in one single year, not long before the Spanish conquest, ten thousand victims were sacrificed to Quetzalcoatl in Tenochtitlan (the modern Mexico City) alone. We have a description of one of the great ceremonies in that city, during which victims were lined up for the length of more than a mile, waiting for their turn on the sacrificial platform. There may be a philosophical lesson in this spectacle of a Mesoamerican Auschwitz. There is also a political lesson: The unity of theory and practice in the Aztec empire was almost certainly a prime cause for its rapid collapse. If it had not been for the Aztecs' radicalization of the sacrificial cult, it is doubtful whether the Spaniards would have had so easy a time enlisting the support of other ethnic groups in the destruction of the Aztec empire. Consistent application of theory can have some thoroughly unforeseen consequences.

It is useful in this context to recall that, at least in so-called advanced civilizations, theories are generally the products of professional theorists—that is, of the kind of people we call intellectuals today. History is not only a succession of power structures but of theoretical edifices, and every one of the latter was first *thought up* by somebody. This is so regardless of who conned whom at any given moment—whether it is a case of intellectuals convincing the wielders of power to carry into practice some particular theoretical scheme, or power wielders hiring intellectuals to concoct theories that will legitimate that particular exercise of power ex post facto. In either case, there are intellectuals in the woodpile.

At Cholula, then, we may contemplate a long succession of intellectuals in action. Toltec priests succeeded Olmec priests, and were in turn followed by the Aztecs, brooding over their calendars and worrying over Quetzalcoatl's feeding schedule. Then came the Spanish priests, theoreticians of empire no less than of the faith, bringing with them a new calendar and a new variety of holocausts. Christian time replaced the Aztec cycles, and the fires of the Inquisition took over from the blood rites of the old gods. And today? In Mexico, at any rate, the sacrifices are less bloody and less visible. But it is still the intellectuals who produce the theories of power, and with them the legitimations, if not of the blood, then of the sweat of others.

Thus the archaeological activities of the Mexican government are not a matter of pure science. Like the Israelis, the Mexicans have an ideological interest in digging up their past. The present regime, indeed, has made a cult of the pre-Columbian past. It has decorated its public buildings with murals idealizing that past (always depicted in sharp contrast with the horrors of Spanish colonialism), and it has built a magnificent monument to the same past in the National Museum of Anthropology in Mexico City. Thus the archaeologists laboring on the great pyramid at Cholula are not *that* far removed from the priests who were once in charge of the structure. Nor is the university next door devoid of continuity with these archaic events. Everywhere today, and particularly in the poor countries, universities are the high temples of the new cult of modernity and progress. Out of the universities come theories that propose the new calendars for human life, including the new schedules for sacrificial offerings (be they in blood or in sweat, or in both). Different gods are still at war, by way of their respective intellectual representatives. All over Latin America today, the universities are the battlefields between the gods of *yanqui* evangelism ("development," "economic growth," "the Free World") and those of the new faith of the left ("revolution," "socialism," "the Third World"). In both camps it is the intellectuals who proclaim the myths and work out the theories, and usually the others who pay the price in sweat and blood. Then as now, intellectuals are generally in a good position to avoid the sacrificial platform, although not always. Recently at the University of Puebla, only a few miles from Cholula, several students were killed in skirmishes between rival ideological factions. And in 1968, at the Tlatelolco massacre, it was mainly students who died under the guns of the Mexican army. There are times when theory is dangerous business even for theoreticians.

Still, on the pyramid mountain at Cholula it is the peasants who continue to carry the stones and who sweat in the hot sun. It is they who labor in the dust, still wearing the straw sandals depicted in Aztec bas-reliefs. In Mexico, since 1910, they have been less silent than they used to be, but it is still mainly others, power wielders and intellectuals, who claim to speak for them. And if sacrifices are to be made (be they as "costs of development" or as "the price of revolution"), it is they who will supply most of the victims.

Octavio Paz, in his essay "Critique of the Pyramid" (*The Other Mexico.* New York: Grove Press, 1972. p. 69 ff.), has suggested that the Aztec pyramid provides *the* clue to the history of Mexico, from the sacrificial cult of Quetzalcoatl to the Tlatelolco massacre. In all likelihood this is giving too much weight to the metaphor. All the same, the metaphor, taken qua metaphor, has implications far beyond Mexico. Thus the great pyramid at Cholula provides a metaphorical paradigm for the relations among theory, power, and the victims of both—the intellectuals who define reality, the power wielders who shape the world to conform to the definitions, and the others who are called upon to suffer in consequence of both enterprises. In speaking of the Aztec system, Paz calls it a "syllogism-dagger." It is not, alas, unique in this quality. What Paz says about it may be applied to situations all over the world today: "What stuns and paralyzes the mind is the use of realistic means in the service of a metaphysic both rigorously rational and delirious, the insensate offering up of lives to a petrified concept."

It is not a question of glorifying peasants. They can be as mindless and cruel as any other group, and their visions of reality have no privileged status in any hierarchy of knowledge. It is even less a question of identifying with peasants, of repeating that peculiar act of self-delusion to which intellectuals have been repeatedly prone since the days of the Narodniki in nineteenth-century Russia. The intellectual will best meet his responsibilities, political and other, if he remains faithful to the intellectual enterprise as such—faithful, that is, to the task of understanding clearly, fully, and honestly. Part of that task is the depetrification of concepts and the debunking of "syllogism-daggers," of whatever form.

Chapter I

༄༅༄༅༄༅

DEVELOPMENT—POLICIES, THEORIES, MYTHS

A FEW YEARS AGO a new song was heard during the carnival at Rio de Janeiro. Its refrain began with the words, "We are the Underdeveloped!" It was a very cheerful song, with a touch of irony, perhaps of defiance.

Words describe the realities of human life. But words also have the power to create and shape realities. The words of the strong carry more weight than the words of the weak. Indeed, very often the weak describe themselves in the words coined by the strong. Over the last two centuries or more the strong have been the technologically advanced nations of the West. As they imposed their military, political, and economic power over most of the world, they also imposed the power of their words. It was they who named the others, in a sort of negative baptism. Who were the others? When the West was still Christian in its outlook, the others were "the heathen." Then they became "the uncivilized," or more optimistically "the less civilized," as Western imperial power came to be conceived of as a "civilizing" mission. Before World War II the most common appellation was "backward." After World War II, with the coming of the United Nations, those others began themselves to participate in the naming game. "Underdeveloped countries" became "developing countries." Since the Bandung conference, in the mid-1950s, the term "Third World" has generated a mystique all its own. Although

9

the ideological implications of all these appellations were shifting, sometimes rapidly, the basic empirical referents have not really changed over the last few decades: The basic division is between rich and poor countries, rich or poor not necessarily in possession of natural resources, but in ability to utilize these resources for themselves. In its broadest sense, "development" is understood as the process by which a poor country is to become richer. Sometimes it is also made to refer to processes by which a rich country becomes still richer.

Just about every commentator on the contemporary world agrees that development is a problem. Some say that it is *the* problem faced by humanity today. But what is "a problem"? Much of human life is unproblematic, in the sense that it proceeds along lines that are familiar, even taken for granted, and that the people in a particular situation believe that they possess the means to undertake at least the essential tasks at hand. A situation becomes problematic when these assumptions begin to break down. Only rarely, though, is this true in the same way for everyone connected with a situation. One man's problem may be another's inherent routine, and vice versa. If one says that development is a problem, one must follow this up with the question, "*Whose problem?*"

Development is a problem for those who make public policy in different countries. Just what kind of problem it is will, of course, depend on what country and what kind of policy maker is involved. In a poor country the problem is likely to present itself in the form of urgent, sometimes desperate, pressures: Something must be done about these pressures, and done quickly. Policy makers in richer countries can generally afford a more relaxed attitude toward a problem that is, in the main, external or even peripheral to their immediate concerns. Also, of course, there are very different kinds of policy makers. There are those who genuinely care about the poverty of their countries, and those who are totally unconcerned as long as their own privileges are preserved. There are compassionate leaders, fanatics, gangsters, and pragmatists, and there are geniuses as well as fools. Almost all policy makers, however, have one characteristic in common: Of necessity, their attention is focused on *action*. Day by day, they must act and make decisions, often long-range ones, on the actions of others. It follows that most policy makers, whatever the intellectual baggage with which they are saddled,

10

are primarily concerned with the practical implications of any theoretical definitions of their situation.

Development is also a problem for various coteries of theorists— people whose principal occupation is thinking rather than acting. Again, there are different kinds of these. Because of the aforementioned relation between the power of words and the more material forms of power, theorists in the rich countries of the West have for a long time been dominant in definitions of the situation—their own *and* that of the "underdeveloped." It was *their* theories that were repeated, taught, and applied not only in the West but in the Western-style centers of intellectual life throughout the world. More recently, theorists in non-Western countries have sought to devise counterdefinitions of the problem, embodying an indigenous perception and often in sharp contradiction with theories emanating from Europe and North America. In addition, theorists are divided into warring tribes along lines of expertise and ideology. Thus the problem of development looks quite different from the perspectives of different social-scientific disciplines, such as economics, sociology, anthropology, or political science. It also looks quite different from the perspectives of different ideological world views—as, say, the world views of social scientists making strategic studies for the United States military and those identifying themselves as Marxist revolutionaries. Finally, there are theorists who are passionately engaged in political activity relevant to the situation they theorize about, and others whose intellectual labor takes place in an atmosphere of detachment.

And, of course, development is a problem for vast numbers of ordinary people, particularly in the poor countries. The overwhelming majority of these people have little or no opportunity to influence policy, and their perspectives on the situation are systematically ignored by almost all theorists. For them, the problem of development is one of everyday life. It manifests itself with pressing practicality as hunger, disease, and early death, the quest for work and housing, and the experience of losing values that used to give meaning to life. It is also evident as a hope for better things to come. The problem here is not in the making of policy or the plausibility of theories, but in coping, from day to day, with suffering and dilemmas caused by often bewilderingly rapid change in the social environment. Yet both policy and theory intrude into this day-by-day experience. The effects if not the intentions of various policies are directly experienced. Politicians make promises. Even the words invented by theorists filter down, by various means of communication, and serve to name what is actually experienced: "We are the Underdeveloped!"

Policy makers and theorists relate to each other in different ways. Sometimes they do not relate at all. There have always been men of action in the seats of power who have had only contempt for theorists and their products, and who managed to get along with "common sense" —which means, in effect, a mixture of old theories established as folk wisdom and ad hoc theories produced in do-it-yourself fashion. By the same token, there have always been theorists in ivory towers, working away at their intellectual constructions in splendid isolation from the sweaty doings of the rest of mankind. In the area of development policy, such segregation is becoming very difficult. There can still be ivory-tower theorists who have nothing to do with policy, but the complexity of contemporary societies virtually compels policy makers to seek out *some* theoretical frame of reference for their actions. Usually, this means dealing with some coterie of theorists on an ongoing basis, be it qua hired hands or qua "consultants." The policy maker commonly intends this relationship to be one in which he remains fully in control. The theorists in his employ are to provide expert information and, perhaps, credible legitimations for his policies. Sometimes it works this way, but, to repeat, words have power. The policy maker may find his actions inextricably interconnected with the theoretical frame of reference he has chosen to explain what he is doing, to himself as well as to others. Words not only describe actions; words also produce or come to dominate actions. In this way, intentionally or not, theorists can acquire considerable power to affect the course of events.

Policy makers and theorists together constitute an elite vis-à-vis the great mass of people in society. This is even true in the highly developed countries of the Western world, despite mass education and the institutions of representative democracy. It is far more true in most of the countries of Asia, Africa, and Latin America, where both groups together are a tiny and usually closely related fraction of the population. This elite almost invariably legitimates its privileged position in terms of alleged benefits it is bestowing or getting ready to bestow upon "the people." The elite is the guardian or the vanguard of the general welfare. Insofar as an elite has been affected by some version of democratic ideology, its members also like to see themselves as "spokesmen" for "the masses." The latter are presumed to be afflicted with great difficulty in speaking for themselves or in understanding their own situation, so the elite very kindly performs these functions vicariously. It must be added in fairness that elites differ in the amount of trouble they take in trying to find out the wishes and perceptions of those in whose behalf they pretend to speak. However, the tendency to arrogate to themselves a superior understanding of the problems of others is just as strong among elites presently in power as among those only aspiring to it. Most social scientists, whatever their country of origin, have this tendency to an advanced degree.

The different theories seeking to explain the facts of the wealth and poverty of nations may today be broadly divided into two competing paradigms or models of theoretical understanding. They are the theory of modernization and the theory of imperialism (though these are not always the exact titles used by their respective advocates). Each paradigm has what may be called "clue concepts"—key explanatory categories, the use of which readily identifies adherents of the two rival schemes. Modernization theorists already give themselves away by the very term "modern" and its permutations, and by categories such as "development," "economic growth," "institutional differentiation," and "nation-building." The other camp employs "clue concepts" such as "dependency," "exploitation," "neocolonialism," and "liberation." Each camp also has a pejorative vocabulary for the respective rival, and a conceptual apparatus designed to liquidate intellectually whatever definitions of the situation emerge from that tainted source. Basically, each camp understands the other as a workshop of ideological smokescreens for conflicting political strategies. It goes without saying that there are also important differences and often fierce controversies within each camp.

The theory of modernization derives its conceptual instrumentarium from a convergence of various streams in the social sciences in Western countries over the last century or so. The most important contributions come from economics and sociology. Economists have provided descriptions and explanations of the enormous transformations that first set in after the industrial revolution in Western societies. Sociologists have done the same for similarly vast transformations undergone by the noneconomic institutions of these societies. There are important differences in the interpretation of the relation between economic and noneconomic factors in this global process of change. There is widespread agreement that the status of the rich countries of the West is best described by their character as "advanced industrial societies" (another important "clue concept"), which character is due to the effects of a number of complex, interconnected, and mainly indigenous factors (indigenous, that is, to these societies). Frequently there is the implication that the poor countries, with whatever modifications necessitated by a different historical situation, will have to replicate the basic steps through which Western societies passed in their ascent from rags to riches. Walt Rostow's notion of "the stages of economic growth" (propounded in a very influential book with just that title, published in 1959) neatly sums up this conception. As far as the poor countries are concerned, the theory of modernization most often eventuates in practical recipes of imitation: "Do as we did, and your problems will be solved." Modernization theorists, as well as their affiliated policy makers, differ in the degree of sophistication by which this general advice is modified to suit particular local conditions.

The theory of imperialism derives in its essential concepts from the Marxist stream in Western social thought. It can be described rather accurately as a gigantic amplification of the classical statement by Proudhon, "Property is theft." The rich countries became rich because they plundered the others, and this continues as the basic relation between the two. Further, this propensity to exploitation is endemic to capitalism as a socioeconomic system—that is, imperialism is a necessary phase in the history of capitalist societies. The rich countries are not categorized as "advanced industrial societies" but as "late capitalist societies" or as "societies in the stage of monopoly capitalism" (again, two important "clue concepts"). Just as the adjective "advanced" used by one set of theorists implies a self-congratulatory attitude, so the adjective "late" used by the other set suggests the gleeful expectation that the system will soon collapse.

Both wealth and poverty among nations are the result of the same global process of exploitation. This conception has been aptly categorized by Andre Gunder Frank as "the development of underdevelopment" (*Capitalism and Underdevelopment in Latin America*, 1969). The problem of the poor countries, therefore, is *not* that they lack resources, technological know-how, modern institutions, or cultural traits conducive to development, but that they are being exploited by a world-wide capitalist system and its particular imperialist agents, both foreign and domestic. The modernization theorists, who focus attention on these other factors, are obfuscating the situation by stressing aspects that, if they are relevant, are only expressions of the prime reality of exploitation. The practical recipes emerging from this interpretation all point in one direction: Imperialism must be defeated, in most instances (at the least) by revolutionary violence. Development, if the term is even accepted, can only take place as an exploited country frees itself from dependency on the international capitalist system. Socialism is the only system within which the problems of underdevelopment may be successfully attacked. Advocates of the paradigm naturally differ as to whether a socialist system worth emulating already exists in the world today.

Theoretical paradigms that have been in contention over a period of time almost invariably "contaminate" each other. This has been the case with the two paradigms in question. Important themes derived from Marx himself and from later Marxist theorists have been incorporated in virtually every discipline of what Marxists like to call "bourgeois social science." Conversely, there are few Marxist theorists who do not employ concepts as well as data from their ideological adversaries. Nevertheless, in most cases, the two paradigms can be clearly distinguished, and there is usually little doubt in which camp any particular theorist essentially belongs.

The two paradigms, of course, occupy different positions in different parts of the world. Marxism in one version or another, and with it a Marxist theory of imperialism, has become the official doctrine throughout the orbit of Soviet power, in China, and in scattered socialist countries of Asia, Africa, and Latin America. The bulk of the social-scientific enterprise in North America and, still, in Western Europe continues to operate within the framework of a non-Marxist theory of modernization in its treatment of the problems of development. Since the late 1960s, however, the other paradigm has rapidly gained in influence among Western social scientists, to the point where in some West European countries (such as Western Germany) it is now an open question which of the two theoretical positions is dominant. Among intellectuals in the countries commonly called the Third World, regardless of the ideologies or policies followed by their governments, the Marxist paradigm (broadly speaking) has become dominant. In Latin America this happened with astonishing swiftness within the span of a few years. Looking at the world as a whole, therefore, an understanding of the problems of development in terms of the theory of imperialism very probably is now the majority viewpoint among intellectuals. It is all the more important to stress, in view of this fact, that *both* paradigms have emerged from specifically Western intellectual traditions and are transmitted by intellectual elites whose formation has been profoundly Westernized. Neither paradigm has grown out of indigenous non-Western traditions, and those whose basic orientations are still rooted in these traditions look upon both as alien importations. Whatever may go on in the circles of intellectuals, this is still true of the great mass of people in Third World countries.

As there are competing models of theoretical understanding, so there are competing models of policy regarding development. Since the interests of policy makers are of necessity pragmatic, the dividing lines between policy models are usually less neat than those between models of theory. It is one thing to worry about the consistency of one's thinking from one book to another, and very different to have to worry whether a country's economy will fall apart the day after tomorrow (or, for that matter, whether one will still be in power then). Thus the different models of development policy are only rarely in a symmetrical relationship with models of development theory.

Still, the major policy models "available" in Third World countries today may be broadly differentiated in terms of the basic options of capitalism and socialism. China represents the most important case of a Third World society embarked on a radically socialist course of development. Brazil may be seen as the most important case of development policy along explicitly and consistently capitalist lines. In Africa, albeit on a minor scale, Kenya and Ivory Coast on the one hand, and Tanzania and Guinea on the other, afford instructive cases of the two alternative options. India, once more on a continental scale, represents a crucially important "mixed model," trying to steer a course between the extremes of the two alternatives. There are other cases of "mixed models" in smaller countries in different parts of the Third World. Unless their paradigms have become completely frozen in ideological rigidity, the theorists are therefore obliged to accommodate their interpretations to a great variety of empirical situations. Their "kit" of concepts and explanatory schemes often makes such accommodation to reality a difficult and painful undertaking. Sometimes the intellectual acrobatics that ensue from their efforts have the character of high comedy.

So far the problem of development has been discussed in seemingly rational terms. The policy makers have rational interests—to develop their countries, to improve the condition of their people, to acquire or to stay in power, or to steal as much as possible. The theorists are trying to grasp a fugitive reality within this or that rationale of thought, be it within some canons of scientific procedure or within the logic of an ideological scheme of interpretation. And ordinary people have their own rational concerns—to stay alive, to get more of the good things of life, to cope with the practical difficulties of the everyday business of living. The rationality of all three groups of participants in the drama of development is very real and must be taken into account. But to view the phenomena in question *only* under the aspect of pragmatic and theoretical rationality is to miss a central fact—the undercurrent of myth.

What is myth? In ancient times, of course, the term had a religious connotation. The Greek word denotes a fable about the doings of the gods or of semidivine heroes, and throughout the world scholars have applied the terms "myth" and "mythology" to the traditions that recount the intervention of supernatural beings or forces in the affairs of men. Since Georges Sorel (*Reflections on Violence*, 1908), however, the concept of myth has attained a more general and at the same time secularized usage within social thought. For Sorel, a myth is any set of ideas that infuses transcendent meaning into the lives of men—transcendent with regard to the routine and selfish concerns of ordinary life. It is through myths that men are lifted above their captivity in the ordinary, attain powerful visions of the future, and become capable of collective actions to realize such visions. In this understanding of myth, therefore, the old religious exaltation is retained, even if any specifically religious contents are discarded. Then as now, the figures of myth touch the lives of individuals with transforming power. Sorel understood socialism as such a myth and sharply criticized the Marxists for their rationalism, which, he felt, made them incapable of grasping the mythic potency of their own ideas. By definition, myth transcends both pragmatic and theoretical rationality, while at the same time it strongly affects them.

17

Men live by myth. If their condition is one of relative comfort, the mythic themes are in the background of their lives and only become actualized in moments of individual crisis. The same is true even for most people who live in a misery that is stable and to which no alternatives have been imagined. The power of myth is most likely to erupt with historic efficacy in situations of rapid change, especially when that change puts in question what has previously been taken for granted, and brings with it, or threatens to do so, a deterioration in the circumstances of life. With varying intensity, this has been the case with all societies undergoing transformations brought on in the wake of the industrial revolution. Today it holds true with cataclysmic intensity throughout the Third World. It should hardly be surprising, then, that both thought and action on the problem of development are permeated by elements of myth.

Development is not just a goal of rational actions in the economic, political, and social spheres. It is also, and very deeply, the focus of redemptive hopes and expectations. In an important sense, development is a religious category. Even for those living on the most precarious margins of existence, development is not just a matter of improved material conditions; it is at least *also* a vision of redemptive transformation. Unless this is understood, much of what is taking place in the Third World today will remain incomprehensible. But development has also become a focus of redemptive aspirations for some people in the rich countries of the West, particularly among intellectuals and the young. There is here a certain vicariousness in the expectations of redemption, a kind of "zionism" with regard to the struggles of Third World societies. Perhaps what is at work here is an archaic mythic motif, that of simpler and purer lands far away, from which some healing secret might be learned. The very phrase "Third World," at least to Western ears, carries a strongly suggestive undertone of myth. One is reminded of the medieval doctrine of Joachim of Flora (in many ways the great-grandfather of all modern Western messianisms), who taught that there would soon come the "third age" (*tertium saeculum,* or *orbis tertius*). This would be the age, or the world, of the Holy Spirit, in which all oppressive institutions would be swept away, all class differences obliterated, and all men would be brothers. It is not implausible to think that these mythic themes still play a role for those Westerners whose imagination has been caught by the Third World. However, large numbers of people in Third World societies have shown a surprising susceptibility to "infection" by Western-

18

inspired messianisms. It is quite possible that the Joachimite doctrine, conceived in a lonely Calabrian monastery in the second half of the twelfth century, continues to engender mythic exaltation in places of which its author never dreamed.

Two powerful myths affect thought and action on the problem of development—the myth of growth and the myth of revolution. It would be a grave mistake to identify these two myths with the aforementioned two theoretical paradigms in a one-to-one fashion. The myths are only imperfectly related to the paradigms—they lurk behind them, as it were. Nor are the myths rigorously discrete with regard to each other. They collide, but they also interconnect and even merge in a variety of ways. Thus, just as a theoretical understanding of the two paradigms is necessarily complex, so is any effort at mythological analysis in this area.

Each of the two myths must be seen in a larger mythological frame of reference; each is a special manifestation of a much more general mythic thrust. The myth of growth first must be seen within the larger context of a mythology of modernity. A "clue concept" in this context is that of "progress": Human affairs are moving in time in an "upward and forward" direction. History, and one's society in particular, thus have a purpose in a future envisaged as a culmination or a series of culminations. The biography of the individual, with its particular hopes and expectations, derives meaning from the societal purpose—the individual's own life is perceived as having *the right* to an "upward and forward" direction. Closely related to the "clue concept" of progress are the notions of technocratic control and productivity. The prime guarantor of movement toward the mythic goal is man's ability to impose ever-increasing control over both the natural and the social environment. This ability, derived from modern science and technology, is expressed above all in the Promethean productivity unleashed by modern industry. In this mythological context, the antiseptic concept of economic growth carries a heavy freight of redemptive hope. As the gigantic power of modern technological production grows, so does the hope for a new world of human fulfillment.

The myth of growth, and indeed the entire mythology of modernity, derives from the specifically Western tradition of messianism. Ultimately, it represents a secularization of Biblical eschatology. Central to all the great transformations of modern Western history, it continues as a centrally important component in the world view of all advanced industrial societies (with particular virulence in America). Its advent in the Third World is, of course, more recent, and is directly traceable to the "evangelistic" effects of Westernization. Its success as a new "gospel" has been enormous. As a result of this, whoever speaks of economic growth in the Third World today is not just engaging in economics, but is rousing a whole array of redemptive aspirations, the ultimate content of which is mythic. It is this content that provides much of the power to sway, inspire, mobilize—and, if frustrated, to enrage.

In recent years the slogan of the governing party in Mexico, the Partido Revolucionario Institucional, has been *"Arriba y adelante!"*— "Upward and forward!" At election times this core formula of the myth of progress can be seen splashed on walls all over the country, from imposing public buildings to the makeshift shacks in the sprawling urban slums, and into Indian villages in the remote countryside. Next to the political slogans, often on the same walls, is the colorful multiplicity of advertising messages holding up the vision of a plenitude of consumer commodities and services. The two sets of communications are related in a very important way. Whatever may be the ideology of those who invent political slogans, the meaning of "upward and forward" for the individual to whom the slogans are addressed is, above all, access to and enjoyment of the fruits of modern technological production. One of the key legitimations of the PRI regime in Mexico has been that its development policies will lead to a better life for all Mexicans precisely in the terms evoked by the advertising imagery. In this the Mexican regime is no different from nearly all regimes in the Third World today (*regardless* of whether they adhere to a capitalist, socialist, or "mixed" model of development). And one of the key propositions of the critics of the Mexican regime has been that the political promise is false and that, therefore, the advertising imagery is a seduction into a false consciousness. The point here is not whether the critics are right or wrong, but rather that the expectations geared to the wonders of modern technological production remain as a constant in both the legitimations and the delegitimations of particular development policies.

In the early decades of this century there arose on various Pacific islands a messianic movement that Western scholars named the Cargo Cult. Indigenous prophets announced that soon would arrive ships, directed by ancestors returned from the land of the dead, bulging with gifts for the islanders. Planes later replaced ships in this vision, but the cargo remained the same—all the wonderful products of Western technology, such as automobiles, refrigerators, radios, canned foods, and so on. The movement is interesting because it represents a curious blend of traditional and modernizing motifs—it is the ancestors who arrive as the bearers of the gifts of modernity. However, if the ancestors are momentarily omitted, the vision provides a perfect metaphor for the myth of economic growth. The latter, in terms of the aspirations it carries, is *always* a "cargo cult"—and not just on the islands of the Pacific.

The theme of technological productivity is closely related to that of technocratic control. Modernity means (in intention if not in fact) that men take control over the world and over themselves. *What previously was experienced as fate now becomes an arena of choices.* In principle, there is the assumption that all human problems can be converted into technical problems, and if the techniques to solve certain problems do not as yet exist, then they will have to be invented. The world becomes ever more "makeable." This view of the world is essentially that of the engineer. First expressed in engineering proper, in the systematic manipulation of nature and of machines, it is carried over into multiple forms of social engineering (including politics), and finally into engineering approaches to the most intimate areas of interpersonal experience (including psychology, qua engineering of the self). Once more there is an important linkage between political and economic propaganda. The political slogans promise participation in the decisions that will shape the future, as advertising promises participation in the benefits of modernity. Both forms of participation entail *choice*—which, indeed, may be designated the modern category *par excellence*. Individual life, traditionally a reenactment of cycles of necessity, now becomes an open-ended series of moments of choice ranging in content from political options exercised through the franchise to the (only seemingly trivial) options between consumer commodities. One of the important promises of the myth of economic growth is, quite simply, that there will be more and more things to choose from.

The myth of revolution is by no means a simple contradiction of the myth of growth. It shares with the latter common roots in the Judaeo-Christian tradition of Western culture, and most of its versions contain elements of the themes of progress, technocratic control, and productivity. Indeed, one recurrent assertion of revolutionary propaganda is that its program can deliver the "cargo" more surely or more swiftly than the gradualistic development models. But if, in view of all this, the myth of revolution must be located in an overall mythological context that is specifically modern, it is also important to understand that the myth contains elements that derive from quite different sources. Indeed, to grasp fully the myth of revolution one must understand the discontents that modernity has generated and the resulting impulses that run counter to modernization. These impulses often taken on mythic qualities.

Modern industrial capitalism was established in Western societies at great human costs. In its early stages it was marked by physical violence and exploitation of singular ruthlessness. This was so in England, the first country to undergo "the great transformation" (as Karl Polanyi called it in his book of that title, published in 1944), and it continued to be true, albeit with varying degrees of brutality, in the other countries that today constitute the advanced industrial societies of the west. Not surprisingly, the transformation encountered all kinds of resistances, some of which were put down by open terror (as in the criminal law of England, commonly called the "bloody code," which at the beginning of the nineteenth century listed over two hundred offenses liable to capital punishment, most of them against property). Again with varying degrees of brutality, physical violence and exploitation continue today as stark realities in some parts of the Third World now undergoing "the great transformation." No great feats of analysis are required to understand that in such situations the victims of oppression are open to revolutionary propaganda, whether or not the latter has mythic components. Indeed, the term "discontents" is hardly useful to describe the reactions to this kind of oppression. Rather, the emotional texture of such situations is marked by fear, rage, and, at times, desperate courage.

People hovering on the edge of despair are always open to messianic myths. It is thus easy to understand why revolutionary movements originating in situations as those just described will readily attract whatever mythic themes of redemption are "at hand" for them. The modernization of societies, however, produces other, more subtle discontents which do not disappear even under conditions that can no longer be adequately described in the vocabulary of oppression and exploitation. These discontents have increased in strength even in the most affluent industrial societies in the contemporary world. They also are open to mythic expression.

Modernization entails the imposition of rationality on ever-increasing sectors of social life—a process that was named "rationalization" by Max Weber. The imperative of rationality is already powerful in the very early stages of capitalism, an economic system that demands procedures and mental attitudes that are calculating, prognosticating, and controlling with precision. The imperative becomes overwhelming with the advent of industrialism. The rationality of the capitalist entrepreneur is now merged with the rationality of the engineer in an immensely potent synthesis. No longer able to be contained within the economic and scientific-technological sectors of social life, it overflows these boundaries with ever-increasing force and finds a new and crucially important embodiment in the institutions of bureaucracy, first in the political sphere, then almost everywhere else. Rationalization means that the individual's life becomes increasingly controlled, administered, "engineered." Rationalization also shapes and reshapes the meaning structures, the world view, of modern societies. Secularization, the progressive "reality loss" by the traditional religious interpretations of the world, is probably the most important result of rationalization on the level of meaning. Its cumulative effects have been cataclysmic.

Modernization operates like a gigantic steel hammer, smashing both traditional institutions and traditional structures of meaning. It deprives the individual of the security which, however harsh they may have been, traditional institutions provided for him. It also tends to deprive him of the cosmological security provided by traditional religious world views. To be sure, it gives him new opportunities of choice—that is, of freedom —but this new freedom is purchased at a high price. Since Emile Durkheim, social scientists have given the name "anomie" to this price— a condition in which the individual is deprived of stable, secure ties with other human beings, and in which he lacks meanings that will provide adequate direction for his life.

The discontents of modernity, apart from the more brutal sufferings that modernization often brings with it, are thus rooted quite deeply in the transformations of human life brought about by industrialism as well as capitalism. Whatever is "irrational" in human beings resists the onslought of rationalization. Very importantly, whatever religious impulses exist in human consciousness suffer profoundly from the impact of secularization—and, if not "allowable" as religious expressions, may seek outlets elsewhere. The loss of collective and individual security carries with it the constant threat of isolation as well as meaninglessness. In their cumulative result, these processes add up to a pervasive condition of "homelessness"—man is no longer "at home" in society, in the cosmos, or ultimately with himself.

There are probably fundamental traits in the constitution of man that render such a condition intolerable. As "homelessness" continues and deepens, therefore, there appear efforts to remedy this condition, to enable man to be once more "at home." Both the oppressions and the discontents of modernity have engendered passionate quests for new ways of being "at home" socially, religiously, and within the individual psyche. The central mythic motif in these quests is the hope for a *redemptive community* in which each individual will once more be "at home" with others and with himself. This motif of a redemptive community is present in the great religious and political movements of messianism since the sixteenth century. It provides the theme of "fraternity" in the triple slogan of the French revolution. It carries the mythic undertone in virtually every ideal of socialism. And it performs the same function with regard to nationalism.

The dream of bringing about a redemptive community necessarily carries revolutionary implications for the institutional order of the status quo. This was so in premodern times and societies. The peculiarly powerful thrust of this dream under modern conditions is due to the confrontation between the dream's vision of "home" and the actually experienced state of "homelessness." In other words, the cry for community comes *de profundis*. But the quest for community, while always antagonistic to the order of modern industrial capitalism in an at least potentially revolutionary way, may take either a "reactionary" or a "progressive" form. This has been so in Western societies, and continues to be so in the Third World today.

The quest is "reactionary" when it locates the longed-for community in the past, be it a real or a fictitious past. Peasant rebellions, movements originating within threatened or declining aristocracies, as well as various forms of romantic nationalism, have this character. In non-Western countries invaded by modernizing forces the same character pertains to the movements subsumed by social scientists under the heading of "nativism"—movements which militantly reassert the continuing validity of traditional ways and values. Redemption from the anomie of modernity is here envisaged as, literally, a *return home*. By contrast, the quest is "progressive" when the redemptive community is projected into the future. Here there is a vision of a "homecoming" that is altogether new —indeed, that is eschatological in the proper sense of the word. Not only the present but the past is perceived as unredeemed; therefore there can be no return, only a movement forward. Even true humanity still lies ahead.

The myth of revolution, as operative in the Third World today, is predominantly "progressive" in this sense, so its affinity with the Marxist stream in Western social thought is quite logical. Marx himself saw the fulfillment of man (his liberation from alienation) as lying in the future, as the goal of that ultimate revolution that will put an end, once and for all, to the oppressive reality of class struggles. As to the past, in the words of *The Communist Manifesto*, "the history of all hitherto existing society is the history of class struggles"—that is, is a history of unredeemed alienation. No one can understand Marxism and its hold over the imagination of large numbers of people who fails to understand this mythic motif. Yet, in looking at the myth of revolution and at ideals of socialism in the contemporary Third World, the "progressive" motif does not always exhaust the observable contents. There are also strongly "reactionary" elements blending with the "progressive" elements of the myth in more or less neat manner. For example, various formulations of "African socialism" or "Arab socialism" have insisted that the social solidarity to be created in the future is, at least in part, a restoration of community as it existed in the past in, respectively, Islamic society and the traditional societies of Africa. In some of these cases, therefore, the Marxist terminology used to define the situation can be misleading. Underlying the "progressive" words may be profoundly "reactionary" dreams. Needless to say, it is an altogether different question whether the partial realizations of such programs of "socialism" do in fact restore traditional forms of community.

There is still another point to be made here on the relation between Marxism and the myth of revolution. While it has been observed that various mythic streams may interweave, the preceding discussion essentially dealt with the myth of growth and the myth of revolution, and the wider mythological contexts of each, as discrete entities. To reiterate: The myth of growth lies squarely within the wider context of modernity; the myth of revolution contains strong countermodern themes. Thus the former myth is fundamentally an ultimate idealization of rationality, while the latter embodies some protests against rationalization. The myth of growth idealizes choice and control; the myth of revolution represents a quest for redemptive community. In consequence, the latter myth is more overtly religious in its social-psychological expressions. The standard-bearers of the myth of growth (its mythological archetypes, so to speak) are entrepreneurs and engineers; those of the myth of revolution are armed prophets. In view of all this, the myth of revolution has greater affinity to archaic, and indeed to "reactionary," imagery and motives; the myth of growth is pure "progressivity." As we have discussed Marxism within the context of the myth of revolution, all these traits may be observed in movements identifying with Marxism, especially in the contemporary Third World. But this is not the whole story.

The peculiar appeal of Marxism comes not just from its relation with the myth of revolution—that is, from its ability to embody and legitimate these particular mythic aspirations. Marxist ideology and Marxist movements also have an important relation to the other mythological complex—that of modernity, progress, and technocratic control—and, in the context of the Third World today, a relation to the myth of growth. What is more: *The peculiar appeal of Marxism is due in important measure to its capacity for mythological synthesis.* Specifically, Marxism has been uniquely capable of merging key themes of the two myths discussed above. Nationalist ideologies have tried to do the same, but the synthesis has been much less articulate. The political creeds associated with capitalist models of development have generally failed to incorporate any significant elements of the myth of revolution.

One "clue concept" for the present considerations is the Marxist term "scientific socialism," which expresses the mythological synthesis with perfect succinctness. "Socialism" is a word triggering all the profound aspirations of the myth of revolution. It evokes the hope for redemption from a miserable and anomic present, and the vision of a future in which there will be true community and in which all men will be brothers. "Socialism" is the condition in which all men will be "at home" with each other. While this is an eschatological condition, movements representing "socialism" offer this experience of life-giving fraternity (by way of a "proleptic event," as some Christian theologians might put it). In the future all men will be brothers; revolutionaries are brothers already (again the compelling parallel with Christian notions concerning the church as an anticipation of the eschatological kingdom). In all of these aspects, "socialism" relates to important countermodern, even archaic, mythic impulses.

But this very socialism is also supposed to be "scientific"! Marx himself denounced those socialists who preceded him as "utopian socialists" because of their unscientific attitude, and later Marxists have invented long vocabularies of denunciation to accuse each other of the same fault. Thus Marxism promises all the good things evoked in the vision of socialism just outlined, and, on top of that, maintains that the necessity of the vision can be scientifically demonstrated and its realization scientifically effected! It therefore appeals equally to the engineer with theological nostalgias and to the prophet who wants to be "hard-nosed" in the eyes of statisticians. Its "unity of theory and praxis" guarantees that no questions may be raised in this harmony of dreams, theories, and actions. And in the end, everybody will have everything— the fruits of progress without the price of alienation, redemption *and* technocratic control, community *and* individual choice. The term "scientific socialism" thus designates the common ambition to have one's cake and eat it too.

A history of Marxism in these terms is yet to be written. Probably it would have to begin at that point in time when Marx himself turned the Hegelian metaphysic on the dry bones of economics and, a wonder to behold, resurrected them as angels of the apocalypse. In this perspective, the development of basic Communist doctrine, from Engels through Lenin to the "dialectical materialism" of official Soviet ideology, represents a purging of the myth of revolution of its countermodern, darkly irrational elements. The apocalyptic angels become salivating Pavlovian dogs. It is not surprising that official Soviet ideology, when applied to the contemporary problem of development, is imbued with the myth of growth, is often downright counterrevolutionary, and is fascinated by the *kabbala* of productivity statistics in a way that puts American corporation executives to shame. This does not mean that this ideology is severed from myth. On the contrary, it fully incorporates some key components of modern mythology, but at a price in motivating power that goes far in explaining the difficulties of Soviet propaganda in the

27

Third World today. The most acute "mythic deprivation" (if this term be allowed) is represented, not by the DIAMAT and HISTMAT ("dialectical materialism" and "historical materialism") of Soviet dogmaticians, but by the "revisions" of Marxism undertaken by Western social democrats. It is this social democracy that represents a redefined Marxism in which all mythic themes, modern or countermodern, have been reduced to a minimum. This fact probably accounts for the difficulties in which contemporary social-democratic parties and regimes find themselves in a number of Western countries.

By contrast with both the scientistic modernism of Soviet Marxism and the mythologically anemic doctrines of Western social democrats, the Marxisms that have had most appeal in the Third World vigorously reiterate the aforementioned synthesis between the two mythic thematics. Most important, they have not made the mistake of allowing apocalyptics to be dissolved in Pavlovian engineering. The dark forces of the revolutionary impulse are preserved. Put differently, the Marxisms of the Third World are more overtly "religious." *This*, rather than any alleged insights into development strategy, is what probably accounts for the wide appeal of Maoism. A French observer of Communist China has suggested that the ongoing application of Mao's Thought to everyday activities is a replication of an essentially medieval, thus premodern, principle—*orare et laborare*—"to pray and to work." The ubiquity of the Little Red Book thus would represent an attitude of "perpetual prayer." One may have one's doubts about the durability of such an enterprise; most people get tired of too much praying. But in a situation of profound mythic yearnings, there are many people ready "to pray," and they cannot be satisfied by being handed growth figures, however glowing. Similar observations may be made about other Third World Marxisms—from Ho Chi Minh's apparently successful attempt to claim a new "mandate of heaven," to Julius Nyerere's doctrine of *ujamaa* in Tanzania (the Swahili word denotes traditional tribal solidarity and is now applied to the development model of "African socialism"), to Fidel Castro's rather less successful notion of "moral incentives" in production. In all these ideological constructions Marxism represents a synthesis of "science" and "socialism," thus of modernizing and countermodernizing themes, but the redemptive and communalistic aspirations are generally much stronger than those of technocratic control. For rather obvious reasons, this dominance is particularly the case with Marxist movements that have not as yet attained power in a country; it becomes more difficult for *successful* revolutionaries, who must turn to the practical concerns of administration and planning. The luxury of being able to dream in a condition of having no practical responsibilities is one of the key characteristics of the New Left in Western countries. Consequently, its socialist visions have been segregated to an unprecedented degree from the reality-referents of either scientific theorizing or engineering praxis. Thus the Marxism of the New Left has been *pure* myth, virtually untouched by the vulgar necessities encountered by those who want to relate mythic aspirations to empirical social reality.

The preponderance of the socialist model among Third World intellectuals, both as theoretical paradigm and as political strategy, cannot be explained in rational terms alone. Conversely, neither can the relative weakness of the capitalist model. The two models must be seen in relation to mythic undercurrents in both. This perspective holds little comfort for the advocates of capitalism. Whoever may have the better arguments, it is clearly the socialists who have the stronger myths. It should be emphasized, though, that this is not *in itself* an endorsement, nor is it, *necessarily*, an expression of rejection. It is possible to conclude, on nonmythological grounds, that capitalism has the better arguments and that what is needed, therefore, is a debunking of the socialist myths in theory as well as in political practice. On the other hand, one might conclude that there are very good reasons, rational as well as moral, for opting for a socialist model of development—in which case its mythic associations can simply be welcomed as a tactical advantage. In other words, the discovery of myth in the context of development, while important to understanding, does not put an end to the debate between alternative theoretical and political positions.

If Sorel is right in stating that myths are indispensable for certain types of collective action, the critique of myths may appear to be an uninteresting or even politically harmful undertaking. Why not leave the myths alone, especially since they are impermeable to rational arguments, and turn instead to the theoretical and practical questions that can be rationally discussed? Why not? For several reasons: Because the theoretical and practical issues are shot through with mythic themes, and without understanding the latter it is not possible to understand the former. Because there are differences to be made among myths, some of which give life, others of which kill. Because myth fosters total commitment, and people who are so committed tend to be blind to mythologically inconvenient facts and indifferent to the human costs of their mythologically legitimated programs. For all these reasons, "demythologization" is both theoretically and politically important in the area of development.

A "demythologizing" approach to the problem of development will, therefore, insist that facts be faced and costs counted. Such an approach will irritate both the social engineers and the social prophets by this insistence. It will be implacably hostile toward what Octavio Paz has called "petrified concepts" and "syllogism-daggers." The myths both of growth and of revolution have produced impressive quantities of such aberrations. It should be clear by now that neither myth, by itself or in synthesis with the other, offers any guarantee for realistic and humane policies. It seems likely that such policies will only be possible if there is skepticism with regard to the pretensions of both the engineers and the prophets.

The critique of myth may stipulate Sorel's position that myths are necessary, but it encourages discrimination and discourages fanaticism. Similarly, the critique of models of theory and policy is not intended to paralyze either enterprise. There are no alternatives to having intellectual and political elites, but it makes sense to prefer theorists who have doubts and policy makers with scruples. This is also not intended to glorify peasants, or others who possess neither theoretical sophistication nor power. Their definitions of the situation are not, in themselves, cognitively or morally superior. All the same, they are entitled to respect, cognitive as well as moral (indeed, the category of "cognitive respect" merits further elaboration).

The critical enterprise, then, to which the preceding may be taken as a preamble, is *not* a general assault on man's mythopoetic propensity, *not* an attack on intellectuals qua myth makers, and *not* a polemic against one or another model of development. Rather, it is a search for nondogmatic approaches to the urgent questions at issue. Answers are difficult to attain in this area; something worthwhile is gained by suggesting certain questions. It becomes plausible in the course of such a critical enterprise that most currently dominant ideological definitions of the situation are inadequate, often irrelevant, always in need of being revised. To the extent that the ideologies are related to political camps, there are practical consequences to such revision. One may even want to transgress the boundary lines between the encampments. And one may wish to think through certain matters from a fresh start.

Chapter II

⟨⟩⟨⟩⟨⟩⟨⟩

AGAINST CAPITALISM? CRITIQUE OF GROWTH

IF ONE WANTED to represent capitalism in visual images, advertising would probably come to mind first. Advertising suggests a garish, neon-lit world of opulence and of promises of more opulence. In advanced industrial societies of the capitalist type, advertising provides a pervasive and highly sophisticated background to everyday life. Part of its pervasiveness comes from the fact that, much of the time, its presence is not consciously registered. Rather, it is integrated into the taken-for-granted texture of ordinary reality. For this reason, its sudden absence comes as a shock. Until very recently such a shock was readily available to any traveler crossing from Western to Eastern Europe. Today, in the wake of various concessions made by European Communist regimes to the dynamics of a consumer market, the difference tends to be quantitative rather than qualitative. But only a few years ago the traveler going from, say, Western Germany to Czechoslovakia would experience the sudden absence of advertising as a deafening silence. Conversely, the traveler returning to the West would be acutely aware of instant reimmersion in the ongoing multimedia cacophony orchestrated by advertising. But the absence of advertising in socialist countries (or, today, its lesser quantity) must not be misunderstood as implying an inferior role for mass communications. The traveler from, say, Frankfurt to Prague will find fewer messages that sell goods or services, but in their place he will be bombarded by innumerable messages recommending ideological and political attitudes. The place of advertising, in other words, is taken by government propaganda.

This difference in the character of mass-communicated messages says a lot about the fundamental differences between these two types of society. There is the difference between an economic principle of competition and an alternative principle of allocation. In the first type of situation pushy salesmen elbow each other to offer me their wares; in the second, government officials allocate to me my share of whatever goodies are available (and usually they are not only *not* pushy, but downright reluctant). Presumably, my relative happiness or unhappiness in either situation will depend on whether I worry more about being conned by salesmen or short-changed by government officials. The difference, though, is not only between economic principles. Indeed, it may be expressed as a sort of trade-off between economics and politics: In one situation "they" want my money; in the other, it's my soul they're after. There will be occasion to return to the theoretical implications of this trade-off, but for the moment one observation may suffice: It is not an accident that the critique of capitalism usually starts with the miseries of economics, the critique of socialism with those of politics. This observation suggests further that anyone interested in developing a truly "critical" social science, one that transcends critical reactions to any single particular or immediate situation, should be able to cope theoretically with *both* sets of miseries.

To return to advertising as a potent representation of contemporary capitalism: The very existence of advertising is based upon two fundamental characteristics of a capitalist economy. Such an economy is dominated by the mechanisms of the *market* and by a built-in commitment to *growth*. Neither dominance is negated by the fact that the market is often modified or "fixed" by both formal and informal restrictions on competition, or by the fact that the rate of growth may differ greatly at different times. It is logical, then, that in most recent attacks on capitalism the critique of the market has been closely connected with a critique of growth. Both critiques are highly relevant to any analysis of capitalist models of development in the Third World today.

33

In Western social science as well as political discourse there recur three key terms in the discussion of the problems under consideration here. These are "development," "modernization," and "growth." In the simplest sense, development refers to the process by which poor countries get richer, or try to do so, and also to the process by which rich countries get still richer. However, the matter is much more complex if more precise social-scientific definitions are desired.

Growth is probably easiest to define, insofar as the term falls squarely within the frame of reference of economics, the discipline that (not necessarily to advantage in all cases) has produced the most precise conceptual instrumentarium among the social sciences. In dealing with growth, economists employ two key measures—rise in the total economic output of a society (gross national product, or GNP), and rise in the per capita output. Both measures have been defined and applied with a great deal of precision.

Under contemporary conditions, economic growth is usually the result of the introduction or improvement in the technological means of production and distribution. But these technological and economic processes do not occur in a vacuum, especially when they take place with the rapidity that is common today. Rather they constitute a turbulent force that affects, increasingly, all the institutions and the entire culture of the society in question. It is this wider transformation that is commonly designated by the term "modernization." In other words, modernization refers to the institutional and cultural concomitants of economic growth under the conditions of sophisticated technology. This usage is now common among social scientists concerned with various noneconomic aspects of society (the economists, as a rule, disclaim competence in this area, even if they concede its importance). While there are many disagreements on specific components of modernization, as well as on its relation to the economic process of growth, there is widespread agreement (at least among non-Marxist social scientists) as to how the phenomenon is to be delineated.

The problem of definition is most complicated with regard to the third term, that of development. Often it is used as an equivalent of one or both of the other two. In that case, the utility of an additional concept is open to question. However, the notion of development, in its general usage, has a much stronger undertone of positive evaluation than is implied by the other two terms. In other words, while growth and modernization can rather readily be defined in a value-free way, such definition is much more difficult with development. Usage of the term usually implies a general improvement in the well-being of the population undergoing the process—if not immediately, then at least as a future prospect. Perhaps this point can be made most easily by giving a negative example: One may readily imagine a society based on slave labor of most of the population, which society nevertheless experiences rapid economic growth and modernizes its principal institutions. Very few social scientists would be prepared to speak of development in this situation (though, in a regrettable number of cases, they have in fact done so if the slavery was a bit camouflaged). Thus the notion of development is at least implicitly one of moral approval and political purpose. Put simply, development means *good* growth and *desirable* modernization.

Concepts are not made in heaven, and all definitions are arbitrary. For the present argument, however, the following definitions will be adhered to: Growth will be understood as an economic category only, in accordance with the conventional usage of economists. Modernization will be understood as the institutional and cultural accompaniment of growth, again following a widespread convention among social scientists. In this understanding, both growth and modernization are value-free concepts, and as such can be meaningfully employed regardless of whether one evaluates these processes as good, bad, or indifferent. Development, on the other hand, will be understood as a political category, and thus as *not* value-free. Development will then refer to such instances (actual or projected) of economic growth and sociocultural modernization as are deemed desirable in the contexts of moral judgment and public policy. Put simply once more: People who speak of growth and modernization may do so in the role of neutral observers. People who speak of development should frankly admit that they are engaged in the business of ethics and, at least potentially, of politics.[1]

There are theories that view economic growth under capitalist market conditions as the fundamental "engine" of development. These theories are linked to policies intended to create, maintain, or improve this "engine." The common assumption of these theories and policies is that development, the desired goal, depends on this kind of economic growth getting ever "bigger and better"—and the last two adjectives are often treated as synonyms. The more growth there is, the more development there will be—if not right away, then in the long run. In this perspective, the problem of underdevelopment is primarily, if not exclusively, *economic*. Since the malady is essentially economic, so is the treatment, even if noneconomic values are part of the projected future. This does *not* mean that noneconomic factors are ignored by either the theoreticians or the practitioners of this model, but rather that noneconomic factors are generally understood as conditions or aids to the underlying economic process. For example, it may be admitted that a particular political system or a particular set of cultural values may either be conducive to development or serve to inhibit the latter. But the political or cultural factors will be viewed in relation to the economic process that is deemed primary, and will generally be evaluated in terms of their helping or hindering this process. Conversely, the idea that the economic process itself might be evaluated as a help or a hindrance for certain political or cultural purposes is unlikely to be conceived at all. It follows that the policy "recipes" emerging from this view of things are economic first, and only secondarily political, social, or cultural. Wherever this viewpoint is established, the pronouncements of economists tend to have oracular status. Since these pronouncements primarily refer to the prognostication of economic growth, any policies that might hinder the latter will be ipso facto ruled out of order. In this universe of discourse, to question the value of economic growth *itself* is to question the basic operative definitions of reality. At that moment, the whole universe of discourse is shaken.

Within the overall assumption of the necessary relation between development and economic growth lie a great variety of theoretical positions, and some sharp contradictions among them. This is not the place to elaborate on all this, although it is important to see that what Marxists like to call "bourgeois social science" by no means presents a united front on many of the questions at issue. Thus, within economics itself, there have been theories of "balanced growth" (also known as theories of the "big push") as against those of "unbalanced growth." The former position (associated with Ragnar Nurske and Paul Rosenstein-Rodan) maintains that the best strategy for economic growth is one of "pushing" the economy as a whole, while the latter (represented by Albert Hirschman) holds that a better strategy is to concentrate on the most dynamic sectors of the economy and rely on the effects of their growth eventually affecting other sectors.

Still within economics, there has been much controversy on the primacy of industrialization for economic growth, as well as strong differences of opinion on what type of industrialization should be given preference.[2] Outside the field of economics, a key point of debate has been a kind of classical chicken-and-egg question: Which comes first—economic growth, or its social, cultural, or even psychological correlates? There have been a number of theories (David McClelland's has been the most sharply debated) holding that a particular personality type is a necessary precondition for both modernization and economic growth.[3] There has been extensive discussion of what cultural values and traits are conducive to economic growth. This question has been of particular interest to sociologists, who have followed up Max Weber's well-known thesis that the so-called "Protestant ethic," with its peculiar values of hard work and discipline, has been a crucial factor in the genesis of capitalism in Europe. A big search has been activated for "functional equivalents" of this ethic in different parts of the world.[4] There has been wide-ranging discussion of the social institutions (including, very importantly, political institutions) that are or are not to be seen as either necessary preconditions or likely consequences of economic growth. American social scientists have been especially interested in whether there is any degree of correlation between economic growth and political institutions along the lines of Western-style democracy.[5] The concept of "political development" has been one of the (probably less than helpful) products of the last-named interest.

From all this, even within the broad confines of capitalist development strategy, has come a great variety of different policy implications. The differences concern not only economic policy proper, but policies in the political, social, or even cultural areas (for instance, in the area of education). Perhaps the most important policy difference has concerned the relative degree to which development strategy should rely on market mechanisms or planning. Put differently, this is the question of the political limits that should be imposed on the market (a question of vast economic ramifications, ranging from monetary policy to policies on health, education, and welfare). Related to this have been different

37

positions on the degree to which planning should be centralized or decentralized (again a question with far-reaching implications, political as well as economic). It should be stressed that all these divergences in both theory and policy may and do exist within the confines of capitalist models of development, though, of course, a number of them entail severe restrictions on the capitalist market economy through public planning and regulation.[6] Logically enough, those with a strong belief in planning and other political interferences with the market have been more sympathetic to socialist approaches to development, as against those with a skeptical or negative attitude regarding the economic role of government.

Yet, despite all these differences in theoretical and policy approaches, it is meaningful to speak of a distinctively capitalist idea of development through growth. In essence this is a universal projection of the "American dream"—a vision of economic plenty in the context of political democracy and a dynamic class society. Closely associated with this vision are the values of personal and political freedom, as expressed in the notion of a "Free World." Thus, especially for Americans, there has been a strong missionary flavor in the promulgation of the capitalist ideal of development. It is especially important to recall this, in view of the fact that there has been for many a souring of this flavor in the recent past. W. W. Rostow, in his basic work originally published in 1959 and aptly subtitled "A Non-Communist Manifesto," waxed eloquent in his depiction of a viable capitalist alternative to the Marxist versions of development. He described the creation of this alternative as "the central challenge of our time," and went on to say: "If we and our children are to live in a setting where something like the democratic creed is the basis of organization for most societies, including our own, the problems of the transition to modern status in Asia, the Middle East, and Africa— the problems posed by the creation of the preconditions and the take-off —must be solved by means which leave open the possibility of such a humane, balanced evolution."[7]

Since Rostow wrote these brave sentences, both the assumptions of the "democratic creed" and the faith in the great moment of "take-off" into "self-sustaining growth" have been severely shaken in segments of American society, particularly among intellectuals. Probably the turmoil of the late 1960s has left its mark on the self-confidence of the society as a whole. Promulgation of the capitalist ideal of development has become more muted, more defensive. It would be a grave mistake to assume, by false generalization from the limited milieus of the intelligentsia, that it has lost *all* plausibility. On the contrary, the ideal continues to serve as a powerful point of reference in the business community, in broad sections of the government, and among large numbers of ordinary people. What is equally important, the ideal continues to be plausible in large portions of the world mentioned by Rostow as the arena of the challenge. One may mention Indonesia, Iran, and most of Francophone Africa in this connection.

It should be noted that, while the interest here is primarily in the capitalist version of the vision of growth, there are also socialist versions. Most important is the Soviet version.[8] This view of economic reality rejects the capitalist market economy, and its specific forms of ownership and social organization. Also, of course, it is based on different theoretical presuppositions derived from Marxism. Despite this, there is a Soviet fascination with economic growth which sometimes shows surprising similarity with at least some features of the "American dream." The Soviets too are great believers in "bigger" economic growth. Their major difference with American fellow-believers concerns the "better" conditions under which the "bigger" growth is to be accomplished—these, of course, being understood as conditions of socialism along Soviet lines. The point to be made here is that, in consequence, various aspects of the critique of growth apply to the Soviet model of development as well as to capitalist models. This fact is of increasing importance in the Third World today, where Western "monopoly capitalism" and Soviet "state capitalism" are now often lumped together as two sides of the same coin —a worthless coin, to boot. While this perception antedates the Sino-Soviet split of recent years (in Latin America, for example, it is originally due to strong Trotskyite influences in the political left intelligentsia), Maoist propaganda in Third World countries has taken up and diffused this interpretation of things with a considerable measure of success.

It is important once more to stress that there is more at issue than a contestation between rational models of theory and policy. There is a mythic substratum beneath the various rationales. Generally there is the myth of growth, embedded in an overall mythology of progress and modernity.

Myths (as far as we know) are transmitted not by divine messengers, but by human "carriers." Who are the principal "carriers" of this particular myth? They are entrepreneurs, engineers, and other technical experts, and various kinds of "social engineers" (most of those in political or private bureaucracies). In capitalist societies this amounts to a broad combination of people from the corporate and state "technostructures" (to use Kenneth Galbraith's term) whose professional background is as businessmen, administrators, and intellectuals. In Soviet-style socialist societies there is a similar amalgam—with the important exception of the entrepreneurs, of course. In the Third World there is everywhere what may be called a "national technostructure," frequently animated by a fervently imitative mentality. Many Venezuelan businessmen look like Midwestern businessmen with improved body rhythm, and some Tanzanian bureaucrats impress one as East European *apparatchiks* in blackface.

It is people of this type who "carry" the myth of growth in the contemporary Third World. They also "carry" a specific set of definitions of reality, a view of the world, which is amenable to description. A central feature of their view is the ideal of productivity, which is commonly linked to certain assertions concerning the nature of man (the assertions, of course, may be philosophically unsophisticated, but this makes them no less potent socially). Man is, above all, *homo faber*. To be human is to work, to produce, to transform and dominate the world. Such a notion of man is almost everywhere in sharp contradiction to indigenous Third World religious and philosophical traditions. It is emphatically Western in provenance, and its ascent in the Third World (even, and perhaps especially, when it is accompanied by virulent nationalist and anti-Western rhetoric) represents a global triumph of Western values. In terms of the history of ideas, this anthropology has two major sources. On the one hand, it goes back to St. Simon's and Comte's vision of the "industrial society"; on the other, it derives from Marx's glorification of "labor." Invariably it has a moral and pedagogic thrust. It not only holds up an ideal of man, but seeks to promote its realization. Practically, it seeks to energize, to mobilize people for the purposes of productive work.

Closely related to this notion of man is the ideal of rationality, which may take the form of faith in a rationally functioning market, *or* in a rational planning process. Whatever may be the mythically grounded legitimations of such faith (be it in terms of the "American dream" or of Marxism), the ideal of rationality fosters an attitude of (alleged) "realism." American corporation executives, who believe that they understand the hard realities of economic life, have at least one important thing in common with socialist planners (who, *mutatis mutandis*, are similarly convinced that they have economic reality by the short hair): *Both* types take pride in their "hard-nosed" approach, and *both* share feelings of contempt for bleeding-heart idealists and fuzzy-minded utopians who refuse to face the tough facts of life. There is the resultant belief that man *does* live by bread, primarily if not alone.

Glorification of productivity and a specific creed of rationality add up to what may be called a materialism of practice, which manages to coexist with various idealisms lurking in the background as mythic inspirations or theoretical justifications. The ultimate purpose of what is practiced may be understood as the fulfillment of the great values of Western civilization, or of Marx's eschatological "leap into freedom"— *in the meantime* let us keep the production lines moving and the GNP growing. Rhetoric aside, this sort of practical materialism forms a remarkably shared universe of discourse for the technocrats of East and West. (For the Russian edition of this book the term PRACMAT will be suggested to the translator, and there will be an appendix containing a mathematical model of this new discipline.) Not surprisingly, such technocrats usually get along very well when they meet (as, increasingly, they do). Augur-like, they wink at each other—"We, who really know what's going on." Their affinity becomes touching in mutual commiseration over the obscurantism of their critics and the superstitious resistances of various target populations.

It is safe to say that this technocratic ethos has been put on the defensive all over the world. In the West there has been a dramatic resurgence of "irrationality" and "mysticism" in youth culture and counterculture. This has found at least partial political expression in the ambience of the New Left. The ethic of productivity and rationality has been directly and profoundly challenged, and its "repressions" have been anathematized as pathological deformations of human nature. In the Soviet orbit there has been a deepening rebelliousness against the "historical materialism" of official Marxism, ranging in expression from the "socialism with a human face" of the effervescent Prague Spring of 1968 to what appears to be a sizable if subterranean eruption of religious interests among Soviet intellectuals and youth. Indeed, it is noteworthy that in both halves of the advanced industrial world the revolt against rationalism has exhibited strong religious components (thus, among other things, posing some serious questions for the view that contemporary man is embarked on an inexorable and irreversible course of secularization). Archaic gods (and, not to forget, goddesses) have been casting strange shadows over the computers that spew out the economic growth rates.

In the Third World there has been a lumping-together (often instinctive rather than reflected-upon) of American and Soviet "materialism." With this has come a political attitude of "a plague on both your houses" and a quest for alternative options. There is a strong idealist emphasis in the self-consciously indigenous socialisms of various Third World countries. Whatever else may be said about the contents of "Indian socialism," "African socialism," or "Arab socialism," they have in common an explicit, often virulent rejection of the "materialism" of *both* the capitalist *and* the Soviet models of development. These ideologies have been dismissed (not least by Western Marxists) as intellectually vague and unsophisticated. Such dismissal sidesteps the crucial point that they express a profound search for alternatives to the theoretical assumptions and practical consequences of the myth of growth. Very often the term "socialism" is misleading in this context. Backing up the term is often a serious effort to preserve or revivify values and styles of life that antedate the cataclysmic invasion of these societies by the forces of modernization and Westernization (and, once again, it is completely beside the point to dismiss these aspirations as "reactionary" or "Luddite"). In Latin America this countermodernizing impulse has expressed itself in an interesting merging of two strands of anti-*gringo* ideology— the anti-Americanism of Marxist ideology, and the much older anti-Americanism of cultural resistance. The latter has commonly been called *Arielismo*. It posits Ariel, the "aery spirit" of a superior Latin civilization, against the crass materialism of the North American Caliban. The United States thus appears as the enemy in a double sense. It is a political enemy in its role as "imperialist metropolis," and a cultural enemy as, classically, the barbarian before the gate.

The widespread appeal of Maoism must be understood against the background of these aspirations. Both in the West and in the Third

World (too little is known about this factor in the Soviet orbit), Maoist China has been perceived as the great and successful alternative to all models of development based on "materialism." The explicitly idealistic components of Mao's Thought (strange indeed when pretending to be within the Marxist tradition) make this perception quite plausible. So do a number of Maoist policies, at least as presented in Chinese propaganda—rejection of economic growth as a goal in itself, emphasis on agriculture as against industrialization, an antitechnocratic and anti-"elitist" egalitarianism, the ethic of "nonmaterial incentives," and the mystique of the communes. To what extent these policies are in fact what the propaganda presents them as being is, of course, an entirely different question. But China is conveniently far away, and information about it is not so readily accessible that its distant admirers cannot select whatever fits their perception. Maoist China thus constitutes a gigantic Rorschach card into which different people can project the solutions to their home-grown discontents. At this point in the argument, these very non-Chinese frustrations and nostalgias are more interesting in themselves than their correspondence or noncorrespondence to Chinese realities.

Reasons for the revolt against the myth of growth and its technocratic "carriers" vary from country to country. It would be a gross oversimplification to *equate* the countermodernizing trends in the West with the aspirations toward a "Marxist humanism" in Eastern Europe, and to equate both with the quest for new alternatives in development in the Third World. Nevertheless, despite all obvious differences, there are important common themes in all these phenomena (which, incidentally, give a deeper credence to the identification with the Third World to be found in counterculture and New Left ambiences in the West). Perhaps it is necessary to penetrate to the mythic substratum to grasp these themes. And perhaps the underlying reason for the revolt can then be stated quite simply: Man does *not* live by bread alone. He also needs the life-giving and meaning-giving sustenance that no "materialist" view of the world can provide. If you will, man needs religion, and if that is so, no technocratic design for human life can be finally satisfactory. This would be the case even if such a design were to be eminently successful in its own terms—that is, in terms of actually delivering the bread. In the Third World there is the additional fact that success stories are rather hard to find.

It is important to understand the "religious" aspects of the aforementioned revolts against technocratic logic. But this in no way exhausts
the subject. There has also been a systematic and highly rational critique
of the theoretical assumptions and policy implications of the models of
development through growth. While this critique is probably fueled by
impulses that reach down into the mythic substratum of consciousness,
it derives intellectual credibility from much more accessible empirical
facts.

The basic fact is this: The models appear increasingly incapable of
delivering on their promises. At the heart of the myth of growth is the
vision of the "cargo cult"—arrival of all the wondrous gifts of modernity
in plentiful supply for all. In many places, however, there has been an
intolerable delay in the arrival of the cargo-bearing ships. In other places
there has been questioning as to whether the cargo is worth the mess it
has made on the beach. Needless to say, the latter question is unlikely
to be raised by those still waiting for the appearance of the ships on the
horizon.

In the West, serious questions have been raised as to whether unlimited growth is a meaningful goal even in economic terms. Can the
economy expand indefinitely, even if one looks upon it as a system
detached from other segments of human society? Economic questions
about unlimited growth have combined with older criticisms of the
sociocultural and even psychological costs of the "bigger and better"
ethos.[9] Recent years have seen a massive attack on the ideal of unlimited
growth because of its ecological results. In the wake of the highly
alarming report of the Club of Rome, more and more voices were raised,
proclaiming that continuing economic growth would lead to a depletion
of planetary resources, ever more catastrophic pollution of the atmosphere
and the oceans, poisoning of the food supply, and eventually the possible
end of life on earth. The ecology movement, particularly in the United
States, combined these prophecies of physical doom with an assault on
the social and cultural "quality of life" in advanced industrial society.
Modern technology, it seemed, has not only poisoned our natural environment but our souls as well. Abruptly, the vision of a New Jerusalem
turned into one of Armaggedon. The most radical policy implication
drawn from all this has been the "zero-growth" ideal: Population growth

must stop; the resources-consuming expansion of technology must stop; indeed, economic growth as such must stop.[10]

It seems likely that the apocalyptic projections of this movement are exaggerated. It is virtually certain that, ecological considerations apart, stoppage of economic growth in the advanced industrial societies would have disastrous social and political consequences. While these matters are important, it is impossible to pursue them here, since none of these considerations touch on the problem of development as perceived in the Third World. This was rudely but aptly expressed by a Brazilian politician, who replied to a question concerning the ecological implications of Brazilian industrialization: "It's *our* turn to pollute now." "Zero-growth," economically, would mean one of two things for the Third World: *Either* the present inequalities between the haves and have-nots of the earth would be frozen forever, *or* some global authority would oversee a reallocation of resources from the haves to the have-nots. The first would be a moral outrage; the second is a politically absurd fantasy.

Not surprisingly, then, ecological considerations have played a small part in Third World criticisms of the models of development through growth. Rather, they have concentrated on economic, social, and political considerations, as these are actually experienced in those countries. The emphasis has been on present disasters rather than on disasters anticipated for the future. The same emphasis will be followed here. Also, while keeping in mind the applicability of some of the same criticisms to socialist versions of the growth ethos, the focus will be on capitalism. Whatever the future may hold, it is economic growth under capitalist auspices, tied to an international capitalist system, that is of central importance in the Third World today. In other words, this particular critique of growth has merged with a critique of capitalism. This is not only relevant for the Third World, for the critique of capitalist development in the Third World has become for many, by a sort of mirror effect, a critique of capitalism as such. In this as in other areas, the Western observer of Third World events comes to the startling conclusion: *Res tua agitur*—it is his own case that is on trial.

The capitalist theory and practice of development have been under attack from the left since their inception, but in recent years this attack has become increasingly influential in the Third World. Today it is probably the predominant position among Third World intellectuals. In Latin America a dramatic change in this regard took place within about a decade. At the beginning of the 1960s development was generally taken as an almost religious goal. By the end of the 1960s the term had acquired a strongly pejorative connotation. "Development" now came to be understood as a term of obfuscation, covering up the realities of the situation, and the ideology advocating it was designated as "developmentalism" (*desarrollismo*, one suggested translation of which has been "growthmanship"). The fullest elaboration of this critique has been in terms of a Marxist or Marxist-leaning theory of imperialism. However, it is important to see that much of the same critique is now part and parcel of a taken-for-granted view of the world among a broad group of people, many of whom cannot be called Marxists or even "leftists" in any conventional sense.[11]

The capitalist ideology of development is geared to the growth of an economy which, at least in its essential character, is based on the market. The critique of this ideology has asked two fundamental questions: *Who benefits?* and *Who decides?* The questions can also be put as: *Whose* growth? and *Whose* market?

The question of who decides is visually presented by almost all cities in the Third World. There is the center of dynamic modernity— a steel and glass world of skyscrapers, traffic jams, well-dressed people rushing around on seemingly urgent business. There are the areas where these people live—a world of quiet streets, with houses that often exhibit luxuries rare in the northern hemisphere (not the least being the plentiful supply of cheap and deferential domestic servants), often a world in which traditional life styles survive surprisingly well in a contemporary setting (feudal graciousness supported by modern plumbing and air conditioning). Both of these zones are typically surrounded by huge rings of human misery and degradation, endless miles of slums, slums, and more slums. The question of who benefits from development can be translated into spatial terms, into the question of how these three urban zones relate to each other.

The ideology of development has long maintained that the benefits will eventually extend to all sectors of society. This tenet has been called the "trickle-down effect," more optimistically the "spread effect." Sometimes it is argued that this diffusion of benefits is already taking place, however modestly. Sometimes the diffusion is held out as a virtually certain expectation for the future. It is argued that the coexistence, in sharp contrast, of wealth and poverty is a necessary stage in the process of development. This is the stage during which capital must be rapidly accumulated in preparation for the "take-off." Once a certain level of accumulation is reached, the benefits will supposedly be distributed in a more equitable fashion, again because of the intrinsic economic dynamic of the development process. History is cited as witness for this argument: The early stages of development in Europe and North America were marked by precisely this kind of polarization, and the misery of the lower classes was possibly even worse than it is today in most of the Third World. Only in the later stages of the process did a much more equitable distribution come about, in addition to a general rise in the standard of living that (apart from the matter of distribution) benefited everyone in the society. In other words, as the economic pie gets bigger, not only do the lower classes get a bigger slice, but they will be much better off even if their slice remains the same. Ergo, the first priority must be to make a bigger pie.

It is obviously difficult to disprove an argument which depends for verification on an empirically inaccessible future. Some critics of development have simply claimed to have the *real* inside information on the future by virtue of a doctrine equally inaccessible to empirical verification. In that case, the issue becomes a contest between true believers. But the critics have done better than that. They have been able to show that the evidence on the Third World to date gives little support to the pious hopes of the "spread effect." In much of the Third World there has been an *increasingly* polarized distribution in income and wealth. That is, the lower classes have been getting *less*, not more, as the process unfolds. Nor has their absolute condition improved appreciably, if at all. There is *more* hunger and *more* disease today than there was some decades ago, not just in terms of absolute figures but even when the increase in population is taken into account. What is more, in much of the Third World there has been an *increase* in unemployment and underemployment. Since present trends give little reason to expect a reversal of the picture, why should one have any hope that such a reversal is in the offing? To so hope can only be the result of an act of faith, and this act, needless to say, the critics refuse to perform.

In Latin America the term "marginals" has been often used to designate those people who live on the edges of the new zones of prosperity. The term is both ironic and obfuscating. Throughout Latin America, with very few exceptions, these same "marginals" are the great majority of the population. If anyone is "marginal," it is the relatively prosperous, and there is no convincing evidence that the border between the two zones is shifting in such a way as to increase the affluent minority. Thus, the situation is marked by what Brazilian economist Celso Furtado has aptly called "growth without development." The growth is real enough, in terms of conventional economic indicators, but it has brought about a possibly permanent coexistence of a relatively well-off and dynamic modern sector and a sector of stagnant or even deepening misery. In these countries, then, there are "two nations" within the territory legally occupied by one, and the future will inevitably hinge on the manner in which these two will relate to each other.

The ideologists of "developmentalism" have frequently cited population growth as the foremost explanation of this situation. Most of the critics are willing to concede some validity to this factor. Population growth in most of the Third World is indeed enormous, and the geometric increase in population puts an increasing strain on scarce resources and thus on any development plans to expand these resources. It would be foolish to deny this, and even the Maoists (who earlier took the classical Marxist position—and perhaps the classically Chinese one— that any amount of population growth is a good thing) have now come around to conceding that the demographers' warnings are not just a bourgeois trick to cut down on the revolutionary masses. Nevertheless, the critics have generally discounted the demographic explanations as being the *primary* explanation of the "two nations" syndrome. Rather, they have insisted, the latter must finally be explained "systemically," that is, as being due to intrinsic characteristics of this type of capitalist growth.

"Growth without development" is based upon the penetration of a Third World economy by foreign capital. This penetration results in a "distortion" of the economy, in the sense that it develops not in terms of internal economic and social forces, but in the interest of the foreign "metropolis" (the country or countries from which the foreign capital comes). The same "distortion" creates an essentially colonial structure for the benefit of the foreign capitalists. It is not quite the same structure as that of the old colonialism, which was largely extractive, taking out raw materials from the colony that were needed for the industries in the home country. The new colonialism promotes industrialization, but of a very peculiar kind. Generally it is capital-intensive rather than labor-intensive, thus actually *creating* unemployment in the "developing" country. Generally it emphasizes durable consumer goods (such as automobiles, refrigerators, television sets, and so on). Their production requires a sophisticated technology which must be imported at great expense, often along with the technicians necessary to operate it (since the Third World countries usually lack this type of personnel). Moreover, these consumer goods can only be purchased by a small minority of the population in these countries, thus deepening the gulf between it and the rest of the population. Allocation of scarce resources to this kind of industrialization actually *prevents* development in other sectors of the society.

In addition, this "neocolonialism" largely exports the profits of the new industrial enterprise back to the home country, leaving the Third World country within which it operates with an increasingly unfavorable balance of payments. The debts incurred as a result of launching highly expensive and (except for the profits of foreign capital) uneconomical industrialization add to this unfavorable balance. The overall failure of so-called "import substitution" (the strategy of developing local industry to substitute for the importation of expensive industrial goods from abroad) is generally cited in support of this argument. The strategy had been widely recommended in the 1950s and early 1960s, in Latin America and elsewhere, as *the* recipe for development. Its application has led almost everywhere to the aforementioned results. "Neocolonialism," therefore, implies increasing impoverishment and ever-greater dependency on foreign forces. In Andre Gunder Frank's graphic phrase, it means "the development of underdevelopment."

The term "dependency" is an important "clue concept" in this critique. It was coined by Brazilian sociologist Fernando Henrique Cardoso and now occupies a central position in efforts by Latin American social scientists to interpret their situation. The term links the economic analysis to a political one. That is, it links the question *Who benefits?* with the question *Who decides?*

Dependency means that the important economic decisions are made outside the country being "developed," in the interest of outsiders. But these economic decisions have political correlates. The economic power of the outside interests can buy political power in the country under penetration. In some cases outside political power can actually be mobilized to support the outside economic interests. In Latin America this would mean political pressure or even military intervention by the United States government, acting in support of United States corporations. As a result of this collusion between foreign economic and political power, not only the economy but also the polity of the dependent country is being distorted. There emerge political alliances between the foreign interests and whatever local strata (usually a blending of the old pre-"development" upper class with new groupings of "national bourgeoisie") find it to their advantage to collaborate with the outsiders. The critique thus includes an analysis of the local political system in terms of the overall dependency syndrome. There is an "internal colonialism," corresponding to the colonial domination from abroad. Just as the "metropolis" exploits the "colony," so does the indigenous colonial class exploit the rest of the population. This parallelism is not just a metaphor; it is intrinsic in the economic and political relations between these groups.

This critique provides an intellectually seductive way of linking, point by point, local with global woes. Fairly clear political goals follow from this. Minimally, the goal will be national independence in decision making on development strategy. Maximally, it will be a severance of ties with the capitalist world system (in most cases possible only through revolutionary overthrow of the existing political setup), followed by establishment of socialism. The minimal goal is just about universally proclaimed in the Third World today, by "bourgeois nationalists" no less than by various brands of Marxists. The maximal goal, of course, is that of the political left in all its shadings. It is easy to see, as this critique becomes plausible, a logical linkage between nationalist sentiment for independence and sovereignty with the aspirations for social justice of the revolutionary left. It may be said that the critique has a powerful built-in potential for political mobilization (which, in itself, has no necessary relation to the critique's claims for scientific validity).

The basic conceptual instrumentarium of the critique is given in the Leninist theory of imperialism. The key formulation of the theory was made by Lenin himself in 1916, in his work *Imperialism as the Highest Stage of Capitalism*. The theory has been subsequently expanded and modified by different Marxist writers, but most differences are marginal to the present concern. The most important proposition of the theory is that all the evils brought on by foreign capitalist penetration are *necessary consequences* of capitalism in its present stage; they are not historical accidents in this or that country, but are "systemic" to capitalism as such. The original growth of capitalism in the West was based on colonial exploitation. For example, the capitalist development of England, including the English industrial revolution, could not have taken place without the plunder of India. But exploitation of colonies continues to be a necessity for capitalism, not so much because of the need of capitalist industry to extract raw materials from the colonies (a widespread pre-Leninist explanation of imperialism), but because capital must expand and the countries now subsumed under the heading of Third World are the most profitable areas into which it can move. In other words, imperialism is not primarily a quest of raw materials but of markets—above all, markets for capital. The "internal contradictions" of capitalist societies (economic, social, and political tensions deemed inevitable in the Marxist view) make it necessary for them to get involved ever more deeply in imperialist adventures abroad.

In this manner the critique of capitalist growth in the Third World is part and parcel of a critique of capitalism as such. This could not be otherwise within a Marxist frame of reference. What is interesting is that today there are many who would not fully identify with the Marxist-Leninist theory, but who nevertheless have become convinced that the evils of capitalism in the Third World necessarily put in question the very nature of capitalism, even as it exists in North America or Western Europe. Thus, by an interesting mirror effect, calls for socialism in Latin America have aided the legitimacy of socialist ideology in the United States. Similar relations exist between Third World socialism and socialist movements in Western Europe.

Again, except for Moscow-oriented Communist parties and the official position of the Cuban government (which cannot afford to antagonize Moscow), many Marxists in the Third World as well as in Western countries have directed elements of this critique against the Soviet Union as well. Indeed, one of the foremost ironies of the recent history of Marxism has been the widespread application of the Leninist theory of imperialism to Soviet foreign policies (thus giving a strange posthumous rehabilitation to Trotsky's heresy). The very use of the phrase "Soviet imperialism" in the context of Marxist analyses (be it by New Left writers, Maoists, or others) is profoundly ironic in itself. It has now become common in the Third World to equate "monopoly capitalism" (the Western system) with "monopoly state socialism" (the Soviet system), applying the same critique and drawing the same political consequences in both cases. In terms of models of development, there is a general critique of the myth of growth which is applicable to both its capitalist and socialist versions.

How is this critique itself to be evaluated? In other words, what would a critique of the critique look like?

For those animated by faith in this area, by what Italian Marxist Antonio Gramsci nicely called "fideistic" motives, there is no problem. The critique is either accepted as the higher truth, or rejected outright as a malevolent deformation of reality. For those who do not look to this particular area for satisfaction of their religious needs, the matter becomes more complicated. There can be neither an easy acceptance nor an easy rejection of this scheme of interpretation. Rather, that most difficult of intellectual operations is called for once more—differentiation.

Except on "fideistic" grounds, the Marxist understanding of capitalism in general and the Leninist theory of imperialism in particular are far from persuasive, if taken as a whole. The general response to both intellectual constructions must be a *no*. Here it is only possible to say this *no* briefly to three cardinal propositions of the Leninist theory.

The proposition that the past economic growth of the West was the result of colonial exploitation will not stand up. To say this, it is not necessary to deny that such exploitation may well have been one of many factors in a complex historical process (as, for instance, in the case of England and India). The major causal factors of this process, however, were almost certainly indigenous to Western societies in an overwhelming degree, rooted in a highly peculiar constellation of social, cultural, and political factors—and also dependent, no doubt, on a good deal of historical accident. For example, if England developed economically as a result of the plunder of India, why did not the plunder of the Americas have the same effects in Spain and Portugal? Anyone looking for visual disproof of the Leninist theory of imperialism in its historical components should pay a visit to the palace of Mafra, the summer residence of the Portuguese kings near Lisbon (various other locations on the Iberian peninsula may serve the same purpose). The Portuguese had available to them for plunder one of the largest and richest empires in human history—and plunder they did. But what did they do with the "surplus value" they extracted from colonies that spanned three continents overseas? They invested it in unproductive luxury at home, drowning their domestic economy in useless gold, to the point where today Portugal is one of the poorest countries in Europe (barely above the indicators of underdevelopment).

By way of contrast, the theoretically oriented tourist might visit some of the little bourgeois towns of Holland, the incredible productivity of which antedated Dutch plunder of the Indies and, the plunder having begun, was able to convert exploitation into even greater productivity. Conversely, it is far from clear that colonialism facilitated worthwhile plunder in all cases; probably it did so in a minority of cases. France, for example, acquired most of its colonial empire *after* its domestic development had reached an advanced stage of industrializing capitalism, and it is an open question whether that empire, taken as a whole, was more of an asset or a liability economically. The same, of course, was true of Germany. As to American capitalism, the theory lacks even superficial credibility for the period of original "take-off."

Apart from historical interpretations, there is the proposition that the *present* affluence of the West results from the exploitation of the Third World. This is an ideologically useful proposition for Third World countries, since it gives a moral legitimacy ("reparations" or the like) to their demands for aid or trade concessions. In terms of the economic facts, the proposition makes little sense. The advanced industrial societies do require certain raw materials available in the Third World, but (with the significant exception of oil) this dependence appears to be declining. A further decline may be expected as a result of technological innovations and the (partially politically motivated) search for alternative resources closer to home. Most detrimental to the Leninist theory, however, the Third World is not an expanding market for capital investment, relative to such expansion within the advanced industrial societies themselves. Thus, for American capital the importance of the Third World as a whole as an area of foreign capital investment is quite insignificant relative to Western Europe and Japan. Indeed, it may be argued that if the Third World in its entirety were closed to Western capital tomorrow, economic readjustments within the capitalist system could be achieved in a short time and without major dislocations. This rather effectively disposes of the third proposition, that imperialism is necessary because of the requirements of capitalist investment. Contrary to the Leninist theory, the affluence of the West is largely due to the superior productive system it has created, a system which by now is mainly autonomous. Also contrary to the theory, expansion of the system is largely internal—in the American case, internal actually meaning domestic; in the case of the international capitalist system, internal meaning within the countries of advanced industrial capitalism. There are, of course, predictions that this state of affairs cannot last, that all the internal markets will sooner or later be exhausted. There is no present way, however, by which the validity of these predictions could be established. So far the evidence very clearly runs in the opposite direction.

It may seem from the last few paragraphs that the intention here is to reject the Marxist critique of capitalist development *in toto*. This is not so. A doctor may diagnose that a patient has the measles, and at the time hold to a theory that measles are ultimately caused by the phases of the moon. It is quite possible to accept the particular diagnosis while rejecting the general theory. The Marxist diagnosis that capitalist development is bad for the Third World makes a lot of sense even if one is unable to subscribe to the full canon of Marxist-Leninist dogma.

Specifically, the way in which the aforementioned critique depicts the empirically accessible effects of capitalist penetration in the Third World today is largely supported by the evidence. The high social and political costs of this capitalism are also a matter of evidence rather than dogmatic faith. Polarization between rich and poor nations, polarization within the latter between relatively affluent factors and sectors of massive misery, growth in the major indicators of this misery (from downright starvation to pervasive unemployment), growing economic dependency of poor nations upon the rich (as reflected in mounting debts, deteriorating terms of trade and balances of payment, vulnerability to decisions made by governments and nongovernmental bodies in the rich nations)—all these are not inventions of Marxist ideologists, but empirical facts readily available to any objective observer. It is, therefore, of the greatest importance that the *no* to various theoretical affirmations of the Marxist critique be balanced by an emphatic *yes* to many of its specific empirical assessments.

Both economically and sociologically, a key test for the critique is the question of the "spread effect" of the benefits of development. There is little disagreement about the present facts. The disagreement rather concerns the projections of these facts into the future. How much of a time span is one to allow for the "spread effect" to become manifest? Advocates of the capitalist model are vague about this. "In the long run," they maintain, all these good things will happen. But as Keynes pointed out in another context, "in the long run" we'll all be dead. The evidence in this matter to date, in most parts of the Third World, supports the Marxist critique rather than the capitalist apologetic. It is difficult to see by what mechanisms this trend is to be reversed, unless one considers *political* mechanisms that are normally excluded by capitalist ideologists (such as, needless to say, the politics of revolution). Nor is there much to be said for the argument that Western history proves that such a reversal must take place. Western history has a number of specific characteristics (economic, social, political, *and* cultural), none of which are present in the same form in the Third World today. The fact that economic benefits came to be more equitably distributed and more widely available in England between, say, 1830 and 1930 thus offers no guarantee that a comparable process will take place in Indonesia or Brazil. To this may be added the fact that, because of the incomparably greater population increase today, these countries cannot afford the leisurely schedule of such a process.

Even more important, the argument from Western history is very abstract and formalistic, and ignores the concrete circumstances in which the Third World finds itself today. The most important circumstance is the very fact of dependency mentioned before. A crucial circumstance of original capitalist development in the West was that it was the *first* such case in history. Conversely, it is decisive for the Third World that it is *not* first, but that a fully developed and enormously powerful international capitalist system already exists—and that the Third World is painfully dependent upon this system. This makes for an entirely different situation, rendering the argument from Western history almost completely irrelevant.

The Latin American critique of "developmentalism," and its parallels in other parts of the Third World, is thus correct in what may be taken as its central proposition—that underdevelopment can only be understood if one understands the basic facts of dependency. Total identification of the two phenomena (*subdesarrollo* = *dependencia*) is clearly an exaggeration (though, within the Latin American context, an understandable one), but their central causal linkage is still valid. It follows that the political goal of independence is valid as well—without such liberation from the dependency syndrome it is difficult to envisage any real development at all. Whether the dependency syndrome is necessarily linked to the fact that the "metropolis" is capitalist, or whether the same syndrome would not be present if the "metropolis" were socialist, or whether the presently dependent countries would be better off if they adopted this or that socialist system—these are altogether different questions, to which it will be necessary to return later. These questions too, it should be stressed, do not in themselves invalidate the main thrust of the critique.

There is yet a deeper level than that of the Marxist critique, another level on which it is plausible to say *yes* to current attacks against the myth of growth. Again, man does *not* live by bread alone. It is this truth which finally invalidates the view that an endless accumulation of the "cargos" of modernity is tantamount to man's salvation. By the same token, it is plausible to say *yes* not only to the critique of capitalist "developmentalism," but also to the extended critique of Soviet development strategy, and to say *no* to the "materialism" of both.

In this connection there should be at least brief mention of another notion that has come to be closely associated with the aforementioned critical attitudes. That is the notion of *participation*. In political usage the term has had quite different meanings, both in the West and in the Third World, and some of these meanings (as in the New Left concept of "participatory democracy") are of no interest here. In the context of the aforementioned critique, however, the meaning is simple: Development is not what the economic and other experts proclaim it to be, no matter how elegant their language. Development is not something to be decided by experts, simply because there are no experts on the desirable goals of human life. Development is the desirable course to be taken by human beings in a particular situation. As far as possible, therefore, they ought to participate in the fundamental choices to be made, choices that hinge not on technical expertise but on moral judgments.

This notion of participation follows logically from the understanding that, unlike economic growth and modernization, development is at root a moral category. As such, morally neutral techniques (be they those of economics or of any other scientific discipline) can claim no jurisdiction on the ends of development, and jurisdiction on the means only to the extent that strictly technical questions arise. Unless one posits experts in the area of moral judgment (and it should be emphasized that, unlike Western advocates of "participatory democracy," many traditional people would do just that), all human beings have equal access to this area by way of their conscience. In any case (no matter whether one accepts such a Western, "Protestant," view, or whether one believes that moral choices should be determined by the authority of traditions), it is clear that the bureaucrats, businessmen, and intellectuals who are the "carriers" of the growth mystique are *not* experts in morality. In this sense at least, the notion of participation is "antielitist": It may, especially in traditional terms, acknowledge other elites, but it will inevitably debunk the moral pretensions of the technocratic elites. Participation, in this context, does not imply any particular political form of expression, and certainly does not imply representative democracy in a Western style.

To call for participation is to render "cognitive respect" to all those who cannot claim the status of experts. As will be elaborated later, such "cognitive respect" is not an arbitrary or even eccentric ideological decision. It is based on the understanding that every human being is *in possession* of a world of his own, and that nobody can interpret this world better (or more "expertly") than he can himself. If one takes with seriousness the perceptions of the nonexperts, one may enlarge the critique of capitalist development (and indeed of modernization in any form) by an important additional dimension by looking at what might be called the "cultural costs" (perhaps even "religious costs") of capitalism. The capitalist ideal of development, by its very nature, fosters individualism and individual competition. However a Westerner might welcome these values, it is crucial to understand that for the great majority of people in other traditions they constitute a threat rather than a promise—or, minimally, a threat *as well as* a promise. The structures of capitalist development destroy the collectivities of traditional culture. Much of the time, what is substituted is a mass of anomic individuals. In any critique of capitalist models that renders "cognitive respect" to the perceptions coming out of traditional non-Western cultures, this fact will weigh heavily. It does so weigh in the "socialisms" of the Third World, often in direct contradiction to the Marxist rhetoric being employed.

It is possible, therefore, to accept substantial portions of the Marxist theoretical critique of capitalist development, without accepting Marxist theory *in toto*. The same holds for Marxist prescriptions for policy. There will be occasion later to discuss the myth of revolution and the socialist models of development emerging from it. However, one implication may now be drawn from the foregoing "critique of the critique": Whether revolution or socialism are or are not desirable in particular situations, they will be so for reasons other than those stated dogmatically in Marxist theory.

It has been argued that the critique of growth, especially as it deals with capitalist models of development, has far-reaching validity. Does this imply an outright rejection of capitalism?

First, an obvious but often neglected point must be made: The question poses itself in different terms in Western countries and in the Third World. A repudiation of capitalism in the Third World does not necessarily imply a similar repudiation in the West. Conversely, an endorsement of capitalism in the West does not in itself mean such an endorsement for the Third World. The necessity for linking the two areas only arises out of Marxist theory, and will thus have no force for anyone not fully persuaded of the latter's claims.

Furthermore, opposition to capitalism is very different in these two parts of the world. In the West, by and large, capitalism *has* been delivering the "cargo." To be sure, there are zones of misery in Western countries, and by abstract ethical standards it is possible to question the equity of distribution in these countries. The fact remains that Western industrial capitalism has produced a better life, materially, for larger numbers of people than any previous or contemporary socioeconomic system in human history. Anticapitalism in the West has been largely ideological. In the working classes of a number of West European countries (notably France and Italy), anticapitalist rhetoric has continued to be employed by political parties and labor movements whose de facto interests are by now more reformist than revolutionary. The most strident anticapitalist rhetoric in recent years has come from upper middle class intellectuals, whose real complaints probably have more to do with the discontents of industrial civilization as such (and their place in it) than with the specific characteristics of its capitalist versions. In the working classes it is an anti-capitalism of graduated and often quite moderate vested interests, in the upper middle class an expression of cultural malaise (and possibly of resentment). To the extent that Western capitalism has fulfilled its material promises, opposition to it often has a strangely "spiritual" quality, and ipso facto a markedly irrational component.

By contrast, capitalism in the Third World has generally *not* been delivering the "cargo," at least not for most people. Consequently, the opposition to capitalism has been capable of enlisting broad popular support, including that of the lower and lowest classes. This has been an anticapitalism of desperation. It may be said that, even in Marxist terms, the relationship between ideology and its underlying "contradictions" has been inverse in the two areas. In the West, the ideology has commonly "invented" the discontents: Upon being told that they are "alienated," some people dutifully experience themselves in this condition. In the Third World such propaganda is largely unnecessary. Because of the amply visible and objective circumstances of their lives, people are desperate long before any propaganda reaches them. An ideology that attacks these circumstances can then express a consciousness that is fully grounded in everyday experience.

This fundamental difference leads to different prognoses for the two areas. It is likely that capitalism, with whatever modifications, will continue to be the paramount form of socioeconomic organization in the West, and certainly in the United States. It is noteworthy in this connection that even Sweden, often cited as the most far-reaching Western "path to socialism," has retained basically capitalist forms of *economic* organization, even as its government has sought to transform various sectors of social life in "socialist" terms. Citing Sweden, of course, immediately raises the question of *what kind* of capitalism is to be prognosticated. This is not the place for such speculation, though the point may be made that there is already no Western country (emphatically not the United States) in which capitalism exists in its pristine, politically unmodified forms. Western capitalism is by no means a monolithic, unalterable phenomenon. Neither, for that matter, is the socialism of the Soviet orbit. If the market is the key category of capitalism and public planning that of socialism, then there have been substantial "convergences" between the two systems in advanced industrial societies. Western capitalism has been greatly modified in a "socialist" sense by the interventions of government. Conversely, especially in recent years, Soviet-style socialism has been modified in a "capitalist" direction by the introduction of market mechanisms to limit the range of centralized planning. Again, this is not the place to speculate as to the degree of "convergence" that is likely in the future.

If one may prognosticate the continued dominance of capitalism, with whatever modifications, in the West, no such prognostication may be made with regard to the Third World. The situation in most Third World countries is highly volatile and ipso facto hard to predict. Nevertheless, it seems likely that a number of these countries will move in a socialist rather than capitalist direction, because socialism continues to activate profound, even mythic, aspirations for community and solidarity, aspirations that are likely to intensify under the pressures of modernization. Capitalism has been singularly unsuccessful in coping with this category of human needs. But mythic aspirations aside, many of these countries are likely to confront an increasingly desperate situation in which socialism will seem to be the only credible program. Even if capitalism might work "in the long run," its short-run social tensions and pressures are likely to become increasingly intolerable in many of these countries. To contain these "contradictions," the prospect is for oppressive political regimes devoid of popular support. While one should never underestimate the durability of unscrupulous oppression, the chances for revolution are great in such situations. Almost invariably, such revolutions will raise the banner of socialism, particularly in countries where capitalist penetration has been strong, as in Latin America. One may quote here a statement by the well-known Mexican churchman Sergio Méndez Arcéo, Bishop of Cuernavaca, who until recently maintained that Christians must not commit themselves to any one social or political program. Upon returning from a conference of "Christians for socialism" in Chile, Méndez Arcéo gave his own endorsement of socialism with these words: *No hay otra salida*—"There is no other solution." This is a conclusion that is likely to spread, and not only in Latin America.

Again, though, the question is *what kind* of socialism it will be. Even in Latin America there is by now a considerable variety of available models, and it would be folly to fail to see the differences among them. In view of all this, apart from the failings of theory, there are very good pragmatic reasons for avoiding doctrinaire positions on either capitalism or socialism. Both are likely to survive in different parts of the world, and both are likely to take significantly different forms.

Socialism is no panacea. No one has been able to improve on H. L. Mencken's classical statement on this subject: "To believe that Russia has got rid of the evils of capitalism takes a special kind of mind. It is the same kind that believes that a Holy Roller has got rid of sin."[12] The socialisms existing today under conditions of advanced industrialism, in the Soviet Union and Eastern Europe, are mostly tempting for already committed believers. But the arguments for capitalism are not exhausted by invidious comparisons. Especially in view of the "left mood" that is currently fashionable among Western intellectuals, it is worthwhile to reiterate some of the positive arguments that have long been made in favor of capitalism.

One important point in favor of capitalism is its productivity. Empirically (and regardless of whether one likes this or not, on ethical grounds), industrial capitalism, based on competition for profit, has brought forth the most awe-inspiringly productive economic machine ever conceived. The contemporary corporation, in particular, is not only an impressive machine for profit making, but is at least equally impressive in terms of its capacity to produce both goods and services. If there is any spurious argument on the left today, it is the argument that capitalism is wasteful. Perhaps this is so on the basis of some a priori moral judgments, but certainly not in terms of economic productivity. Indeed, if wastefulness applies anywhere, it is to the socialist economies of the Soviet orbit, whose malfunctions have forced precisely the aforementioned modifications by way of market mechanisms and even profit motives. Acknowledgment of the productive superiority of Western capitalism is nicely expressed in a recent Soviet joke, one of the "Radio Erivan" series, in which questions are asked of a fictitious radio station in Soviet Armenia. Question to Radio Erivan: "Is it possible for an advanced industrial society to be truly socialist?" Radio Erivan replies: "In principle, yes. But it is not very good for the industry." If, in a particular situation, the imperative to produce is deemed primary (and that decision, of course, is political and moral, not economic), it is hard to find a better alternative to capitalist modes of production.

Another point in favor of capitalism is its capacity, under favorable conditions, to lead to a high degree of prosperity for nearly all levels of the population. Nowhere has socialism been able to match this feat, not even where conditions have been very favorable (as, for example, in Eastern Germany or in Czechoslovakia). It should be stressed that degrees of prosperity have no necessary relation to the state of equality. Thus there has been little change in recent decades in Western societies (including the United States) in the *distribution* of economic benefits. Income distribution, for instance, has remained fairly constant, with both the highest and the lowest income groups retaining pretty much the same portions of the total economic pudding. However, while the benefits of the lower groups have not changed appreciably relative to the higher groups, they have improved steadily in absolute terms. Put simply, people have not become more equal, but, on all levels, they have become increasingly well-off. In this, as already pointed out, the situation is quite different in the Third World.[13]

A third point in favor of capitalism (and perhaps most important in the present context) is its linkage with individual freedom. To be sure, this has not been without its price. As Karl Polanyi and others have pointed out, the major price was that of the old solidarities. Capitalism destroyed or gravely weakened the traditional structures of community which had sheltered the individual from both economic and psychological isolation. In sociological terms, the main cost of capitalist freedom has been anomie. This, indeed, was the major burden of conservative critiques of capitalism long before the socialist attack made its appearance. Still, there has been an important historical connection between the economic market and political democracy—that is, between economic and political choices. Capitalism, by its innermost economic logic, has freed the individual from collective restraints and opened up large new areas for individual options. To a great extent this is still true today. Capitalism posits individual achievement and competition as against collective ascription and allocation. In this important regard, socialism, with its ascriptive and allocative thrust, is much closer to the collectivism of most traditional cultures than is modern capitalism.[14]

Similarly, capitalism posits an "agonistic" ideal of society, in which individuals and groups struggle with each other for economic success and social status. If you will, capitalism posits an "adversary model." By contrast, both socialism and most premodern traditions posit an ideal of society in which harmony prevails, a harmony preestablished by the political order. Even leaving aside the more elevated questions of individualism and freedom, the empirical consequence of this is that capitalism has a strong *pluralistic* thrust, while socialism (even in its most anti-totalitarian versions) has a built-in tendency to contain plurality and especially to "harmonize" conflicts. Minimally, capitalism has a "private sector" not directly under the aegis of the political order, while it is of the very nature of socialism to incorporate that sector within the political order.

The ultimate questions are those of value. Is productivity a viable goal? If so, for how long and at what noneconomic costs? Is the sheer quantity of economic benefits available to all more or less important than the manner in which these benefits are distributed? In other words, is general affluence more important than relative equality? And most importantly, which values are given moral priority: Individual freedom or collective security? Pluralism or community? Enterprise or harmony?

There are no easy ways to answer these questions, and no ways at all of doing so on the basis of social-scientific evidence. The ultimate desirability of either capitalism or socialism cannot be scientifically "proven." It one comes out on one side of the above value options (especially the last three sets of paired options), then a bias in favor of capitalist models of development is both morally and intellectually credible—contrary to what is currently fashionable among Western intellectuals. In that case, *other things being equal*, one might prefer such models to succeed as against socialist ones, even in the Third World. One might also hope then that the evils of capitalist development can be remedied this side of the abolition of capitalism.

However, other things are *not* equal in the Third World. There is a certain appeal to taking positions that are contrary to current fashions (*épater les gauchistes* can be a rewarding pastime—they are so easily shocked!), but intellectual responsibility forbids taking this course. The hope for a morally and humanely acceptable capitalism in much of the Third World appears tenuous today. Therefore, even those with a value commitment to capitalism, and/or a vested interest in its survival, would do well to forego the rhetoric of the "Free World" in the style of the 1950s. They will be better advised to examine the socialist options in an open and nondoctrinaire manner.

NOTES

1. The notes for this chapter are not designed to provide full references in accordance with scholarly conventions. Their main purpose is to indicate to the reader where he might go to pursue some arguments that could only be made here very briefly. The present position on the definition of terms was previously taken in Peter Berger, Brigitte Berger, and Hansfried Kellner, *The Homeless Mind—Modernization and Consciousness* (New York: Random House, 1973), pp. 3 ff. For a good introduction to the economic problematic of growth, the reader may consult Robert Heilbroner, *The Great Ascent* (New York: Harper & Row, 1963). For a basic and more technical presentation of the same, see Simon Kuznets, *Modern Economic Growth* (New Haven: Yale University Press, 1966). On definitions of modernization and development outside the field of economics, see C. E. Black, *The Dynamics of Modernization* (New York: Harper & Row, 1966); Myron Weiner, ed., *Modernization* (New York: Basic Books, 1966); Marion Levy, *Modernization—Latecomers and Survivors* (New York: Basic Books, 1972).

2. For a discussion of some of these issues, see A. N. Agarwala and S. P. Singh, eds., *The Economics of Underdevelopment* (New York: Oxford University Press, 1963).

3. See David McClelland, *The Achieving Society* (Princeton: Van Nostrand, 1961); Everett Hagen, *On the Theory of Social Change* (Homewood, Ill.: Dorsey, 1962).

4. See S. N. Eisenstadt, ed., *The Protestant Ethic and Modernization* (New York: Basic Books, 1968).

5. See Gayl Ness, ed., *The Sociology of Economic Development* (New York: Harper & Row, 1970); Jason Finkle and Richard Gable, eds., *Political Development and Social Change* (New York: Wiley, 1966).

6. For a strong representative of the planning position, see Gunnar Myrdal, *The Challenge of World Poverty* (New York: Pantheon, 1970). For the other side, see P. T. Bauer, *Dissent on Development* (Cambridge, Mass.: Harvard University Press, 1972).

7. W. W. Rostow, *The Stages of Economic Growth* (Cambridge: Cambridge University Press, 1965), p. 165. It is noteworthy that in 1959, when this was written, Latin America was taken for granted as a (presumably non-problematic) part of the "Free World"!

8. See Charles Wilber, *The Soviet Model and Underdeveloped Countries* (Chapel Hill: University of North Carolina Press, 1969).

9. See E. J. Mishan, *The Costs of Economic Growth* (New York: Praeger, 1966).

10. See Peter Passell and Leonard Ross, *The Retreat from Riches* (New York: Viking, 1973).

11. For an overview of this position, see Robert Rhodes, ed., *Imperialism and Underdevelopment* (New York: Monthly Review Press, 1970). For its economic aspects, see Paul Baran, *The Political Economy of Growth* (New

York: Monthly Review Press, 1957), which is a basic text for recent formulations of the Marxist theory of imperialism. Important applications of this approach to specific regions are Andre Gunder Frank's to Latin America (see his *Capitalism and Underdevelopment in Latin America,* New York: Monthly Review Press, 1967) and Samir Amin's to Africa (to date available only in French). The best currently available critique of the Marxist theory is a recent book by Benjamin Cohen, *The Question of Imperialism* (New York: Basic Books, 1973). Most of the sociological analyses coming out of similar positions are not presently available in English, notably the works of Pablo González Casanova (Mexico) and Fernando Henrique Cardoso (Brazil). For an idea of this type of analysis, see James Petras and Maurice Zeitlin, eds., *Latin America—Reform or Revolution?* (Greenwich, Conn.: Fawcett, 1968).

12. Alistair Cooke, ed., *The Vintage Mencken* (New York: Vintage, 1956), p. 233.

13. It is interesting in this connection that the income distribution in Eastern Europe and the Soviet Union is similar to that of Western societies to an embarassing degree—embarassing, that is, for Soviet ideology. The decisive differences in this matter, it seems, are not between East and West, but between North and South—not between socialist and capitalist societies, but between advanced industrial societies of either type and the Third World.

14. The classical formulation of these arguments has been made in the works of Georg Simmel, F. A. Hayek, and, more recently, Milton Friedman.

INTERLUDE

TABLEAU IN GARBAGE—
CHILD, WITH VULTURES

S ALVADOR: First city founded by the Portuguese in Brazil, in 1549. Salvador: Capital of the state of Bahia, in the northeast, with a population of about a million. Brazilians usually call it Bahia, after the bay along which it stretches—Bahia de Todos os Santos, "Bay of all the Saints." The city is also called "the heart of Brazil." More than any other it has produced poetry, music, and that painfully pleasurable nostalgia known as *saudade*.

On the surface the old and the new appear to coexit harmoniously in Salvador. The colonial city climbs up a mountainside, oddly (or rather, not so oddly) reminiscent of Lisbon. A tropical Lisbon, invaded by blacks, the hot African rhythms of the *samba* superimposed upon the gentle melancholy of the *fado*. Afro-Lusitania—a splash of colors, human and otherwise, a pervasive sensuality, languor that contains potential violence. One may walk down narrow, twisting alleys toward the harbor. In the hot sun, bells ring from the steeples of ornately baroque churches. Late in the evening, fountains splash in quiet squares where time seems to have stood still for at least two hundred years. None of this, on the surface, seems swallowed up by the bustling activity of the new. There are all the signs of the "Brazilian miracle," including government posters that proclaim it as the economic wonder of the century: "A task for all of us—a country that transforms and constructs itself." There are the steel-and-glass office buildings, sprawling industrial parks, and traffic jams. As usual in Brazil, all the economic growth indicators point upward. "Are Bahians really different?," asks an article in an illustrated magazine, part of a series entitled "The New Northeast." (Yes, they are, the article suggests in a rather sparse text squeezed between pictures of luxuriously endowed beach beauties. Like all Brazilians today, they are busy building a modern society, yet they have retained the old graces. All the beach beauties, incidentally, are white.)

In addition to the old graces, Salvador also possesses one of the largest slums in Latin America. Known as the Alagados, it covers about two square miles along the bay and is inhabited by about one hundred thousand people. Except for its size, and the physical fact that part of it consists of huts erected on stilts in the water, it looks like a typical *favela* or squatters' settlement. There are some solid constructions, but most of the houses are "auto-constructed" with wood, tin, and other flimsy materials. An important place in the Alagados is occupied by garbage. Part of the area is the main garbage dump of the city of Salvador. The garbage is dumped into the bay, creating new landfill. Since this is new land, belonging to nobody, it is ideal for squatters. New huts are built on top of the landfill. Thus the garbage is welcomed by the inhabitants of the Alagados, for this reason as well as because all sorts of usable and vendable objects can be retrieved from it. Indeed, the garbage is an important economic as well as ecological factor for the community. Local politicians promise the inhabitants more and better garbage in exchange for their votes. As the garbage trucks arrive in the dumping zone, they are met by crowds of people, including large numbers of children, ready to pounce upon the contents. The inscription on the trucks reads "A developed people is a clean people."

Statistical data on a community such as this are notoriously unreliable. Such data as exist tell a typical story of misery. Unemployment is high, and has been increasing. The lines between unemployment and underemployment are hard to draw: Is a man working a few hours a week as a relief elevator operator employed, unemployed, or underemployed? The employment that exists is mostly in the lowest-paid categories of unskilled labor. The minimum monthly salary in the state of Bahia (in 1973) is two hundred forty cruzeiros—about forty dollars. For most people in the Alagados, the legal minimum is in fact the maximum salary; many earn below that. A kilogram of cheap meat (in 1973) costs eight cruzeiros. As part of its campaign to control inflation, the government has a very tight wage policy. Wage increases are permitted only to reflect cost-of-living increases. Local people dispute government figures on what the latter have in fact amounted to. Perhaps the government figures are computed on a national basis, or perhaps they include indicators that are irrelevant to the inhabitants of the Alagados. The most relevant inflation locally is that in food prices, and these, it appears, have increased far beyond the government figures. The result is simple: The real income of large numbers of people in the area has actually declined.

Nutrition is sparse and unhealthy. The people eat a lot of starch, and in consequence they look well-nourished. This appearance is deceptive. Medical services are inadequate. Infant mortality is high. A local pediatrician says that not a week goes by in which he does not have a case of death that can, quite simply, be diagnosed as death by starvation. In the hottest period of the year many babies die of dehydration, being unable to retain the bad water in the area.

The first impression of any *favela* like this one is of chaos. At least in the Alagados, this would be a false impression. In fact, the community is amazingly well-organized—from within itself, not by outside agencies. There are sixteen neighborhood associations, known as *sociedades*, which take care of internal problems and also serve as the community's representatives in dealing with the outside (including government). Except for one small area in which a tough element has settled, crime in the community is minimal. Only six policemen are assigned to the Alagados.

Government policy toward the Alagados appears to have been shifting. The original intention apparently was to relocate the entire population elsewhere. At least according to the community's version, this intention was abandoned because of the determined resistance of the *sociedades*. Yet, after a good deal of international publicity, something had to be done. The official policy now is to rehabilitate the area with the population remaining in the same location. Following a decree of the federal government, the National Housing Bank (itself an agency of the federal government with jurisdiction over the bulk of "urban renewal" programs throughout the country) launched an extensive study of the area. This study is to be the basis of future government action.

The headquarters for the study is in a converted residential building. There are files full of papers, charts, maps, and photographs (even aerial ones). A spokesman for the project explains everything in great detail. There is a sense of accomplishment, though it is emphasized that so far no action has been taken; indeed, those undertaking the study have no responsibility for any implementing actions. The spokesman is very frank about the problems of the area, yet one must wonder about this frankness when one compares his statements with other sources of information. The study purports to have statistics on ownership of durable consumer goods, and its computers have concluded that, given these figures, income must be underreported in the area. It is true that one notices a surprising number of television antennas in the community. Is it possible that people whose children are starving invest in television sets? Or are these different groups? The spokesman shows glossy photographs taken in the community, some showing people engaged in various leisure-time activities. "They don't look hungry, do they?," he asks. A little later he comments, "You see poverty in this area, but not misery. People are quite happy."

On the next day the American visitor is taken on a field trip to the Alagados. He goes in an official car, with three women connected with the study. Latin Americans always exhibit friendly curiosity about one's family status. "Are you married?," "How many children?," "How old are they?," and so on. This ritual is gone through before the trip begins. One of the women, who serves as the main guide, admits to one daughter. The woman is the wife of a professional; as with her two friends, one obtains the impression that this sort of "social work" is a socially acceptable form of employment for middle-class housewives. "Let me show you a picture of my daughter," she says, then stops herself: "Oh, I'm so sorry—I don't think I have a picture here." All the way out to the Alagados, and occasionally during the time spent there, the three women keep chattering away on common acquaintances, their illnesses and accidents, and similar topics. This chatter is sometimes punctuated by observations such as "This is quite depressing, isn't it?," or "How can these people live like this?"

The high point, literally, of the trip is a walk up a hill, from which one can see most of the area. Directly underneath the hill is a new landfill of garbage. In the tropical heat, the smell is trenchant. A number of big, black vultures are circling over the garbage, occasionally swooping down into it. A little boy, dressed only in a pair of short pants, runs back and forth on the landfill. He is perhaps three or four years old. He has a big hat which he uses to chase the vultures. The women exclaim: "Look at the boy with his big hat!," "How cute!," "Look, he is chasing the vultures!" The smell is very bad indeed, and the visitor lights a cigarette. The woman who serves as the main guide opens her handbag to look for her own cigarettes, then says excitedly: "Oh, I have a picture of my daughter after all. Here—this is my daughter." She shows a plastic foldout with three photographs of a little girl, about seven years old. All the photographs appear to have been taken at a birthday party or similar event, with other children crowding around. The girl is wearing a white party dress.

What is an "acceptable" model of development?

Chapter III

⟨⟨⟨⟨⟨⟩⟩⟩⟩⟩

AGAINST SOCIALISM? CRITIQUE OF REVOLUTION

REVOLUTION is a word with emotionally potent promise. The word provokes a vision of salvation after an act of purifying violence. It is, in other words, a vision similar to that of war, except for the detail that the imagined actors are, so to speak, out of uniform.

This is hardly the place to discuss the questions (recently raised by Konrad Lorenz and others) as to whether lethal violence is a biologically built-in human trait, and whether murderous fantasy normally carries the aforementioned emotional freight. Whatever may be the answers to these questions, it appears that the fascination with revolutionary violence has some peculiar characteristics. If war is defined as the use of "official" violence between societies, and revolution as the overthrow of a societal order by way of "unofficial" violence, then revolutionary fantasies relate to militarism as pornography relates to the public morality. Possibly this accounts for the peculiar satisfactions that these fantasies seem capable of providing.

Revolution is not a vision with equal contents or force in all parts of the world. Once more it is important to distinguish between the Third World and the advanced industrial societies, as was done previously in the discussion of the appeal of socialist models. In the Third World today revolutionary rhetoric commonly expresses desperation about conditions that, by any reasonable standard, can be described as humanly

71

intolerable. In the West, by contrast, revolutionary rhetoric reflects discontents of a much more subtle and thus less readily comprehensible kind. It is not difficult to understand that a landless peasant in some Asian country, whose life expectancy is forty, whose children are starving, and whose realistic chances of improving his condition are close to nil, will want to go out and kill somebody. It is a little harder to understand the same ambition in a tenured university professor in America, and even harder to grasp the assertion that the professor and the peasant share a common state of oppression. Be this as it may, the one part of the word in which virtually nobody seems to be turned on by revolution talk is the orbit of Soviet power. That is not difficult to understand at all: In these societies the rhetoric of revolution has for decades been part and parcel of what Zbigniew Brzezinski has nicely called "the bureaucratization of boredom," thus making it impossible for anyone to get a high from the rhetoric.

Intellectuals have always had the propensity to endow their libidinal emotions with philosophical significance, in sex as in politics, and in both areas one often suspects that the need for philosophy arises from an unfortunate combination of strong ambitions and weak capabilities. The writings of Frantz Fanon, among others, have provided philosophical justification for the dreams of violence of many individuals whose empirical lives take place in settings of pacific tranquillity. It is safe to assume, in most cases, that the dreams antedated the discovery of the justification. Again, this is not the place to discuss why intellectuals are particularly susceptible to revolutionary visions, as they are to socialist ideologies. In all likelihood both susceptibilities may be explained by the discrepancy between what intellectuals think they have to offer and what society (at any rate "bourgeois society") is prepared to offer them by way of power. Whatever the explanation, intellectuals have a dangerous facility to imagine themselves occupying the seats of power in the wake of, so to speak, the revolution of their choice. With revolutionaries as with generals, one ought to beware of those who manage to philosophize about their lust for battle; in this connection, incidentally, Fanon could be described as the Clausewitz of revolution.[1]

Revolution, like war, involves the killing of human beings. The most elementary moral sense, therefore, suggests a strongly "repressive" attitude toward the libidinal components in both cases. It is all the more important to stress that rejection of the libidinal intoxication with violence is *not* necessarily tantamount to a rejection of violence as such. It is one thing to condemn the glorification of war by militaristic ideologists, and quite another to be a pacifist. Similarly, one may understand the psychopathology of much revolution talk and still not take an antirevolutionary stance in every given political situation. The foregoing has the character of a cautionary note, and is by no means intended to rule out the revolutionary option a priori.

Revolution in itself is not linked to any particular political program. There have been revolutions of the "right" as well as revolutions of the "left," and discussions about the "genuineness" of this or that revolution are typically exercises in quasi theology that only make sense to true believers. Thus both Italian and German fascism originated in revolutionary movements, the Spanish Falange struggled to power in what may be described as a traditionalistic revolution, and the Third World has experienced a long series of nationalist revolutions that are often difficult to designate as either "left" or "right." Today, however, people speaking about revolution usually (though not exclusively) have in mind revolutions of the "left." That is, the revolutionary rhetoric tends to be anticapitalist and the political programs in view tend toward socialism. This is clearly the case in most of the Third World (though it is noteworthy that regimes that are clearly capitalist in policy have also arrogated to themselves the term and the mystique of "revolutions," as in Brazil or South Vietnam). By and large, then, advocacy of revolution implies a socialist vision of the future. The great alternatives in the Third World are commonly posed as development through capitalist growth or liberation through revolutionary socialism. Enough has been said previously about the different mythic undertones of the two goals of development and liberation. The important political fact today is that the latter goal is charged with redemptive expectations that are generally absent in the context of capitalist development policy.

Precisely because of these "religious" themes it is important to be clear about what one means by socialism (leaving to rival Marxist camps the dreary business of denying each other the claim of being "genuinely" socialist). The conventional definition of socialism has been of a system in which the basic means of production are under public ownership and administration. Putting the same thing negatively, socialism has been defined as a system in which the basic means of production are not in the hands of private enterprise. This definition has been used by both

73

adherents and opponents of socialism, by Marxists and non-Marxists, and has the great advantage of simplicity. The advantage is not diminished by the fact that, within this definition, one may distinguish a variety of different versions, and that there are cases in which one may question whether they are to be subsumed under the category as defined. Similar problems of classification pertain to any definition of capitalism, and indeed to any other social phenomenon that one may wish to delineate.

The interest here is in the critique of "left" models of development, with "left" implying the alternative political goal of liberation through revolutionary socialism. Needless to say, this alternative is by no means unified. There are the massive Soviet and Chinese models, with a considerable diversity of other cases ranging (at least at the time of writing) from Tanzania to the "people's democracies" of Eastern Europe (whose systems are by no means identical with that of the Soviet Union or, for that matter, with each other), from Peru to North Vietnam, from Cuba to Yugoslavia. As in the previous discussion of capitalist models, it would be quixotic to attempt here a detailed analysis of all these cases. Rather, the interest will be in a critique that pertains to the socialist alternative on a broad level of generality.

The alternative, of course, is generally coupled with a critique of capitalism, as discussed in the previous chapter. The purpose now is not to reiterate this discussion, but to look at the proffered solution. One point to notice first is that this solution is usually presented as the only possible one. For example, this is how it is put by Andre Gunder Frank (after he rejects the position of Brazilian economist Helio Jaguaribe, who raises the possibility of "autonomy" for Third World countries in distinction from both the present state of dependency as well as the revolutionary solution): "The Latin American lumpenbourgeoisie can only resort to military strength to impose its 'alternative of autonomy' and 'development strategy,' both of which were devised by the ideologists of individual autonomy and institutional dependence. As they modernize Latin America's dependence by means of reforms within their alliance for the progress of imperialism, the contradictions of lumpendevelopment in Latin America are deepened and can only be resolved by the people—with *the only true development strategy: armed revolution and the construction of socialism.*"[2]

The strident style of this formulation is as typical as its doctrinaire claim to exclusiveness. It is easy to be irritated by these qualities, thus

74

making it all the more important to undertake the critique of this position without succumbing to the temptation of being equally combative. Clarity of perception is rarely arrived at in a stance of combativeness. The critique of the socialist alternative must be able to make the same kind of differentiations that are essential for a critique of capitalism. The critique must also ask the same basic questions—that is, *Who benefits?* and *Who decides?* In other words, here too there must be a sober assessment of costs.

In terms of such a critique, the two components of the alternative can be separated. There is a question of the costs of revolution, and another question of the costs of socialism. In creedal statements such as the one quoted above, of course, the two are inextricably linked. It also seems likely that in much of the Third World the only possibility of establishing socialism is by way of revolutionary upheaval. Nevertheless, it remains useful for analytic purposes to consider the two components separately.

With few exceptions, revolutions demand a high toll in human suffering. Revolutionary warfare, certainly in this century, has been marked by atrocities and a general brutality, on both sides of any particular conflict, that easily match any achievements in this regard by those who wage "conventional" war. Indiscriminate bombing and shelling of civilian populations, massive destruction of the material basis for life of large numbers of people, and the "generation" of refugees are as characteristic of revolutionary wars as of other types of warfare. But revolutionary warfare produces peculiar horrors of its own, all connected with the strategy of terrorism of the revolutionaries and the (seemingly inevitable) counterterror of their opponents. Revolutionary movements almost everywhere have deliberately sought to create chaos by violently disrupting the ordinary business of social life, a strategy that inevitably entails the killing and maiming of large numbers of innocent bystanders. Counterrevolutionary forces have regularly responded by massacres of equal nondiscrimination. The counterrevolutionaries commonly have an advantage in terms of firepower, so that their massacres have tended to be the larger ones. The revolutionaries have generally tried to offset this advantage by the ferocity of their own terror.

Revolutionary warfare (contrary to the ideology of revolutionary intellectuals) is very largely *not* a matter of "winning the hearts and minds of the people," but rather a competition as to which side can make more people afraid of it. This "balance of terror" (which, in cases of successful revolutions, eventually shifts to the side of the revolutionaries) includes the particular horrors of assassination and counterassassination, the taking and the killing of hostages, brutal reprisals against the families of political opponents, and systematic torture of prisoners. On the crest of the "left mood" of the late 1960s, and in the context of the protest against the American-sponsored counterrevolution in Indochina, these horrors have generally been highlighted in the West when perpetrated by the counterrevolutionary forces. It is important to stress (and was, or would have been, equally important to stress in the late 1960s) that precisely the same horrors are habitually practiced by revolutionary movements, limited only by the means available to the latter rather than by any humanitarian scruples. Indeed, both revolutionary tactics and the doctrine of so-called "counterinsurgency" have one fundamental proposition in common—for all practical purposes, there are no innocent bystanders.

In view of all this, there can be no question of the validity of asking whether the human costs of revolution are either necessary to the achievement of the revolutionaries' goals, and/or morally justified in terms of the putative benefits achieved by a successful revolutionary regime. The great moral merit of the peace movement of the late 1960s was its vigorous opposition to the human horrors committed by the United States and its allies in Indochina. The equally great moral blemish was its general failure to denounce or even to acknowledge any horrors brought on by the other side. In this capacity for selective outrage the opponents of the American war in Indochina were fully equal to its apologists. Dead Vietnamese children were always brought up in the argument—if the *other* side was responsible for their death. One of the enduring lessons of this period should be (and, alas, is most unlikely to be) the insight that the corruption of moral vision knows no political boundaries.

However important these questions are, they must be differentiated from the critique of socialist models as such. If socialist systems have been erected at the price of great human suffering, so have capitalist systems. Not only revolutions cause suffering and death; the status quo can also kill, often by hunger rather than by bullets. The longer the historical time span one considers in this connection, the clearer is this point. The construction of capitalism in Europe, during the period aptly called "the great transformation" by Karl Polanyi, was marked by massive brutality, including the brutal application of physical violence. Friedrich Engels' classical work, *The Condition of the Working Class in England* (written in the 1840s), is still most useful in making this point. In other words, one cannot dismiss the question of the socialist alternative by pointing out (however truthfully) that socialist revolutionaries have been murderers.

In asking about the human costs of revolution, it is also important to distinguish between those costs resulting from revolutionary warfare and those exacted by a revolutionary regime that has attained power. Both in terms of practical necessity and of possible moral justification, there is a great difference between acts of terror undertaken against armed (and possibly equally terroristic) opponents, and terror imposed on opponents who have been disarmed and are fully under the control of a revolutionary regime. This distinction is at the basis of whatever progress has been made in recent centuries in the international law of war. It applies equally, and for exactly the same reasons, to the warfare of revolutionary movements (although this application has not yet been elaborated juridically).

A critique of revolution per se, as distinguished from a critique of the alternative of revolutionary socialism as a model of development, would have to deal extensively with these matters. There will be occasion later to return to some of them. The immediate interest, however, is different. It is the critique of established models of socialism, rather than of the revolutions that established them. Therefore, the focus will have to be on the costs of socialism rather than on the costs of revolution.[3]

To reiterate: In the Third World today the two great alternatives appear to be development through capitalist growth or through the establishment of socialist regimes. Both alternatives have been subjected to critical analysis. What are the key features of a critique of the second alternative?[4]

There is, first, the question of what may be called the internal economic costs of socialist models. Essentially, this revolves around the ability of these models to deliver the promised "cargo."

The case of the Soviet Union is very important with regard to this question. Soviet propaganda in the Third World, as elsewhere, rests largely on the claim that the Soviet model of socialism has demonstrated its capacity to move a large country out of underdevelopment into the ranks of advanced industrial societies. This alleged fact is then taken as the decisive legitimation of the model, sometimes including the costs of Stalinism (which then appear as a tolerable or even necessary price of the achievement). It is noteworthy that this argument is widely accepted by outside observers, who may not necessarily sympathize with Soviet ideology or even be socialists. The argument, in other words, is that the Soviet Union has shown that socialism "works" in terms of development.

An argument such as this, involving a vast mass of historical evidence, cannot easily be either proven or disproven. But doubts have been entered on every one of its assumptions. To begin with, it is not clear that Russia on the eve of the Bolshevik revolution was an undeveloped country. It contained a sizable industrial sector, it had made considerable strides in modernizing various areas of the country, and it is even possible that it had gone beyond the point of economic "take-off." More importantly, it has been questioned whether the economic achievements of the Soviet Union have been all that remarkable as compared with other countries— and, therefore, whether the sacrifices of the Stalinist period (when, as everyone agrees, the most rapid economic development took place) made that much of a contribution to what has been achieved. The interesting further question (unanswerable in principle) is whether Russia under a different, and perhaps less costly, system might not today be in exactly the same, or perhaps an even better, economic position.

For example, Zbigniew Brzezinski cites data to the effect that the Soviet Union has not surpassed any country except Italy in per capita GNP since 1917. Soviet production of steel (a key factor in the economic indicators of development) during the Stalin years increased only slightly faster than in Russia before World War I—and, even more interestingly, increased at about the same rate as steel production in Japan during the latter's period of rapid industrialization. As to the benefits of Soviet economic growth, the data show a rather mixed picture. In 1967 the Soviet Union was first among developed countries in the number of doctors per one hundred thousand population (though it is not clear that the definition of who is a doctor is held constant in these statistics), and also first in per capita annual social security expenditures. By contrast, in 1960 the Soviet Union ranked thirty-ninth among one hundred twenty-four countries in educational benefits, and thirteenth among seventy-nine countries in life expectancy.[5]

The Soviet model emphasized industrialization (it still does), and heavy industry at that. Whatever may have been its achievements in this sector, one of the great weaknesses of the model has been in the sector of agricultural production. In the early 1940s agriculture was collectivized rapidly and at an immense human price, setting up a production system that has essentially survived to this date. Yet today it is widely believed that lack of agricultural productivity is the Achilles heel of the Soviet economy. It is not unreasonable to think that this is directly related to collectivization. In the early 1960s, for example, 99 percent of the cultivated farmland of the Soviet Union was under "socialist modes of production," in collective or state farms. Only 1 percent of the farmland was in small family plots, which have been tolerated as (supposedly insignificant) remnants of private production. This private sector provided *30 percent* of the total agricultural output of the country, with *60 percent* of its potatoes and *nearly 50 percent* of its vegetables.[6] Since the question of agricultural productivity is absolutely central for most Third World countries today, failures of the Soviet model in this area are of great importance.

Are the people of Russia better off today than they were before the Soviet regime? The overall answer is almost certainly yes, at least in terms of economically measurable benefits. But are they better off because of, or perhaps despite, the socioeconomic system established by the regime? This question is very much harder to answer.[7] Be this as it may, Soviet-style socialism as a model to be emulated in the Third World today is less than compelling in its achievements, even if one rigorously excludes noneconomic considerations from the assessment.

The unfortunate fact is that there is no comparable case to regard. A number of Soviet-oriented countries in Eastern Europe have made great economic strides in recent years (notably Eastern Germany, Czechoslovakia, and Hungary), but they were anything but underdeveloped when they established socialist systems. China is still a desperately poor country, economic data about it are sparse and suspect, and in any case the socialist experiment is so recent that apologists for the regime can argue with some plausibility that its benefits cannot as yet be fairly judged. The same is true of other socialist models in the Third World. Consequently, statements and projections concerning the economic achievements of socialism in the Third World are largely "fideistic," to use Antonio Gramsci's useful term—that is, they depend on an act of faith, or its absence.

However, one general question suggests itself on the basis of such data as exist. This is the question of the relationship of socialism and the *motives* for productivity. The intrinsically allocative orientation of socialism almost certainly inhibits individual efforts to achieve. Where the allocative principle has been realized most fully (as in the Chinese and Cuban policies of "moral incentives"), the decline in productivity appears to have been sharp (in both cases forcing a revision of the policy). The aforementioned Soviet data on agricultural productivity strongly suggest that peasants work better for private than for collective gain. Closely related to this is the bureaucratic centralization that has come with socialist systems everywhere, generally creating a top-heavy colossus administering the economy with sometimes surrealistic inefficiency. Thus it has been argued that, if capitalism has introduced a dynamic principle of rationality into economic production, socialism has a built-in tendency to revert to the awkward and inefficient economic habits associated with premodern social systems. Pierre Bourdieu has spoken of "socialo-feudalism" in this connection, and S. N. Eisenstadt has coined the apt term "neo-patrimonialism" to designate similar phenomena.[8] Both terms denote a system in which putative benefits are allocated, with whatever degrees of benevolence or corruption, to a population that has little to gain from individual economic effort. Put differently, in such a system the emphasis is on political rather than economic activity—with foreseeably negative effects on economic productivity.

An example might make this critical point more relevant to the policy options in the Third World today. An East European social scientist (who, at any rate "officially," identified himself as a socialist at the time) recently told about his research in an African country. He pointed out that socialism in Africa meant simply that all significant economic activity was government-run—and in Africa, he added, this means that the government official in question hires all his cousins. To illustrate this, he recounted how this particular African government had instituted on office for space research, presumably in anticipation of the time when its development plan would have succeeded to the point that it could launch a national space program. The director of this agency was, of course, a relative of the minister for economic development. Other than employing a small bureaucratic staff, the sole activity of this office was the following: Once a week a truck drove out to a hill near the capital city. A number of individuals were put in barrels, and then the barrels were rolled down the hillside. This exercise was supposed to constitute preliminary training in weightlessness. The individuals in the barrels were on the payroll, and, needless to say, were all relatives of the director of the office of space research. After the audience for this story had duly laughed, it was pointed out that, after all, such cases of corruption were not unknown to capitalism. "Yes," was the reply, "but in capitalist enterprises there is at least a certain tradition of firing people for inefficiency."

If one economic point in the critique concerns the internal effects of socialism, another deals with the external relations of socialist economies. Establishment of socialist systems in the Third World today entails at least a relative severance of relations with the international capitalist system. This is necessary both because of the ideological and political pressures originating within the country in question, and because of the probable retaliatory measures to be taken by capitalist governments and/or corporations and credit agencies in the wake of any real "steps toward socialism" in that country. Both factors could be seen in operation in Chile during the Allende period. But whether this progressive rupture between a socialist regime and the international capitalist system is the result of internal policy decisions or external sanctions, or both of these, it is clear that there are costs to such a rupture.

Generally speaking, the critique at this point posits two equally disagreeable options. One is to balance the disaffiliation with the capitalist system by an affiliation with the "socialist community of nations." In effect, this means affiliation with the economic system dominated by the Soviet Union, since there exists no other socialist complex of economic power capable of providing any significant assistance to a Third World country (whether in terms of aid or of trade). What this further means, however, is a simple exchange of one dependency for another. The case of Cuba is a graphic illustration of this point. Now, this does not necessarily mean that the Cubans have no reason to prefer dependency on the Soviet Union to their previous dependency on the United States. If nothing else, it may be better to be economically dependent on a country on the other side of the globe than on one just ninety miles away. Also, for political and military reasons, the Soviet Union may have a less exploitative interest in Cuba. Neither of these facts, though, has anything to do with the Soviet Union's being a socialist system and the United States a capitalist one. Indeed, the logic would be precisely the reverse with a country located in close geographical proximity to the Soviet Union (one need only talk to Czechs or Hungarians to grasp this point).

The record of the Soviet Union in its external economic relations with weaker partners is not reassuring for those who think of the "socialist community of nations" as an alternative to dependency. This record shows that the Soviet Union is motivated by economic self-interest in much the same way as any capitalist country—*unless* there are non-economic "reasons of empire" intervening as restraints. The latter proviso applies equally to the United States, and to any other country with "imperial" ambitions (be it France in Western Africa or China in Eastern Asia). A Third World country "penetrated" by Soviet economic power will show very much the same "deformations" as those previously discussed in the case of capitalist models, even if some details will be different (for instance, Soviet "penetration" will hardly manifest itself in a proliferation of luxury consumer goods). The essential similarities are these: Crucial economic decisions are made outside the country, and in the interest of foreigners. As "development" proceeds, dependency on the foreign "metropolis" increases. The immediate symptoms are an unfavorable balance of trade and mounting indebtedness. The long-range syndrome is an economic situation unfavorable to development.

If these facts are less visible today than those associated with Western "imperialism," this is not due to any altruistic economic policies of the Soviets, but rather to their relative inability to undertake "penetrations" of comparable magnitude. The ability of the Chinese for such "imperialism" as of now is close to nil, which puts them in an excellent position to moralize about the wickedness of both the West and the Soviets. It is possible that the time will come when the Chinese economy will be strong enough to penetrate other countries in a significant way. To those who believe that the Chinese record will be different from that of other advanced economies, one might well say, "If you believe this, you'll believe anything."

The other option posited by the critique is to forego external capitalization and seek economic "self-reliance" (a term that has been particularly popular in Eastern Africa). A common way to describe such a strategy is "sweating capital out of one's own population." The image is disagreeable, as are the probable consequences of the strategy. It means to forego any immediate alleviation in the condition of large numbers of people, and envisages a long-range, possibly indefinite, prolongation of the period of maximum sacrifice. Even assuming that it is politically feasible, this is a strategy of very high human costs.

In terms of the question *Who benefits?*, then, there is a good deal of ambiguity about the socialist alternative. It is doubtful whether the population as a whole benefits more under existing socialist systems than under capitalism. It is even doubtful whether such benefits as pertain are more equitably distributed. For example, income distribution data from the Soviet Union show inequalities of a high order between the upper and lower reaches of the system (even leaving aside the acute poverty of the rural population). It is likely that a much higher degree of egalitarianism exists in China. At this point, though, this is largely an equality in poverty, and it is an open question whether a similar egalitarianism can be maintained by the Chinese as their economy advances.

If the question *Who benefits?* can only be answered ambiguously, what about the other question? *Who decides?* This leads to a consideration of the political costs of socialist models.

Marxism-Leninism, in all its versions, maintains that socialism can only be established and preserved through the "dictatorship of the proletariat." The dictatorship part of this formula is clear enough, and it has a high degree of plausibility. If socialism entails a massive reshuffling of power and privilege in a society, it is not difficult to see why democratic political forms are likely to break down in this process. One of the most noteworthy recent attempts to construct a socialist society while retaining the political structures of "bourgeois democracy" was that of the Allende regime in Chile. The character of its failure makes it difficult to draw clear-cut lessons from this experiment. Contrary to the Leninist implications currently being drawn by many on the left, the major lesson of this particular case is quite simple: If a regime wants to preside over a social revolution *and* to continue playing by the rules of democratic politics, it must have a majority of the votes.

A good argument could be made for the proposition that development out of a state of severe poverty will probably require some form of dictatorship *regardless* of the model chosen. The basic reason for this is simple: Such a process requires sacrifices, not only by the few but by the many. In other words, large numbers of people will have to make strenuous efforts and forego immediate relief from their miseries. It is unlikely that, apart from short periods of collective enthusiasm, people will *vote* such sacrifices for themselves. The hard decisions as to what sacrifices are necessary to attain specific development goals, therefore, are much more likely to be the result of political leaders having dispensed with the business of popular voting (under whatever guise of "real democracy").

Socialism by way of dictatorship? Yes, this seems a plausible proposition. But dictatorship of the *proletariat*? That is an altogether different question, and one that has troubled Marxism all through its history.

In the Marxist myth of revolution, it is the working class that takes over power from the bourgeoisie in a great act of liberating violence. Marx, of course, expected this to happen in the most advanced countries of the West. The expectation was disappointed, as the Western working class refused to play the redemptive role assigned to it in the myth. Marxism has had to come to terms with this great disappointment, and subsequent Marxist theoreticians have redefined Marx's prophecy in various ways so as to salvage its basic ingredients. Since the empirically available working class would not make the revolution, it could not be the "true" working class. Much of Marxist theory during this century has been a quest, often quixotic, of the "true" working class. The mythic category was shifted to the peasantry, to the urban underclass (which Marx contemptuously called the *lumpenproletariat*), even to racial minorities and disgruntled intellectuals, and most importantly (in the Leninist theory of imperialism) to the exploited peoples of the colonial countries. However, no matter to what societal location the "true" revolutionary class was shifted, there always remained one constant assumption —that of the "mass" character of the revolution. The revolution that is to bring in socialism must be a movement of "the masses"; otherwise the revolution would not be authentic in terms of the myth. The category of "the masses," however, has had its empirical problems, too.

The problems are less acute during the period of struggle preceding establishment of a revolutionary regime. In most cases, some degree of mass support must be obtained by the revolutionary movement if it is to be successful, in the later stages of the struggle if not earlier. During this period it may be said that people vote with their fists, and to the extent that the victory of a revolutionary movement is brought about by a large number of fists punching in the same direction, there is a rough plausibility to the assertion that "the masses" have acted. The problems become much sharper after the revolutionary regime is established. The notion that some sort of permission by "the masses" is required to carry on the program of the regime is obviously inconvenient. Indeed, such a notion is pejoratively assigned to "bourgeois democracy" by Marxist theory. The regime already knows what "the masses" want, even knows it better than "the masses" themselves, and any institutional arrangement to ascertain the wishes of the populace in an ongoing fashion and thus to impose checks on the actions of the regime is ipso facto a counterrevolutionary trick. In order to make this redefinition of "democracy" plausible, an additional category is required. This is the category of the "vanguard."

The concept of the vanguard has a long history in Marxism, and even precedes it. In its essence the concept means that a particular group of people, by virtue of unique qualities ascribed to it, is the "embodiment" of "the will of the masses." As this "embodiment," it has no need for the kind of representative mechanisms characteristic of "bourgeois democracy." Even if "the masses" don't know it yet, the vanguard already represents them. It was Lenin who refined this concept of the vanguard in his doctrine of *partiinost* (roughly translated as "partyhood"): The Communist party is the vanguard of the proletariat. It embodies the will and the revolutionary destiny of the proletariat. The dictatorship of the proletariat, therefore, means the dictatorship of the Communist party.

To believe this one must perform a considerable sacrifice of intellect. For the believer, though, the doctrine will be plausible up to the clearly definable point at which there are rival claimants to the status of vanguard. From this perspective the Roman Catholic church has been fortunate since papal infallibility was proclaimed a little over a century ago. While there have been challenges to the doctrine of infallibility, there have been no rival popes! Marxism has been less fortunate. Trotskyites, Titoists, Maoists, and others have set up *alternative* vanguards, confusing the believers much more than those who simply challenged the notion of the vanguard as such. In consequence, the Marxist universe of discourse has been full of excommunications and counter-excommunications, with popes and antipopes reading each other out of the "true" revolution.

Be this as it may, a key political element of the critique of socialist models can be put in terms of a simple question directed toward any one of these putative vanguards: *Who elected you?* To say that this question is "bourgeois" is an anathema, not an argument, for the question does not imply the assumption that "election" can only occur through the mechanisms of Western representative democracy. Thus a Bedouin sheik could give a very credible answer to the question. So could a peasant revolutionary such as Emiliano Zapata. Perhaps even Ho Chi Minh could, at least in the early days of his regime. The present rulers of the Soviet Union or China would have a very hard time indeed. The critique, as an exercise in nonbelief, will give an answer to its own question: Nobody elected you. Indeed, you have done everything possible to stamp out any procedures by which you or your policies could be elected through collective acts of choice. Yet you claim to represent the will of the people. This claim is fraudulent, and that fraud is at the very root of your system.

A basic contradiction of most of the existing socialist systems is precisely this political fact—the contradiction of a dictatorship that defines itself as a democracy. Marxist legitimations of this fact have largely involved a gigantic debasement of language. It can be much better described in other terms: These systems are ruled by political elites which, whatever the original circumstances in which they came to power, have progressively suppressed any actual or potential checks on that power. This thrust toward absolute power carries with it a growing threat of arbitrariness and corruption. As Hannah Arendt has convincingly shown, it is necessary to distinguish between dictatorship and totalitarianism. The latter category only makes sense in a situation in which the state has absorbed into itself all other significant institutions. Not all dictatorships are totalitarian, and it would be false to say that all the socialist regimes in the world today are totalitarian. Socialism need not imply totalitarianism. But socialism contains a built-in *tendency* toward totalitarianism, for a very simple reason: Socialism, by its very nature, will seek to absorb the economy within the state, thus vastly increasing the totalitarian potential of the latter. This totalitarian tendency, with all the attendant risks of unchecked and tyrannical power, must be counted as one of the possible political costs of socialism. It is a high cost indeed.

In this connection it is necessary to raise the issue of terror. This often ambiguous term should be employed precisely and economically. In such usage, terror refers to large-scale application of physical violence by a government to the population under its control. Terror, then, must be clearly distinguished from the terrorism employed by a revolutionary movement not yet in power, as well as from the human costs of civil war in general. Terror must also be distinguished from lesser "repressive" measures of governments (such as infringements on various liberties associated with Western-type democracies). Even if physical violence is employed by a government, the term "terror" had best be avoided unless the violence is massive in scope and is a matter of policy rather than merely sporadic. However careful one is in the use of the term, there is an uncomfortable correlation between terror and regimes of revolutionary socialism.

The most important cases are those of the Soviet Union and China. The worst period of terror in the former was under Stalin in the 1930s, during the drive to collectivize agriculture and the subsequent waves of "purges." Robert Conquest, a British historian who has painstakingly collected evidence on this period, probably has the most reliable estimates on the victims of this terror.[9] He estimates that three and one-half million people perished in direct consequence of the collectivization campaign, by direct killing and through a deliberate policy of starvation. For the most intensive "purge" period, 1936–1938, he estimates one million deaths by execution and two million deaths by starvation, disease, and maltreatment in the forced-labor camps. The physical suffering of millions of people who did not die in the camps and prisons of the regime are not susceptible to such quantification; neither is the mental anguish of fear and grief. The full dimensions of the Stalinist terror only became visible after the revelations that followed the Twentieth Party Congress of 1956. There has been no such event in China as yet. It is clear, however, that the dimensions of the terror there bear comparison with the Stalinist era. (In this connection there is a grisly significance to the fact that the Maoist regime has steadfastly refused to repudiate Stalin, while Khrushchev, the instigator of de-Stalinization, ranks high in the Maoist demonology of "revisionists.") For 1949–1955, the period of agricultural collectivization and of the most massive "rectification" campaigns in China, the probable figure of outright executions runs in the millions. By comparison with this period, the violence of the Cultural Revolution was moderate. Again there is no easy way to quantify the physical (let alone mental) suffering of millions of Chinese even now confined in "Reform through Labor" camps and "May 7 schools," exiled to remote rural hinterlands, or subjected to other forms of forced labor.

Every assessment of the Soviet or Chinese models of socialism that ignores these hecatombs of victims is morally contemptible. Neither can the human costs of terror be ignored in the case of any other model that defines itself as an emulation of the Soviet or Chinese "paths to socialism." There will be occasion to return to this point later. There has been a type of critique (perhaps rare now in academic circles in the West) that would *identify* socialism with this kind of terror. Such an identification is inaccurate and unfair. Socialist models exist in which terror has been minimal, and in some there has been no terror at all. Even in dealing with the Soviet Union and China, it is necessary to point out that the Stalinist period has come to an end in the former (whatever else one may still hold against it) and that even in China, where some of the leaders who preside over the earlier terror are still in control, there has been no repetition of the massive killing of the 1950s. It is also important to stress that terror exists as a large-scale reality in a number of emphatically nonsocialist countries. However, it is not possible to dismiss the question of terror when dealing with the socialist alternative in general. The totalitarian tendency is a constant threat in any full-blown socialist system. Once totalitarian structures are erected, with the elimination of all viable political checks on the elite's exercise of power, terror is an ever-present possibility. This too must be reckoned as a political cost.

Related to the question of political costs, though not identical with it, is the question of the more general social-structural costs of socialism. Even if one brackets the aforementioned totalitarian tendency, there is an antipluralistic tendency in socialism—a leveling, uniforming thrust. This too is rooted, of course, in the integration of political and economic institutions under socialist systems. This tendency seems to produce a cultural drabness, a sense of dreary sameness. But perhaps more importantly, it imposes severe restraints on individual variety and initiative. It may possibly be a design for societal stagnation.

An episode may illustrate the point. Some time ago an American visitor overheard a conversation at a party in Tanzania. At first he could not make sense of the conversation. It seemed that one of the persons present, a newspaper editor, was trying to persuade another, a university official, that a young man working at the university should have a job on the newspaper. Upon inquiry, the situation was explained to the visitor. In Tanzania, as in several other African countries, university students are on government stipends. In return for this they have the obligation of working for the government for a certain number of years. A person working for the government, or for a government-related agency, may change his job only with the consent of his superior, hence the conversation between the two persons at the party. So far, all of this appears to be a thoroughly fair procedure, not at all peculiar to Tanzania (except perhaps for the quasi-military discipline imposed on government personnel) and having nothing to do with the Tanzanian socialist model.

But one further item must be added: *There are virtually no jobs in Tanzania other than government jobs*—at least none to which an individual with even secondary education would aspire. There is no "private sector" offering alternative career possibilities. There are three structures within which desirable careers are possible—the state bureaucracy proper; the government party, TANU (there is no other party); and the so-called "parastatal organizations," which are government-controlled agencies regulating the various sectors of the economy. All three structures are, in effect, government. This is not to say that this system is particularly inhuman or corrupt. On the contrary, one of the most cheering qualities of the Tanzanian system, when compared with other African situations, is its humaneness and lack of corruption. It is a system, all the same, which subjects the individual to an all-embracing bureaucratic colossus. This has far-reaching consequences both for the individual and for the society as a whole.

Socialism purports to do away with the inequalities and the savage competition of capitalist class societies. Even in its mildest forms, however, socialism creates new inequalities and new forms of competition. These inequalities are not the result of "class struggle" but of the hierarchical order of bureaucracy. The competition is an endless maneuvering for position within the bureaucratic hierarchies. Stated sociologically, stratification comes to be dominated by political rather than economic criteria. Put less elegantly, while under capitalism your bank account goes far in determining what you can fix in city hall, under socialism you are on city hall's payroll and the position you have managed to get there determines the size of your bank account. There may be advantages to the socialist alternative, but there are also tangible costs in terms of a "closed" social structure.

Finally, there is a quite different line of attack taken by some critics of the socialist alternative. This is not so much a critique of the alternative as such, but rather an argument that the differences between capitalist and socialist models are fundamentally irrelevant, because the real forces of modernization have nothing to do with this dichotomy.[10] These forces are understood as technological, demographic, and social-structural processes which are deemed to be present in all societies that have reached a certain phase of development. Consequently, these societies "converge" in their basic characteristics, regardless of whether they call themselves capitalist or socialist.[11]

There are complex sociological issues related to this argument. These cannot be taken up here. However, this much may be said: Even if the argument has merits, it is not relevant to the concrete options now before Third World countries. In other words, it is difficult to deduce policy decisions from global societal trends which, if valid as alleged, will take generations to mature.

The critique of the socialist alternative thus takes different forms and has different foci of attention. Generally, its stress is on the political rather than economic miseries of the socialist model. In this, of course, it reverses the emphasis of the critique of capitalism. This reversal is logical in view of the primacy of the political order posited by the very principle of socialism. This is the crux of the critique. There is an underlying paradox to the myth of revolution and to the socialist ideal. The myth promises a great liberation for humanity (Marx's "leap into freedom") and, quite often, the empirical reality of revolutionary movements can be fairly described as liberating. Socialist systems established in the wake of successful revolutions are, therefore, accompanied by high expectations of a quasi-millennial intensity. History shows that such expectations are invariably doomed to disappointment. But socialism has a built-in disappointment factor, built-in precisely because of its principle of politicization: *What begins as a liberating community ends up as the all-embracing state.* To anyone who takes seriously the Marxian view of man, this is doubly paradoxical: The revolution is to free man from his "alienation" and socialism is to be a society making such freedom possible—yet it is hard to imagine any social structure more deeply "alienating" than the modern totalitarian state.

If one concedes that even a portion of this critique is valid, does this imply an overall rejection of socialism? Must one say *no* to the socialist alternative of development? Once more: What can be said by way of a "critique of the critique"?

It is again necessary to distinguish among socialist models as they present themselves in different parts of the world. Much of the afore-mentioned critique is based on the large, established socialist systems, especially those in the orbit of Soviet power. It is not valid to generalize from this case. There is as little reason to assume that a socialist society set up in Latin America must follow Soviet (or, for that matter, Chinese) lines as there is to project that capitalist countries in Africa will eventually look like Switzerland. A disadvantage in the discussion of socialist models of development is that, once one has removed from the discussion the Soviet orbit and China, there are not too many examples left. This theoretical disadvantage, however, points to a political advantage: Socialism in the Third World is something new, largely untried, containing manifold possibilities. There is hope in this fact. Yet on each of the major points of the critique, an easy *no* is as hard to pronounce as an easy *yes*.

In the matter of what was called the internal economic costs of socialist models of development, the critique is largely valid in having shown up the negative correlation of socialism and productivity. To the extent that continuing and perhaps even rapid economic growth is a presupposition for development, this is a grave criticism of the socialist option. Whatever may be the moral beauties of socialist egalitarianism, the wealth must first exist in order to be equitably distributed. The notion that this goal can be achieved by *redistribution*, which means expropriation of the wealthier classes, may have a certain (probably illusionary) plausibility in the richer countries. In the poor countries of the Third World the notion is palpably false: There simply is not enough *there* to be expropriated. If the new socialist society is to involve something better than equitably shared poverty and stagnation, there must be economic growth. And economic growth presupposes economic productivity.

All the same, there is enough evidence to indicate that there are possibilities of modifying the inertia-generating propensity of socialism. This is possible on the level of both individual motives and bureaucratic functioning. Indeed, the Soviet Union and the socialist countries of Eastern Europe have gone a long way (at least in the urban sectors of the economy) to create incentives for individual effort and achievement. Even Maoist China, in the years since the Cultural Revolution, seems to have taken steps in the same direction. In other words, it is not intrinsic to socialism to provide for an "equality of result" that stultifies the individual's motives to produce. What is more, similar tendencies may occur under capitalist conditions, in consequence of various government policies, labor union activities, or even cultural trends. As to the stagnation brought about by the overbureaucratization of the economy, this has been recognized as a problem by virtually all socialist theorists. Even in the Soviet Union, where the problem has been most severe, a number of modifications of the economic system have tended toward decentralization. In China such decentralization in economic decision making appears to be deliberate policy. The so-called Yugoslav model is often held up as an illustration that a clearly socialist system can permit initiative and productivity of decentralized economic units. Similar efforts are now under way in Peru, under the heading of "cooperativism" as differentiated from "statism." While it may be a valid concept that socialism carries with it an ever-present danger of economic inefficiency brought on by overbureaucratization, this is not an inexorable destiny, and various measures are possible to counteract this tendency.

In this connection, a "critique of the critique" should pronounce an emphatic *yes* to all those socialist propositions that dethrone economic growth from its tyrannical primacy in development thinking. To say this, as should be clear by now, is *not* to dismiss the importance of economic growth; neither is it an endorsement of the fantasies of the "zero-growth" rhetoric of recent years. Rather, it is to debunk the idea that economic growth *as such* is the be-all and end-all of development, and the faster the better. Socialism has insisted for a long time that economic growth unrelated to social justice is antidevelopment—and social justice in this context refers to all the issues that have been touched upon under the question, *Who benefits?* If there are capitalist ideologists and institutions who are beginning to say this today (Robert McNamara and the World Bank are probably the most illustrious cases), it is largely in response to attacks from the "left" on the earlier "growthmanship" of the same circles. This *yes* includes acceptance of the proposition that the rapidity of economic growth must be assessed in connection with other factors, and that, in consequence, a slower rate of growth may sometimes be indicated by social rather than economic considerations. A *yes* may also be pronounced to the emphasis on agricultural development at the expense of rapid industrialization that has been characteristic of some socialist models. In this regard the Maoist ideology has almost certainly been more insightful than its Soviet rival, for economic as well as social reasons. However, this agreement with the proposition that development is likely to be empty unless it is based on a firm agricultural foundation definitely does *not* imply agreement with the socialist fixation on the collectivization of agriculture. Even if one leaves aside the human havoc that this fixation has caused, available evidence suggests that it is an absurdity in purely economic terms as well. Unfortunately, the point is one on which most socialist ideologists have shown an unbending rigidity.

As to what (perhaps awkwardly) have been called the external economic costs of socialism, the critique has effectively pointed out what is probably the basic Marxist error in the analysis of underdevelopment— to wit, the error of ascribing to capitalism alone certain conditions that are endemic to any relations between richer and poorer economic entities. In terms of logic, this error is a fallacy of *pars pro toto*. The Marxist-Leninist theory of imperialism is correct insofar as it serves to show how Third World countries are economically exploited by this or that capitalist "metropolis." Such exploitation is real enough, and under conditions of capitalism it takes distinctively capitalist forms. Unfortunately, relations between economically unequal partners are almost invariably exploitative, and this has nothing to do with capitalism. A socialist "metropolis" is just as capable of exploitative relations with Third World dependencies, as Soviet economic policy has painfully revealed; it is not at all clear that Third World countries whose internal system is socialist are necessarily in a better condition to resist such exploitation. When a poor country has economic dealings with a rich country, it is almost always supping with the devil—and the devil has the much longer spoon.

On the other hand, it is possible, despite the aforementioned critique of socialist models, to say *yes* to the proposition that development hinges on at least a relative independence from domination by foreign economic power (it is doubtful whether any country in the world today can be fully "independent"). Minimally, it must be a goal of policy that the basic decisions concerning development are made within a country, and not outside it. A comparable *yes* is deserved by the proposition that development hinges on the abolition of domestic structures of exploitation. In addition, the critique has been unable to invalidate the demonstration by Marxist analysts that, in many instances, the foreign and domestic exploiters are linked in international networks of economic and political power.

In all likelihood, both the goals of even relative independence in national development policy and of domestic programs directed against exploitation will involve a high degree of state intervention in the economy. In many cases this intervention will deserve the designation of socialism. The ideological and political dynamics of most Third World countries today make it likely that, whatever other options exist theoretically, there will be a bias toward the socialist alternative. The critique suggests that there will be economic costs to this. One question that socialist development planners in the Third World should ask themselves is: If capitalism, whatever its evils, has superior productive capacities, what are the practical possibilities of controlling rather than abolishing it? In other words, can you make the beast work for you? To throw out capitalism, and especially foreign capital, from a Third World country requires an exercise in political power. If the Marxist-Leninist view of revolution is clear about anything, it is clear about *this*. One may ask, then, whether such political power, once in existence, cannot profitably be used to control rather than destroy the capitalist entities. Put simply: If you are strong enough to throw the rascals out, are you not strong enough to force them to play by new rules set up by yourself? And may you not be better off doing this, in terms of developing your country?[12]

On the political costs of socialism, the plausibility of arguing that development is unlikely to come about under nondictatorial regimes has already been discussed—and, however reluctantly, conceded. This point is not directly related to socialism; it applies with equal force to capitalist models of development, and therefore cannot be used as an argument against either. More serious is the charge that socialism has a built-in tendency toward a totalitarian expansion of the state. For the reasons stated before, this is an element of the critique that must be taken seriously. All the same, similar responses in defense of the socialist alternative can be made to this as were cited in connection with the productivity-inhibiting tendencies of socialism: Many who favor socialism in the Third World are aware of this danger; if nothing else, the growing disinclination to emulate the Soviet "path to socialism" has brought the danger into sharp focus. Demonstrably, there exist socialist systems that, so far at least, have successfully avoided the drift toward totalitarianism. Indeed, there are others that seem to be trying to emerge from totalitarianism toward a greater measure of political decentralization.

In all of this discussion, it is important not to be hypnotized by broad categories. It is one thing to say that there is a trend toward dictatorship in the Third World, another to view all Third World dictatorships as being of the same character. This may even be said of narrower categories such as military dictatorships. Thus, for example, both Brazil and Peru may be described as military dictatorships. Yet, in terms of just about every relevant political, social, and economic reality, what is presently happening in one country could hardly be more different from what is happening in the other. Similar differentiations must be made with the category of one-party regimes.

American observers particularly must try in this area to overcome what may be called a residual Wilsonianism—that is, the belief that any political system not measuring up to the standards of Western-style representative democracy is some sort of loathsome tyranny. Although this belief leads to unfortunate distortions of perception with regard to "right" as well as "left" regimes, there is a realistic foundation to this bias toward democracy. Unchecked power is almost always a source of corruption and cruelty. There are different ways in which checks can be institutionalized, and it is naive to be doctrinaire about any one way. But it is valid to be suspicious of any development model that depends on the benevolence of an elite exercising power without any institutional limits. Conversely, it is valid to seek some sort of "countervailing" mechanisms in any model. To the extent that socialist models are "elitist" in the power they give to the revolutionary "vanguard" (however it may call itself, and however much it may camouflage its power by a participatory rhetoric), the critique is correct in erecting danger signals at every juncture.

The one political component of the critique that is virtually impossible to gainsay is the debunking of those "vanguards" that pretend to speak for "the masses." Almost invariably, this pretension is mendacious. The most appalling aspect of this mendacity is in the relation between Communist revolutionary movements and the peasantry. Beginning with the Soviet Union, and repeating itself in China, North Vietnam, and elsewhere, the pattern has been the same: The revolutionary movement sets out by promising the land to the peasants. This promise is a key factor in mobilizing peasant support for the revolution. The peasants are encouraged to understand the promise in the sense of what, all over the world, has always been their deepest aspiration—individual or family ownership of land. The revolutionary movement, insofar as it is animated by a Marxist ideology, of course never intended to keep the promise at all. At best, individual ownership of land, following whatever expropriation takes place, is understood to be a temporary phase in the march toward collectivization. Whenever the moment is deemed ripe after the revolutionary regime is safely installed, there is a *second* expropriation. The newly propertied peasants are deprived of their property and forced into collective structures. Not surprisingly, the peasants react to this treachery with outraged resistance—hence the brutality of the collectivization process (massive brutality in the three cases cited). All this would be bad enough in itself, both in moral terms and in view of its effects on agricultural productivity. The crowning immorality as well as "false consciousness," however, is the fact that the same "vanguard," which is responsible for the betrayal and coercion of the peasantry, continues to designate itself as the spokesman of their "true" aspirations. Perhaps a minimal moral as well as cognitive demand that one may make in such situations is the acknowledgment of a certain difference between submission to rape and consent.

United Nations statements in recent years have presented a reiteration of the demand that development involve "participation." Needless to say, different member nations have understood this term differentially. If, for instance, one understands participation to mean popular mobilization behind the programs of the government, then Nazi Germany was one of the most "participatory" societies in this century. A meaningful concept of participation will have to include some kind of sharing in the decision-making processes relating to development. Somewhere along the line people must be *asked* their views of the issues at hand, and there must be some political mechanisms by which these views feed into the decisions of those in charge of development policy. Participation understood in this way is pretty much the opposite of mobilization, and clearly will be easier to achieve on the local or regional level than on the level of national development planning and policy. But on whatever level it occurs, the effort to institutionalize participation will imply at least the possibility of *opposition* to projects emanating from the national power centers. Without this possibility, participation will be a farce. For this reason, it is not just a matter of naive Wilsonianism if one has a bias toward such "bourgeois liberties" as the protection of free expression and criticism, be it in the press or elsewhere. The cavalier manner in which Marxist ideologists habitually dismiss these matters does little credit to their mode of analysis. The interesting question as to just what are *non*bourgeois liberties cannot be taken up here.

None of the above, *in any way whatever,* implies an acceptance of terror. Whatever may be the indications for dictatorship, or whatever the difficulties of institutionalizing participation in a situation of rapid social transformations, or indeed whatever the human costs of revolutionary struggle—none of these can be used to legitimate the imposition of large-scale physical violence on a population that is already under political control. This point will be taken up once more at a later stage in this book.

The social-structural costs of socialism need not be discussed further here. The critique, to the effect that socialism tends to be inimical to pluralism and hence to be leveling in its sociocultural influence, must be conceded. This, too, however, is something of which many who favor socialist models are conscious, and in this matter, as in that of over-bureaucratization, efforts have been made to modify socialism in a pluralistic sense. Again, Yugoslavia and Peru may serve as illustrations.

In the critiques of both capitalism and socialism, the attempt has been to weigh costs and benefits in a nondoctrinaire, open manner. An interesting parallel between the two models should be pointed out (one that will have implications for a later part of the present argument). More precisely, the parallel is between the ideological techniques that legitimate the economic miseries of one model and the political miseries of the other. This is the parallel between the functioning of the notions of the "spread effect" and (to use Marx's own term) of the "withering away of the state" in the respective ideologies.

Candid advocates of the capitalist models of development will admit that, as far as the evidence goes, their version of development brings on polarization, unemployment, and some of the other dislocations that have been discussed in the previous chapter. They will then go on to advise patience; these unfortunate phenomena, they will tell us, are only temporary. Eventually the "spread effect" will take place, and everyone will benefit from the fruits of economic growth. This argument bears an uncanny similarity to the classical Marxist method of explaining away the less edifying aspects of the "dictatorship of the proletariat," except that the phenomena that need explaining away in the latter case are largely political rather than economic. Thus the more candid advocates of socialism will not deny the sordid dimensions of various revolutionary regimes. Of course, they will admit, there have been acts of unnecessary cruelty, even whole institutions supporting such acts (in Communist parlance, these aberrations are usually referred to as "mistakes"). But one should not lose the overall perspective because of these regrettable details. Overextension of the state in the wake of the revolution is only temporary. Eventually there will be, if not a "withering away" of the political institutions, then certainly their democratization. At that moment there will be no more "repression," and there will be a merging of the benefits of social justice and political liberty.

In both cases there is a legitimation of present evils in terms of putative future remedies. In both cases these remedies are expected because of alleged necessities of the societal process—the necessities of the laws of economics in the first case (after a certain level of economic growth is reached, a distributional dynamic allegedly sets in), the necessities of the dialectic of history in the other (after the expropriators have been finally and irrevocably expropriated, there will be no more need for a coercive state apparatus). In both cases alleged knowledge of the necessities of the future brings the assurance that present trends will be reversed. Finally, in both cases there is great vagueness as to *when* the happy consummation may be expected.

The future is empirically inaccessible. Predictions, however scientific in manner, are disputable. More or less plausible hypotheses, however, are not enough to legitimate the kind of human suffering that is at issue in both cases. The predictions must therefore be elevated to the status of dogma. Thus, in both cases there is a strongly "fideistic" element in the advocacy of the respective ideological propositions. Not everyone has the same capacity for faith.

It is important to stress once more that the critical questions bearing on the two models cannot be answered in scientific or technical terms alone. There are fundamental value alternatives involved. Social-scientific analysis can clarify situations, criticize interpretations, and point out probable consequences of certain courses of action. It can never resolve the underlying value conflicts.

The value conflicts between the two models are clear. There is the primacy of the individual as against that of the collectivity. There is freedom as against belonging. There is acceptance of an "adversary model" of society as against the ideal of "harmony." Now, clearly, the counterposition of these values is rarely absolute. Few who advocate socialism would like to see total eradication of individuality in the collective. Few of even the most enthusiastic advocates of the hurly-burly of free-enterprise competition would carry their enthusiasm as far as a Hobbesian jungle of the war of all against all. The values are typically posited in relative terms—they are favored, "other things being equal." Yet, even with such relativization, there are many situations in which the alternative presents itself quite sharply.

One pejorative concept that often enters the discussion of these values is that of "ethnocentrism," most commonly directed against those who uphold values of individual freedom as against collective well-being and order. There is a measure of validity to this charge. It is primarily in Western civilization, through a confluence of cultural traditions going back to ancient Israel and Hellas, that a unique value has come to be attached to the individual and his liberties. In that sense, emphasis on the individual is not only "bourgeois" but European, Western, and Judaeo-Christian. But exactly the same is true of the emphasis on such rights as social justice, equality of access to the good things of life, deliverance from hunger and disease, and hope in a better future for all. The critic of "ethnocentrism" cannot have his cake and eat it, too. If the value of individual freedom is to be rejected as "ethnocentric," then one may also reject such Western hang-ups as the notion that some people should not starve while others gorge themselves, or that human beings have the capacity and the right to shape a better future for themselves. *Both* of the ideologies at issue here originate in specifically Western traditions. *Neither* can plausibly charge the other with "ethnocentrism" without including itself in the charge. The question of whether non-Western values can be accomodated within *any* model of development will occupy us later in the argument, but it is not relevant to the two critiques under discussion.

Whether or not one believes in the possibility of a value-free social science (the author of this book believes in it), and whether it is incumbent on a social scientist to explicate his own values every time he opens his mouth (the author is not so persuaded), it is certainly important that one's mind be clear about one's own value commitments. Indeed, such clarity is doubly important for anyone who strives for value-free perceptions of society. To have values, however, means neither to see reality through spectacles colored by one's value-based wishes, nor to distort or demonize the values of others. In other words, neither objectivity nor fairness need be casualties of strong moral commitment. For this reason, in comparing different designs for social change it is a good rule to try to compare the *best* rather than the *worst* instances of a particular design. It is not valid, either intellectually or morally, to base a critique of capitalism on the worst cases of the dislocations caused in the Third World today by capitalist penetration. It is equally invalid to make the socialist alternative bear the full burden of the hecatomb of victims caused by the Maoist terror. Critique, therefore, is never enough. There must always be the corrective of a critique of the critique, and the readiness to remain open minded in both intellectual operations.

The concept of costs is of strategic importance in any such attempt at critical thought. Indeed, if there is any one general principle that ought to be impressed on anyone working in the area of development policy, it is the principle that everything in human history has a price. This can be economically illustrated by a joke: It seems that the ruler of an Arabian oil sheikdom was puzzled by what was happening to him and to his country as a result of the new wealth. He invited ten of the world's foremost social scientists to come to his capital city, and asked them to prepare a memorandum of ten pages that would explain to him the mysteries of economic growth and development. The team of experts worked hard and produced the desired memorandum. The sheik read it, said regretfully that he still did not understand, and asked them to boil down the statement into one page. Again the experts worked very hard, and produced another memorandum of only one page. Still the sheik shook his head, still he did not understand; he asked them to say everything they had to say in one sentence. In a final burst of mind-boggling teamwork the experts did produce this one sentence. It read: *There are no free lunches.*

Left-leaning social scientists have made much in recent years over the alleged need for a "critical theory." Even if one does not share their assumptions on the methodology of the social sciences, one may agree with the moral thrust of their position that the products of the social scientist should have bearing on political efforts to improve the human condition. "Critical" then means the quality of being able to criticize the status quo, but this quality cannot be—or, more accurately, should not be—selective. The foremost intellectual weakness of Marxist "critical theory" has been its general failure to provide the tools for a critique of any socialist status quo. Some time ago, in a seminar at an American university, a student presented a paper on certain aspects of the Chinese situation that was uniformly accepting of the interpretations put forth by the Chinese government. In the discussion the student (a very intelligent individual, it should be added) was challenged as to the objectivity of his sources. He asserted that he was indeed objective in his presentation. Asked to define what he meant by objectivity, after a moment's reflection he replied: "Well, by objective sources I mean those sources that are basically favorable to the Chinese experiment, and that's how I am objective." However such an intellectual attitude is to be described, it is *not* "critical theory."[13]

Only if "critical" is understood in a sense that is, in principle, universal in applicability will it be possible for Marxist and non-Marxist social scientists to have meaningful converse with each other. Much more importantly, only a "critical theory" that can include within itself the critique of *all* empirically available models of development will have political utility. Such an approach will be sober in its assessment of both the gains and the costs of the different models. It will not be blinded by the labels "capitalism" or "socialism," and will not waste energy on futile discussion of when the adjective "true" may be prefixed to either label. It will be more interested in the questions "*What kind* of capitalism?" and "*What kind* of socialism?" Both types of socioeconomic organizations, with whatever modifications, are likely to continue existing

101

in different parts of the world. Advocates of each side will therefore be well advised to remain open to the possibilities of development inherent in the alternative posited by the other side. However, while such a growth in "ecumenical" tolerance is desirable, an even more important consequence that might follow such an attitude of openness is the possibility of thinking about development in categories that *go beyond* the capitalist/socialist dichotomy.

NOTES

1. See F. A. Hayek, "The Intellectuals and Socialism," in *The Intellectuals*, George de Huszar, ed. (New York: Free Press, 1960), pp. 377 ff. For the credulity of Western intellectuals with regard to Soviet socialism, see David Caute, *The Fellow-Travellers* (New York: Macmillan, 1973).

2. Andre Gunder Frank, *Lumpenbourgeoisie—Lumpendevelopment* (New York: Monthly Review Press, 1972), p. 145 (emphasis added). For a good introduction to this ideological position, see Irving Louis Horowitz et al., eds., *Latin American Radicalism* (New York: Vintage, 1969).

3. For a discussion of the costs of revolution, see Peter Berger and Richard Neuhaus, *Movement and Revolution* (Garden City, N.Y.: Doubleday, 1970). Particularly relevant is Neuhaus' attempt to outline a theory of "just revolution" analogous to the classical theory of "just war." A related question that cannot be pursued here is whether modern revolutions conform to common and predictable patterns, so that there is a commonality in the human costs they exact. See Clarence Crane Brinton, *The Anatomy of Revolution* (Englewood Cliffs, N.J.: Prentice-Hall, 1952).

4. For an overall critique see Zbigniew Brzezinski, *Between Two Ages* (New York: Viking, 1970). With special reference to the appeal of socialism in the Third World, see I. Robert Sinai, *The Challenge of Modernisation* (New York: Norton, 1964); John Kautsky, *Communism and the Politics of Development* (New York: Wiley, 1968). For a critique in terms of economics, see P. T. Bauer, *Dissent on Development* (Cambridge, Mass.: Harvard University Press, 1972), especially pp. 69 ff. and pp. 164 ff. One of the urgent research needs in this area is for comparative studies of socialist and nonsocialist cases of national development. There is very little material of this kind. Samir Amin tried to do something along these lines, from a Marxist point of view, for West Africa (*L'Afrique de l'ouest bloquée*, Paris: Editions du Minuit, 1971). For an interesting non-Marxist rejoinder, see Jon Woronoff, *West African Wager* (Metuchen, N.J.: Scarecrow, 1972), which compares Ghana and the Ivory Coast (whose then leaders, Kwame Nkrumah and Félix Houphouet-Biogny,

made a wager in 1957 as to which of the two countries, following socialist and nonsocialist models respectively, would be farther ahead after a decade). Amir and Woronoff come to generally opposite conclusions.

5. Brzezinski, *Between Two Ages*, pp. 131 ff.

6. Data from Raanan Weitz, *From Peasant to Farmer* (New York: Columbia University Press, 1971), pp. 34 ff.

7. For a balanced assessment see Paul Hollander, *Soviet and American Society* (New York: Oxford University Press, 1973).

8. Bourdieu mentioned the term in conversation and apparently has not used it in print so far. Eisenstadt developed his term in his "Traditional Patrimonialism and Modern Neo-Patrimonialism," a mimeographed document published at the Hebrew University of Jerusalem in 1972.

9. Robert Conquest, *The Great Terror* (New York: Macmillan, 1968).

10. This position is taken forcefully by Marion Levy, *Modernization—Latecomers and Survivors* (New York: Basic Books, 1972).

11. So-called "convergence theory" has been particularly relevant to the comparison of American and Soviet societies. For a critical approach, see Hollander, *Soviet and American Society*. Related to "convergence theory" is the idea that all societies can be viewed as being on a continuum of degrees of development, culminating in "postindustrial society." See Daniel Bell, *The Coming of Post-Industrial Society* (New York: Basic Books, 1973).

12. This point of view has been represented in recent years by, for example, the spokesmen of the Velasco regime in Peru. It seems that Peru is succeeding, due to its position in the Andean Community set up by the Treaty of Cartagena, in persuading other Latin American countries of the viability of this position, and, even more interestingly, in persuading various North American corporations that this is a definition of the situation with which they can live.

13. Recently, perhaps partly as a result of disillusion with the latest gyrations of Chinese foreign policy and the first hints of suspicion that the Chinese utopia may turn out to be as shaky as the Soviet one, there have been interesting calls by Western Marxists for a critical approach to socialist societies. The December 1972 issue of the West German leftist journal *Kursbuch* was an important first stab in this direction.

INTERLUDE

A TALE
OF TWO SLUMS

"DRINK Inca-Cola—It's Ours!" proclaims an advertising poster at various intersections in the city of Lima. Would the slogan be the same if Inca-Cola were a subsidiary of Pepsi? In any event, its brash assertiveness is typical of Peru under the "Revolutionary Government of the Armed Forces." The young officers who sit in all government offices (in uniform, to boot) seem to speak the same language as the young intellectuals—nationalist in tone, socialist in content. The bookstores are bulging with Marxist literature of all descriptions—even the bookstore in the close vicinity of the gleaming new Sheraton hotel. "Neither capitalist nor communist" is the official self-definition of the regime. What is it then? Socialist? Presumably, but the officially favored term is "cooperativist." The meaning of the term is not completely clear as yet. Its major empirical point of reference is the formation of what the regime calls "social property": Both in the agricultural sector and in urban industry there is a welter of new legislation seeking to transfer ownership of the means of production from the "bourgeoisie" (foreign or national private enterprise) to local units of peasants or workers. The policy, while clearly anticapitalist and socialist in inspiration, also wishes to be "nonstatist": The state is intended to be a "transmission mechanism" which will transfer but not retain economic control.

On the outskirts of Lima is being constructed what is proudly described as "the first cooperativist city in Peru." It is called Villa El Salvador. The concept is gigantic; so is the physical realization.

Lima, like nearly all Latin American cities, is ringed by a huge agglomeration of squatters' settlements (called *barreadas* in Peru). Within less than two years about one hundred thousand people were moved from these settlements into El Salvador. Government offices were working overtime for months organizing the logistics of the move. The government surveyed the land, designed the future city in blueprints, and provided transportation and other assistance during the move. The government also provided building materials and architectural supervision. But then, in the style of previous *barreadas*, the people built their own houses, within the specifications of the architects. As the city was being constructed, the government provided basic municipal services—water, sewage, electricity. Schools and health centers went up. SINAMOS, the organization for "popular mobilization" set up by the regime, started to gather the population into political units. Perhaps it may serve as validation of the "nonstatist" ideology that some of these units soon came into conflict with various government agencies.

The land belonged to the government before construction began, and will not be transferred to individual ownership. Legal arrangements are not fully worked out as yet, but ownership will be vested in various "cooperative" units, possibly set up on a neighborhood basis. Nor will private enterprise be allowed to move into El Salvador. A large piece of land on the edge of the new city has been designated for industrial use. Private companies offered to build factories there, to utilize the huge labor force now concentrated in the area, but the government refused permission. The factories, when they are built, will also be "socially owned," with the initial capital investment provided by the government. Studies are being made to determine what type of industry should be set up in El Salvador, in terms of the labor skills available and the economic needs of the Lima region. In the meantime, people travel long distances to work—if they have work.

On a small hill in the center of El Salvador stands a large statue of Christ, hands outstretched in blessing. From the hill one can look over the new city sprawled over a vast area all around. The vista may be sociologically impressive; it is hardly so in aesthetic terms. The houses are arranged in endless rows, neat and orderly, but wretched in appearance. There are houses both in brick and in wood. Dust swirls through the streets. Everywhere there are small stores, set up in wooden huts and stalls—groceries, mechanics, shoemakers, barbershops. People stand in long lines waiting for a bus.

Driving back to Lima, in the company of two enthusiastic young SINAMOS functionaries, one is taken through another *barreada*—supposedly for the sake of contrast. It is a much older settlement, the houses are almost all in brick, and some are larger than those in El Salvador. The streets are narrower, less neat, and dirtier. The people here did not want to move to El Salvador (the government apparently made no effort to force them), and they even refused to be organized by SINAMOS. "You will see," says one of the functionaries, "everything here is chaos—very different from El Salvador." She adds that there is much crime and prostitution here. The chaos is not visible to the naked eye. Neither is the alleged contrast. But this doesn't prove anything; sociological facts are often inaccessible visually. At the same time one wonders why the people of this *barreada* refused to be organized in accordance with the government's design. Were they just suspicious of the government? Or could it be that they already had their own organization, one with which they were reasonably satisfied?

The young functionaries do not seem troubled by such questions. It is clear to them that one place represents hope for the future, the other a sterile past. They are proud of El Salvador. Standing near the statue of Christ on the hilltop, one of them looks over the panorama, beaming with pride, and says: "I'm sure there is no other place like this in the world."

Well, there is. And it is, as it happens, in Brazil.

When construction began in the 1950s on Brasilia, the new capital of Brazil deep in the interior, the squatters' settlements (*favelas*) grew faster than the "official" city. Brasilia is still ringed with favela-type "satellite towns" (as they are described in government parlance), but they have been removed from the immediate proximity of Brasilia proper toward the outer limits of the Federal District. Thus it is possible to admire the science-fiction architectural marvels of the new capital, its miles and miles of soaring steel-and-glass edifices, and its heroic monuments, without being disturbed by the sights and smells of the poor. Yet it is not correct to say that the government has done nothing to improve the conditions of the capital's proletariat. Its most grandiose effort is Ceilandia, a new "satellite town" about a half hour's drive from the center of Brasilia.

Ceilandia's name derives from the Portuguese words "Campaign for the Elimination of Invasions"—the title of the government program to do away with favelas. The similarities with the Peruvian project are striking. They include the physical dimensions and the time span: Here, too, a population of about one hundred thousand squatters was resettled in less than two years. It is not clear whether any coercion was used in the process, but people were collected from existing favelas and put down into Ceilandia in a massive and rapid transfer. Here, too, the government provided architectural advice and building materials (indeed, small plants to produce building materials were set up within the new community), but the people built their own houses. Here, too, as the houses went up, the government provided basic municipal services. And here, too, there are schools and health services. The Brazilian government also has its own version of "popular mobilization," though the rhetoric is nationalist without the leftist flavoring. MOBRAL, the agency for the promotion of literacy, has an intensive program in Ceilandia. Indeed, it seems that everybody is going to school. Most of the work available to residents is in construction. Brasilia is still being built. Only now, for example, has work begun in earnest on the area that will house all the foreign embassies. No one seems to know what the people will do when construction of the capital has been finally completed.

Visually, at least to the eye of a nonarchitect, Ceilandia in its details looks very much like El Salvador: Rough constructions in brick and wood; long, dusty streets, in orderly arrays of intersecting straight lines; small shops and stores scattered through the area; ramshackle buses carrying people to and from faraway places of work. Here, too, there are young functionaries, apparently full of enthusiasm for what they are doing. A brand-new day-care center has just been opened. The proud director insists on showing the visitor every corner of the building. The children, here as in El Salvador, are curious about any newcomers. Here they are Afro-American rather than Indo-American. Afro-American children smile more readily than their Indo-American contemporaries. The same difference may be detected as between, say, Venezuela and Mexico. It has nothing to do with political systems.

An essential difference, however, is in the respective concepts of ownership. No talk of "social property" in Ceilandia—needless to say. All land in the Federal District belongs to the government, so that there were no problems with land titles. Here, as all over Brazil, urban resettlement is under the auspices of the National Housing Bank, itself a government agency. As soon as a family settles in Ceilandia, it receives the title to the land on which it is "autoconstructing" its house. The BNH holds the title in mortgage. Each plot is divided into two parts. At first a wooden house is built in the rear part, while the part closer to the street is left empty. As the family is able, the front part is used to build a brick house and the wooden construction is eliminated. At this point there are only a few brick houses.

The concept is to foster private ownership and the family security that, supposedly, comes from it. "Private home ownership is a matter of principle with us," says a government official in explaining the program, "it is the basis of our program of social rehabilitation." When translated into U.S. currency, the monthly payments on the mortgages (varying by size of house) are very low; translated into Brazilian wages, they are not quite that low. If payments are kept up, the mortgage can be paid off, in most cases, in about five years. Not surprisingly, government spokesmen and their critics differ on the facts in this matter. The BNH claims that its program is working and that it is creating a vast new class of propertied workers. Critics claim that large numbers of people are unable to keep up the payments (because of inflation and unemployment), and that many thousands have lost their houses once more. A critical American resident speaks of the entire BNH program as "one big ripoff." It is difficult for an outsider to judge the merits of these claims.

There is a starkly modernistic television tower in Brasilia, with a plush restaurant and, on top of that, an observation platform. From it one can view the immense panorama of the new capital, including the boulevard with all the ministries and the surrealistic national cathedral (no hint of transcendence in the latter—one goes inside and feels that one is in but another ministry). At the end of the boulevard stands the Plaza of the Three Powers—Congress, Supreme Court, and Presidential Palace—creating a visual harmony with an ironic relationship to present political realities. One must turn around and look in the other direction in order to see Ceilandia, an unimpressive expanse of low buildings in the far distance. The two vistas are counterpositioned visually. Whether they are also contradictions socially is a matter of interpretation.

It was suggested earlier that a critique of different models of development ought to compare the best, not the worst, examples. El Salvador and Ceilandia represent two concepts, the difference between which is actually brought out more sharply by the similarities in their respective realizations. Each concept, in its "official" formulation, embodies the best aspirations of the two models of national development. Many critical questions can be raised with regard to both concepts. The questions will be much more urgent in the Brazilian case. One *must* raise, in discussing any aspect of Brazilian development today, the question of government terror. Whatever is or is not happening in Brazil must be seen against a background of police intimidation, mass arrests, torture, and assassination. Perhaps even more seriously, it must be seen in conjunction with wage and employment policies that deliberately postpone the alleviation of brutal misery for the sake of economic growth. More specifically, one may raise questions such as those asked by the critics of the BNH program—which add up, finally, to the question of whether the whole concept of property formation may not be illusionary.

In terms of human urgencies, the questions suggested by El

Salvador are of a milder sort. There is no terror in Peru and the development policies of the Velasco regime deliberately subordinate economic growth to social reform. Yet one may question the ideological fixation on "social property," which denies the people of El Salvador present employment opportunities offered by private industry in the name of a rather hazy future ideal. This question leads logically to the broader question to be asked about the Peruvian model (a question previously suggested in the discussion of socialist models)—whether, in the end, the model will eventuate in a shared poverty, that is, in a condition that might then be described as "social impoverishment." One may also raise questions about the future prospects of a political system that substitutes government-run "mobilization" programs for the electoral process.

To see the two concepts in sharp relief, however, it may be a useful exercise to bracket all of the above questions, at least for a moment. *Suppose* it were possible to realize the concept of El Salvador without the aforementioned economic and political risks. *Suppose* the concept of Ceilandia were realized in a Brazil that would still be capitalist but freed from its present terror and the inhumanities of its present economic course. In that case, for which of the two concepts would one opt? If one makes this kind of supposition, a host of empirical questions are bracketed. The value alternatives then emerge with great clarity. Sooner or later, they will have to be faced.

Chapter IV

"CONSCIOUSNESS RAISING" AND THE VICISSITUDES OF POLICY

IN THE EARLY 1960s, before the military coup, Paulo Freire and his collaborators experimented with a new method of literacy education in the Northeast of Brazil. The basic idea of the new approach was simple: Teaching literacy was not to be an isolated activity, but was to be part of a larger enterprise of broadening the intellectual horizons of the previously illiterate. An important aspect of this was political. The illiterate were to learn reading and writing at the hand of topics (Freire called these "generative themes") that concerned their everyday social experience. For the impoverished rural proletariat of the Northeast, this was to a high degree an experience of deprivation, exploitation, and oppression. The educational purpose was to combine "alphabetization" with the inculcation of a deliberate awareness of the facts of oppression, as well as an understanding of the forces (economic, political, social-structural) that supposedly caused these facts. This political awareness, rather than literacy for its own sake, was what Freire was primarily interested in fostering. His method was thus, in essence, one of political education—more precisely, of education for political activity. It is hardly surprising that, after 1964, the military regime put a prompt stop to the

111

program, forcing Freire to leave the country. The present literacy program of the Brazilian government, MOBRAL, has retained some of the strictly technical innovations of Freire's method, but has completely stripped it of its political content, and thus of its essential purpose.

From a purely pedagogical viewpoint, Freire's method has shown itself to be very successful, not only in Brazil but in other places where it has been tried more recently. It has been demonstrated that adults of average intelligence can be taught literacy in about six weeks. The clue to this success is in the motivation. People learning to read and write around topics that relate directly to their everyday experience will do so more easily than if they use texts that have nothing to do with their own lives. The learning process will be further stimulated if its results are directly related to actions desired by the learner—in this instance, political actions designed to alleviate his overall condition. For Freire and his collaborators, however, these pedagogical results are not the real justification of the method. The political themes are not dragged in to help with literacy training. On the contrary, literacy training is but a useful tool for expansion of political consciousness and for political activation of the individual.

It is this essential political purpose, rather than the technical innovations in literacy education, which has created world-wide interest in Freire's method. He called his method *concientização*—literally, "making conscious." This name has caught on internationally—as *concientización* in Spanish-speaking Latin America, as *Bewusstmachung* in the West German left, and (a very apt translation) as "consciousness raising" in the United States. In most current usage of the term the original educational context has been left behind. Rather, "consciousness raising" is the method by which any oppressed group is taught to understand its condition and (in a unity of theory and praxis) to be activated politically for the revolutionary transformation of this condition. In its left context, "consciousness raising" is the cognitive preparation for revolutionary action.

This wider usage raises some interesting questions on the relationship of theoretical understanding and political practice. Indeed, this usage calls for a critique. Such a critique may be undertaken even if one has great sympathy with Freire's original intentions in Brazil—and also if one concedes that there are situations in the world that call for revolution, and that any viable revolution presupposes something like revolutionary consciousness. Even if these propositions are stipulated, the concept of "consciousness raising," as currently used, implies some highly questionable assumptions. To wit, it implies philosophical error and political irony.

A good way to begin a critique of the concept is to concretize it sociologically: *Whose* consciousness is supposed to be raised, and *who* is supposed to do the raising? The answer is clear wherever the term is used in political rhetoric: It is the consciousness of "the masses" that must be raised, and it is the "vanguard" that will do the job. But who are these people? "The masses" are, of course, whatever sociological category has been assigned the role of the revolutionary proletariat by the ideologists of the putative revolution—industrial workers (in countries where this particular assignment still seems plausible), peasants, landless rural laborers, even white-collar "wage slaves" or students. The "vanguard" consists of the aforementioned ideologists—typically intellectuals, who may be defined for our purposes here as individuals whose major preoccupation in life is the production and distribution of theories. Such individuals have usually passed through a long period of formal education, and usually come from the upper middle or upper classes of their societies. The concretization, therefore, may be put this way: "Consciousness raising" is a project of higher-class individuals directed at a lower-class population. It is the latter, *not* the former, whose consciousness is to be raised. What is more, the consciousness at issue is the consciousness that the lower-class population has of *its own situation*. Thus a crucial assumption of the concept is that lower-class people do not understand their own situation, that they are in need of enlightenment on the matter, and that this service can be provided by selected higher-class individuals.

One side benefit of such concretization is the insight that the concept is not necessarily linked to the political left. In the United States, for example, a left-wing ideologist may be convinced that he understands the real interests of the working class much better than most workers do themselves. But a right-wing politician or a middle-of-the-road liberal social worker may be animated by precisely the same conviction in dealing with other clienteles. "They don't understand what is good for them" is the clue formula of all "consciousness raising," of whatever ideological or political coloration—and "we do understand" is the inevitable corollary. Put differently, the concept allocates different cognitive levels to "them" and to "us"—and it assigns to "us" the task of raising "them" to the higher level. Coupled with this epistemological arrogance is a recurrent irritation with "those people" who stubbornly refuse the salvation that is so benevolently offered to them: "How can they be so blind?"

Although one may find this stance morally offensive, there is a philosophical error here that has nothing directly to do with morality. The error lies in what one may call the hierarchical view of consciousnesses. There is something medieval about this, rooted perhaps in the old scholastic notion of the "chain of being"—the mind of God is at one end, that of the dumb animals on the other, and in between are we humans, carefully stratified in terms of proximity to either pole. The divine pole is hardly visible in the universe of discourse under consideration, but the animal pole certainly is. Even Freire himself, a man reputed to be personally unpretentious, has this to say about the consciousness of peasants (in his rather unfortunate essay "Cultural Action"): "This level of consciousness . . . corresponds to such a dehumanized reality that existence in it, for men, means living like animals. It is often impossible for such men to recognize the differences between themselves and, say, horses." One may wonder about the ethnographic data on which such an assertion is based. But there is no ambiguity about the implications for the "consciousness raising" program: Someone, whose consciousness is on a less than human level, is raised to the level of humanity by someone else—who, by definition, is more human already.

There is, of course, an affinity between "consciousness raising" and the Marxist concept of "false consciousness." There, too, the intellectual identified with the "vanguard" lays claim to a cognitively privileged status: He and only he has reality by the shortest possible hair. This cognitive superiority, which allows him to designate other people's consciousness as false, is ipso facto a human superiority: The cognitively superior individual is, by virtue of his consciousness, at a higher level of freedom, and thus of humanity. It cannot be our task here to pursue these conceptions to their roots in the inner recesses of the Hegelian metaphysic, nor can we undertake a critique of the latter here. But it is possible to make some fairly simple observations.

If the hierarchical view of consciousness simply referred to levels of information on specific topics, there would be no need to quarrel with it. For instance, we might stipulate (at least for purposes of this discussion) that one of Freire's young people—say, a university student from a bourgeois background—knew more about the economic structure of Brazil than a peasant to whom he was teaching the alphabet. One might further stipulate (even if one sometimes wonders) that bourgeois intellectuals as a group know more about economics than peasants as a group. If the process of imparting information from the first group to the second is called "consciousness raising," there would be nothing more wrong with the term than a certain maladroitness in choice of words. But the term, of course, is not that innocent. It implies the aforementioned cognitive and indeed ontological hierarchy. For that, however, there is no evidence whatever—at least not for anyone who has not performed an act of faith. Intellectuals may be superior to peasants in their information and perspectives *on specific topics*. If one wishes to extend this superiority to information and perspectives *in general*, plausibility disappears, for peasants very clearly have far superior information and perspectives on *other topics* —such as plant and animal life, soil conditions, the weather, and a multitude of manual skills and material artifacts (not to mention the intricacies of kinship and the true significance of dreams).

It is possible to argue that the intellectuals' information "kit" is superior in its usefulness for certain purposes, such as, for example, political action; but the peasants' is just as obviously superior for other purposes. It is *not* possible to claim intrinsic superiority to either body of information. Furthermore, even if it were, there is no way of demonstrating that superiority of information is also a *human* superiority. To assume such an identity is to exhibit the most obviously self-serving myopia of the individual who has invested his life in the gathering and theoretical organization of information, and who then claims that this activity, more than any other, defines what is truly human. Almost any peasant who has even a vestigial relationship to the mythology of his tradition can easily turn the tables in this argument: It is the soil that gives life, he may say, and to be human is to adhere to the soil. By the same logic, the member of a hunting society will define the hunter as the only fully human being, and little boys with pimples will maintain that only very superior types have this particular trait.

The philosophical error implied by the concept of "consciousness raising" is closely related to its political irony. Those who employ the concept in their rhetoric usually see themselves as genuine democrats, close to the throbbing life of "the masses," and emphatically "antielitist." In the same essay in which Freire tells us that peasants cannot distinguish themselves from horses (on the very next page, no less), he denounces the allegedly reformist activities of the higher classes: "The more representatives of the elites engage in paternalistic action, the more generous they consider themselves. The practice of this false generosity . . . requires men's misery, their alienation, their docility, their resignation, their silence." It is hard to find a better description of the stance of "consciousness-raising" intellectuals. And it is hard to imagine a more "elitist" program (and, for that matter, a more "paternalistic" one) than one based on the assumption that a certain group of people is dehumanized to the point of animality, is unable either to perceive this condition or rescue itself from it, and requires the (presumably selfless) assistance of others for both the perception and the rescue operation. The elite that Freire had in mind in the above passage (imagine, say, a group of social workers committed to the status quo in Latin America) is just as sure as Freire's preferred elite of revolutionary intellectuals that *it* has a consciousness superior to that of the peasants. It only differs in the ideological contents of this consciousness—and perhaps it even has a slight moral advantage in not deluding itself that *its* consciousness embodies the true will of "the masses."

The critique of the concept of "consciousness raising" is important because it may serve as an introduction to a very different approach to the relationship of theory and policy. Such an approach may begin with a *postulate of the equality of all empirically available worlds of consciousness.*

Every human being lives in a world. That is, he is conscious of reality in terms of specific cognitive structures that give cohesion and meaning to the ongoing flux of his experiences. No individual has a world identical with that of any other, but human groups do live together in shared worlds, and indeed society would not be possible otherwise. Thus the world of a middle-class intellectual differs greatly from that of a peasant, and so do the consciousnesses of these two social types. It is possible to argue that the one consciousness is superior, or on a higher level, than the other in terms of specific contents. In other words, people know different things, and one body of knowledge may be more useful in a given situation than another. It is also possible to make moral judgments concerning different worlds and consciousnesses. For instance, one might propose that the intellectual's consciousness is superior in compassion, but that the peasant's is on a higher level of personal integration (peasants, that is, tend to be callously indifferent to the suffering of outsiders, while intellectuals are a notoriously neurotic lot). Such moral evaluations, however, are debatable. How is one to decide on the weight of these two traits, compassion and integrity, in a hierarchy of consciousnesses? One thing is clear: No objective, scientific analysis of empirical data will help in making a decision.

Moral judgments apart, every human world must be deemed, in principle, as being equal to every other human world in its access to reality. Perhaps one might want to modify this proposition with respect to very young children or mentally deficient individuals. The proposition nevertheless holds for any world that gives meaning to the lives of any collectivity of adults. In the nineteenth century, in sharp opposition to the Hegelian metaphysic of progress, the historian Leopold von Ranke insisted that "every age is immediate to God." Thus Western civilization could not view itself as the pinnacle of human history—nor, in principle, could any other civilization or era. *Mutatis mutandis*, the same proposition may be made against any attempt to order different human worlds hierarchically: "Every consciousness is immediate to reality." Human beings have produced an immense variety of ways in which they have sought to relate to reality, to give order to experience, and to live meaningful lives. There is neither a philosophical nor a scientific method by which this variety can be arranged in a hierarchy from lower to higher (or, more precisely, there are many different hierarchies in terms of which, with equal plausibility, the empirically available structures can be arranged).

On the level of meaning, every "inhabitant" of a world has an immediate access to it which is superior to that of any "noninhabitant." Thus the peasant knows his world far better than any outsider ever can. Now, this does *not* mean that the outsider may not have information and perspectives bearing on the peasant's world which are not in the peasant's possession. Such information and perspectives may be transmitted, conceivably to the peasant's benefit. What is involved in this kind of transmission is the "exportation" of the cognitive contents from one world to another. What *may* be involved, moreover, is that eventually one world swallows up the other. Empirically, this will mean that the "inhabitants" of one world impose their particular modes of perception, evaluation, and action on those who previously had organized their relationship to reality differently. This kind of "cognitive imperialism," as one might call it, is a crucially important component of modernization.

117

The process may be welcomed or deplored. But it is not very helpful to call it "consciousness raising." A better term would be *conversion*, and a very good way of understanding anyone claiming to raise the consciousness of other people is to see him as a *missionary*. A peculiar mixture of arrogance ("I know the truth") and benevolence ("I want to save you") has always been the chief psychological hallmark of missionary activity.

The individual human mind is probably limited in the contents it can hold. It is certainly limited in its capacity to focus—or, to use the phenomenological term, in its "attentionality." If one is attentive to one aspect of reality, one will be less attentive to other aspects. An individual who devotes himself to politics will probably not become an accomplished musician. The same principle of selectivity applies to the worlds "inhabited" by human beings collectively (and thus to their consciousnesses). If a society puts collective emphasis on the manipulative conquest of nature, it will probably neglect the arts of contemplation—and vice versa. Now, if one society "converts" the other to its order of priorities, there will be a shift in the contents of consciousness. People will become attentive to one set of data (such as the data of science and technology), and they will "forget" another set (such as the data obtained from mystical exercises or from other forms of "irrational" intuition). Again, the term "consciousness raising" is misleading when applied to this change. It immediately implies a value judgment; if one makes such a judgment, one should so label it. To designate a rearrangement of cognitive contents more objectively, one may call it a *trade-off*. There will probably be different opinions as to who made the better bargain.

Put simply, no one is "more conscious" than anyone else; different individuals are conscious of different things. Therefore there is no such phenomenon as *concientização*, unless one is reviving someone who's just been hit over the head. All of us are moving around on the same level, trying to make sense of the universe and doing our best to cope with the necessities of living. No one is in a position to "raise" anyone else; some of us try to convince others that our *modus operandi* makes more sense than theirs. Such efforts may or may not be laudable, but they are, in principle, transactions between equals.

The critique of the concept of "consciousness raising," then, may be undertaken on a theoretical, even a philosophical, basis. It could be expanded considerably by way of a detailed phenomenological analysis of human consciousness. Our interest here, though, is in the moral and political implications of the critique. These are particularly relevant for intellectuals who provide theories with policy applicability. The moral implication is exceedingly simple: It is tantamount to a lesson in humility. The political implication is essentially an injunction to be skeptical of any outsider's claim to superior knowledge of an insider's world. What people say about their own social reality must always be taken with great seriousness—not only because this is morally right, but because failure to do so may lead to great and sometimes catastrophic practical consequences. The area of development policy is full of cases in which costly disaster could have been avoided if the policy makers had paid less attention to alleged experts brought in from the outside—and correspondingly more attention to what the insiders in question had to say. There will be occasion to return to this point later on.

Perhaps the category of "cognitive respect," introduced earlier in our argument, makes better sense now. It is an attitude based on the postulate of the equality of worlds of consciousness. The term leads to another—that of "cognitive participation." There has been much discussion of political participation in development policy. Essentially, what is at issue is the ability of those at whom the policy is aimed to participate in the decisions that have to be made. In other words, at issue is participation on the level of praxis. There is also, though, a problem of participation on the level of theory. One of the most-quoted maxims of sociology is the statement by W. I. Thomas—"If people define a situation as real, it is real in its consequences." All action in society depends upon specific "definitions of the situation." A crucial question, therefore, is: "Who does the defining?" Every "definition of the situation" implies specific theoretical presuppositions, a frame of reference, in the last resort a view of reality. Once a situation has been defined in certain terms, a number of practical options are ipso facto foreclosed. It is a very limited notion of participation to let an elite define a situation in complete disregard of the ways in which this situation is *already defined* by those who live in it—and then to allow the latter a voice in the decisions made on the basis of the preordained definition. A more meaningful notion of participation will include a voice in the definitions of the situation that underlie this or that decision-making option.

Put simply again: There are different ways of understanding participation. An individual, by virtue of his power or his status, can say to a group of people that what they need right now is to repair the roofs

119

of their houses, and he can then ask them to vote on different methods of doing this job. One may say that they are thereby participating in the decision-making process. But the decisions that will now be taken are all based on the predefinition of the situation, to the effect that repairing the roofs is the need of the moment. It is quite possible that this group of people is perfectly satisfied with their roofs, and greatly concerned with their ancestral shrines. Does the individual with the power and the status allow them to propose a different order of priorities? Can they be different perhaps not only in terms of perceptions but of values? If he does, whatever one calls the resultant process, it will be participation of a more fundamental and ample sort.

Two issues which have had large significance for the methodology of the social sciences are also relevant for anyone who wants to understand any human problem or situation. These are the issues of "ethnocentrism" and "value-freedom." Both are relevant to development, in terms of theoretical understanding as well as policy.

"Ethnocentrism" is a pejorative term, coined in the early years of this century by William Graham Sumner. Since then it has acquired wide usage outside the social sciences as well as within. The term refers, of course, to an attitude that is narrowly bound by the cultural or social biases of an individual. It has long been a truism of social-science training that this attitude is bad for the scientist; largely in conjunction with the diffusion of liberal ideals of tolerance, it is now widely assumed that the attitude is bad for anyone. The good social scientist, and by extension the good liberal citizen, will constantly seek to overcome his "ethnocentric" prejudices in dealing with people or situations outside his own sociocultural background.

In the area of development, the label of "ethnocentrism" is commonly used to denigrate the imposition of Western perspectives and Western values on non-Western situations. For example, for a long time American political scientists tended to view the political side of development as a progressive approximation to Western institutions of representative democracy—the closer a society could be placed to the latter, the more developed it was pronounced to be. This viewpoint has been criticized in recent years (vigorously so from within the discipline of American political science) as an ideological expression of "ethnocentrism." Of all social scientists, it is probably the anthropologists who have for the longest time and with the strongest emphasis placed the battle against "ethnocentrism" at the heart of professional training. The anthropologist must rigorously discipline himself to suspend his socio-cultural bias and to immerse himself, in complete openness, in the alien situation he is studying.

As far as development is concerned, however, the injunction against "ethnocentrism" has recently taken another turn: It is no longer just a methodological caveat against the imposition of Western frames of reference, but is, in addition, a moral attack on Western values as such. The difference between these two variants of anti-"ethnocentrism" must be clarified.

An extreme example might serve for such clarification. Suppose an anthropologist is studying a cannibalistic society. In order to understand this society, it will be essential that he try to suspend or control his own horror and moral outrage, at least for the duration of the study. Unless he does this, he will be incapable of accomplishing the act of under-standing. Thus he knows that he himself could participate in a canni-balistic ritual only by fighting down intense nausea, and that he would be plagued with terrible guilt feelings afterwards—but he must refrain from projecting such nausea or guilt onto the actual participants. Indeed, a crucial step in his acquiring understanding of the situation will be the insight that there are people who can eat other people in perfect equanimity. Needless to say, this does *not* mean that the anthropologist must cultivate moral approval of the practice, recommend it to others (including his own home society), or enthusiastically join in it. But suppose now that the same anthropologist is called upon to contribute to the formation of development policy in this particular society. Suppose further that the nationalist leadership of that society is quite willing to build cannibalism into the development plan (perhaps for purposes of population control?). Is the anthropologist meekly to assent to this, in the name of anti-"ethnocentrism"? Is he perhaps even to express a sense of inferiority about his Western soft-heartedness, and admiration for the healthy robustness of the other society's moral code?

Actually, the example is not that extreme. The Third World today is blessed with a number of development strategies that calmly include (implicitly or explicitly) the sacrifice of large numbers of human beings, be it by direct violence or by policies that deliberately refrain from alleviating suffering. Criticisms of these strategies are routinely turned back by negative reference to Western "ethnocentrism." If the strategies are by right-wing regimes, the critics will be labeled "bleeding-heart Western liberals." If it is left-wing regimes that are engaged in the "cannibalism," the critics will be denounced for their "Western bourgeois morality." In both instances the anti-"ethnocentric" proposition will be that "there is a different attitude to the value of individual life in society X." This proposition is put forth not only as an empirically valid description, but as a moral justification.

Some basic confusions are involved in this expansion of the notion of "ethnocentrism." Most basically, there is no ready nexus between methodology and morality: To accept a fact as empirically existent is by no means to accept it as morally right. Within the moral universe of discourse, furthermore, it is not consistent to apply Western values to one set of facts and denounce such application as "ethnocentric" in relation to other facts. For example, one cannot quiver with moral indignation at exploitation of the peasantry in society Y, but reject as "ethnocentric" Western bias any indignation about mass executions in society Z. If "ethnocentrism" is bad in the realm of moral judgment, the only proper attitude toward *both* situations is moral acceptance of the fact that these people just happen to have different values. Indeed, in society Y it will then probably be plausible to reject as Western prejudice the notion (outlandish within the cultural context of Y) that peasants have any function in life *other than* being exploited.

Western civilization has produced historically unprecedented values concerning human rights, human dignity, and human freedom. These values are today at the heart of *all* politically relevant ideologies of development and liberation. If it is "ethnocentric" to adhere to these values, we would suggest that one be "ethnocentric" with enthusiasm. The currently fashionable denigration of Western values is as intellectually confused as it is morally distasteful. To hold values, however, means ipso facto to engage in moral judgments. If one believes that human beings are entitled to certain fundamental rights simply by virtue of being human (a Western value *par excellence*), then one is constrained morally to condemn situations in which these rights are denied. If, on the other hand, such moral judgments are deemed impermissible, then they will be impermissible in all cases—and, logically, the only political attitude possible will be one devoid of any morality. Such an attitude, we would contend, is tantamount to dehumanization.

"Cognitive respect," then, means that one takes with utmost seriousness the way in which others define reality. It does *not* mean that one makes no moral distinctions among these definitions. Similarly, "cognitive participation" means that one tries to safeguard the right of others to codefine those aspects of reality that are relevant to policy. It does *not* mean that one accords the same moral weight (and, if one has the power, the same political support) to the definitions of the cannibals and of those who would do away with cannibalism. Put simply: To understand is *not* to choose, but to accept as facts the choices of others. To act politically *is* to choose—and that means, whether one sees this or not, to choose between moral alternatives. Such choice, when there is power behind it, inevitably means *imposing* some of one's values upon others; after all, there may be those who stubbornly insist on going on with their old custom of eating their fellow-men.

The intrinsic relations among theory, policy, and morality may be further clarified by a consideration of the concept of "value-freeness." This concept was coined in Germany by Max Weber at about the same time that Sumner was teaching his American students not to be "ethnocentric," and there was a similar intention behind it. The ideal of "value-freeness" is that the scientific observer of human affairs should subdue his own values for the sake of understanding. It is virtually identical with the notion that science should be objective.

In Weber's time there was an intense controversy over this matter, most of it centering on the question of whether "value-freeness" was possible in the first place. In American social science there has been a reiteration of the controversy in recent years, most of it based on misinterpretations of Weber and most of it marked by a lack of methodological sophistication. One interesting aspect of the recent debates is that the *same* people who have rejected "value-freeness" as an ideal for social scientists have also been exhorting the latter to divest themselves of their Western "ethnocentrism"—a rather remarkable contradiction. This cannot be the place to review either controversy, but a few basic clarifications will be useful for our argument.

"Value-freeness" is an ideal for theoretical understanding. It does *not* imply (and was never intended by Weber to imply) that the social scientist who aspires to it is himself free of values, is unaware of the values operative in the situation he is studying, or has the notion that one can engage in policies devoid of value consequences. To the extent that all these implications have been falsely deduced from the term, it is perhaps poorly chosen. In essence, "value-freeness" means that one tries to perceive social reality apart from one's hopes and fears. This does not mean that one has no hopes or fears, nor does it mean that one refrains from acting to realize what one hopes for or to avert what one fears. "Value-freeness" in science is, therefore, perfectly compatible with the most intense value commitments and with intense activity springing from these commitments.

The value-free analysis of situations pertinent to development means that one tries to understand even if that understanding is contrary to one's wishes. It especially means that one tries to gain a detached view of the probable consequences of one's favorite policies—including the probable unintended consequences. It also means that one carefully observes the interaction between values and facts, regardless of whether one adheres to the values in question. In all this, "value-freeness" pertains to the theoretical attitude; it cannot pertain to action. One may aspire to value-free science; value-free policy is an absurdity.

The recent controversy about "value-freeness" has to a large extent been an exercise in shadow-boxing. Any honest observer of a social situation will try to see it "as it really is," not as he would like it to be— even if he adheres to a methodological position that rejects "value-freeness." The real debate has been about something else—to wit, the question of who is served politically by the social scientist, and who *should* be served. In the United States, revelations about Project Camelot and utilization of the social sciences in "counterinsurgency" research have brought this underlying question into sharp focus. But it is a moral rather than a methodological question, and it would be helpful if it were dealt with as such. It is a moral, not a methodological, principle that a social scientist is responsible for the political uses to which his findings are put. And if, in a given situation, one says that social scientists should support the revolution rather than those trying to suppress it, then one is making a moral judgment rather than taking a philosophical position on the possibilities of scientific understanding.

We would take for granted that being a scientist does not absolve an individual from moral responsibility for his actions. We would stipulate that an individual, even if he is a scientist, would favor actions in accordance with his values—and, given the means to do so, would want to participate in such actions. The question remains how the individual can be most useful qua social scientist. We would answer *this* question in terms of an ideal of objective understanding (even if in practice this ideal is often hard to attain). Take the case of a social scientist committed to a revolutionary movement. He may want to shoulder a gun—but others can do this. He may engage in propaganda and agitation—but others are probably better at this task. Even in terms of his usefulness to the revolutionary movement, the social scientist will be best employed in the task of objective understanding: What is the situation really like? How can its future course be projected? What is the strategy by which the movement is most likely to succeed? What are the probable consequences of this or that action? All of these are questions of fact, not of value, and the answers most useful to the revolutionaries will be, precisely, value-free answers.

In the area of development, a social scientist may be propelled by his values in different directions. He may want to advocate socialism, to search for capitalist alternatives, perhaps to find methods that will resist modernization and preserve traditional ways of life. Given favorable circumstances, he may want to engage in any number of actions that will foster these value commitments. However, his greatest usefulness qua social scientist is going to be the calmer business of clarification. Probably the most useful statements he can make will be in an "if/then" form: "*If* your development policy is based on such-and-such values, *then* these are some of the likely consequences." Or: "*If* you take action A, *then* you are implicitly choosing value B over the alternative value C." Or: "*If* you take this action, *then* you should be aware of these particular side-effects that you did not originally intend or foresee." Such statements are, if you will, value-neutral—but they are not value-blind. Nor do they preclude the addendum: "This is all I can tell you as a social scientist—but here is what I believe you ought to do, given that both you and I adhere to value C." Or: "If you do this—give me a gun, I want to join you." Or, for that matter: "I regret that, for reasons of conscience, I must herewith submit my resignation—and I've already given a copy of my report to the opposition."

"Cognitive respect," therefore, is a category very close to that of "value-freeness." It is, as it were, a theoretical virtue. "Cognitive participation," however, is a political rather than theoretical category. As such, it cannot be divorced from considerations of value, since politics is never value-free. Thus one will seek ways to *deny* participation, cognitive as well as active, to those who would define reality in terms of cannibalism, or of racial hatred, or of the right of one group to enslave another. It will be helpful if, in doing this, one is clear about the clash of both values and power—that is, if one does *not* delude oneself that the values one is seeking to impose are "really" their values as well.

A critique of the concept of "consciousness raising" leads to the proposition that there can be no such thing, because all of us are, in principle, equally endowed when it comes to having consciousness. At best, we differ in terms of the quantity of information we possess about certain topics. In looking at the information on which policy is typically based, however, even this last statement has to be modified. In this connection, we would propose the *postulate of ignorance in the formation of policy*.

To be sure, policy makers differ in the amount of information available to them and in the seriousness with which they look upon these data before plunging into a particular course of action. Perhaps too much information can actually inhibit policy making, and two political scientists, Warren Ilchman and Norman Uphoff (in their book *The Political Economy of Change*, 1971), have even proposed a principle of "optimal ignorance." If governing is choosing, and if a plenitude of information increases awareness of all possible choices in a given situation, then there may well be a point of diminishing returns, after which any new input of information will simply paralyze those who have to make the political decisions. The Ilchman-Uphoff principle thus introduces the simile of Buridan's Ass into political science. Nevertheless, it remains generally plausible to say that the usual problem of the policy maker is too little, not too much, information.

Social scientists are in the habit of preaching the necessity of bigger and better information to policy makers, a recommendation which clearly involves vested interests. Typically they say that "there ought to be a study," and this means funds, jobs, status, and patronage for social scientists. Nevertheless, vested interest or not, it is usually impossible to quarrel with the logic of the recommendation in its own terms: Most policy makers would undoubtedly profit from more reliable information on the problems facing them. Even granting all this and even stipulating that social scientists are always capable of producing the sort of information that the policy makers asked for (a generous stipulation if there ever was one!), one crucial element is left out in this approach—the time element. Social-science research takes time. Adequate social-science research on larger issues of national policy takes many years (apart from being enormously expensive). But the policy maker rarely has that much time available to him. He faces immediate pressures, often of an overwhelming force. He must act now, or at least very soon. Therefore, even if he may agree with the recommendation that "there ought to be a study," and even if he is able to dig up funds for such a study, his most pressing question will be: *What do I do in the meantime?* The above postulate gives a simple answer to this question: "In the meantime" he will have to act in a state of ignorance, to which a small addendum may be made: At least on the level of large-scale national policy, this answer pertains to virtually all cases.

Daniel Patrick Moynihan (in his book *The Politics of a Guaranteed Income*, 1973) has written an instructive account of this dilemma in the setting of American government. In the years preceding the first Nixon administration there took place an enormous growth of the welfare rolls. No one could really explain this phenomenon. Information was inadequate and contradictory. Yet it was obvious that something had to be done—the existing situation was politically and fiscally intolerable. The government *had* to act—and it had to act in a state of considerable ignorance. The proposed guaranteed income policy was an attempt to meet the dilemma. Since no one really understood the problem, no one could predict the outcome of the proposed policy. Thus there was a *double* ignorance. But even those who saw this clearly (among them, no doubt, Moynihan himself) were not in a position to forego action on this account. It may be added that the subsequent political defeat of the proposal had little to do with this state of ignorance.

Moynihan does not develop the point, but it is clear from his account that the case of welfare is not all that unique in terms of national policy problems in the United States. If one ticks off some major problems of recent domestic policy (such as poverty, unemployment, education, or racial justice), while there are large bodies of social-science data on each one, it is amazing how much contradiction there is in the literature concerning the alleged basic causes of each—and, therefore, how ambiguous is the usefulness of the available information for the policy maker. If all this is so in the United States (and, by extension, in other Western countries), the point can easily be made *a fortiori* for the countries of the Third World. It is a crucially important point with regard to the formation of any development policy.

In most Third World countries, the amount of reliable information available on any area of national life is very much less than in Western countries. Government statistics, beginning with basic census data, are much more limited and unreliable. Nongovernmental research is minimal or nonexistent. Often data are processed in the capital city with modern techniques of cybernetic science, but no one has the vaguest idea how seriously these data ought to be taken. Local officials in many Third World countries are not beyond "correcting the truth" in the information they send to the national government (even assuming that this custom is not practiced by the latter, too). It is quite possible, then, that the data fed into shiny new computers (possibly purchased with USAID funds) in the nation's capital have the scientific validity of folk tales or bazaar rumors. A few years ago an American visitor was shown through the premises of a government agency for economic research in a Latin American capital. Large numbers of people were busily engaged in entering data on agricultural productivity on IBM cards and feeding the cards into very up-to-date sorting machines. The visitor and his guide, a young man employed at the agency, were contemplating this activity for a few minutes. Then the guide smiled and said: "All science fiction!"

Such a state of affairs might, at first glance, give added cogency to the recommendation "there ought to be a study." In actual fact, it does the opposite. For one thing, the funds for the kind of study recommended are typically unavailable. Recently USAID sent an American expert to an Arab country for the purpose of making a study of health needs, which study was to provide the basis for a reorganization of public health policy in that country. At a preliminary meeting in the ministry of health the American expert outlined his plan for the study and gave a cost estimate. An evidently angry young government official was furiously scribbling on a pad during the presentation and then produced his calculation that the funds required for the study would be sufficient to equip two new hospitals. He suggested that, in view of his country's health situation, that would be a more plausible expenditure. Beyond the shortage of data and the unavailability of funds to produce more data, however, there is an additional fact that must be considered in the Third World context: The problems facing the policy maker are usually much more pressing than those faced by a Western government. Put simply: *There is less time.*

In the dilemma described by Moynihan, at least nobody was actually dying. In many Third World countries the policy decisions literally involve questions of life or death for large numbers of people threatened by hunger and disease. Such a condition produces desperation—and desperation often results in overwhelming political pressures (if not in the immediate prospect of violence). Few Third World governments, therefore, can afford the leisurely pace that large-scale research by social scientists presupposes. Political decisions and action, by necessity, must concentrate on short-run solutions.

Take by way of example a question, discussed earlier in this book, which is crucial for development policy—the question of socioeconomic polarization. In terms of available data, it is fairly safe to state that, at least under capitalist models of development, one early result of rapid economic growth is polarization of the population into a small sector of relative affluence and a large sector of continuing if not worsening misery. Even this statement is not unassailable. The data on which it is based are insufficient either in scope (there are many countries on which we have little or no data at all in this matter) or in detail (it is quite possible that important variables have been left out of the data). Worse, there are very few so-called longitudinal data—data that record changes over an extended period. Thus we may be in a position to state that there is a sharply polarized situation in country X *today*—but if we compare this situation with the one that existed, say, twenty years ago, is there more or less polarization? In other words, are matters getting worse or better? Most serious of all, there can, logically, be no data for the future—yet every policy must make assumptions about the future. As we have seen, advocates of capitalism, mainly on the basis of historical data from Western societies, maintain that the polarization process will reverse itself after a certain level of economic growth has been reached. We have argued that they are probably wrong. *But we don't know this.*

129

What is more, *there is no possible way of knowing.* "In the meantime" there is hunger, disease, early death—and deepening desperation. "In the meantime"—what is to be done?

If our postulate of ignorance holds for most policy-making situations, at least on the national level, it holds doubly for development policy in the Third World. It should be emphasized that this not only applies to the policy decisions of governments, but of any individuals or groups who seek to replace existing governments. In other words, not only the statesman but the revolutionary must act in a state of ignorance. In most situations, neither has enough information, and what information he has is likely to be of dubious reliability. Neither can foresee the future—and this particularly grave ignorance also pertains to the future consequences of his own actions. Such a condition of ignorance, coupled with the pressing necessity to act, produces both theoretical and moral problems.

The theoretical problem lies in the fact that policy is, at best, based on probabilities. Given at least a certain quantity of trustworthy information, and a reasonably objective attitude on his part, the policy maker may be in a position to make some intelligent guesses about the relation of what exists and what he intends to do. Perhaps the most important result of this insight should be an interest in the *probable limits of policy*. This, too, will be, first of all, a theoretical interest. No realistic actor on the historical stage (as, indeed, on the ministage of individual life) has any reason to suppose that his projects will be realized in the way he originally imagined them. Social reality is hard, obstreperous, resistant to our wishes. Any situation of policy making should embrace as clear an awareness as possible of the likely limits this reality will set to the intended projects. In view of the postulated state of ignorance, it will be advisable to define these limits narrowly rather than broadly, thus possibly reducing the probability of failure. In other words, since we know so little it is wiser to act toward goals that are relatively proximate and therefore relatively calculable, than toward goals that are so broad and remote that all calculations break down. It is easier to save a village than to save the world. It is easier to alleviate specific miseries than to bring about a condition of general happiness. However, the more general are the aims of a policy, the greater will be the responsibility of the policy maker to be aware of its probabilistic context and to reckon with the likely limits to his intentions. Otherwise he will be open to the charge that he is indulging his personal or "religious" ambitions at the expense of the sweat and blood of others. For those others, objects rather than subjects of policy, a simple rule of thumb eventuates from these considerations: "Be suspicious of all those, be they in power or still seeking it, who claim absolute certainty about what they propose to do!" Conversely: "Trust those who evince consciousness of the limits of action and of their own limits!" Indeed, if the concept of "consciousness raising" has any merit, we would recommend that it be employed for any enterprise that teaches a consciousness of limits.

The moral problem implied by the postulate of ignorance should be clear from everything that has been said in this chapter. It is the problem of the *probable costs of policy.* Whoever acts politically with a measure of effectiveness (that is, with real consequences flowing from his actions) is gambling with the lives of others. Not only is it morally imperative that he be cognizant of this fact (if the concept of "false consciousness" has any merit, it would be as a description of a state of mind that *lacks* this recognition), but that he carefully calculate the probable costs of his actions. In terms of development policy, such calculation will include many topics already discussed in the preceding chapters—economic, political, and social-structural costs of different models of development. To a degree, all responsible discussion of development policy deals with these, so to suggest that some variant of costs/benefits analysis be applied to development policy is hardly an original idea. Perhaps the closest to an original contribution we can offer in this matter is the recommendation that any such analysis be undertaken with a healthy consciousness of our degree of ignorance.

But there are two facets of "cost accounting" that, we would contend, have been neglected in the largely "technical" analyses of development policies. One is the facet of human suffering: How much sacrifice, and by whom, does a particular development model presume to either inflict or accept? The other is the facet of values: Human beings do not live by bread alone—how much destruction of the values by which men must live does a particular development model imply? And further: What new values does the model have to offer in exchange for those it is about to destroy?

Any approach to the problems of development (and, indeed, to the politics of social change in general) that claims to be moral in intent will have to face up to these questions. In addition to the "merely technical" (and ipso facto value-neutral if not value-blind) accounting of the probable costs of different policy models, there must be added a moral accounting. Needless to say, this cannot be an exercise in pure science; from the beginning it will entail value considerations and at least the possibility of moral judgment. We would suggest, in what follows, two essential steps in such a moral accounting of the probable costs of policy—a calculus of pain and a calculus of meaning.

INTERLUDE

A MATTER OF
SHINING SHOES

IMAGINE an international conference on development problems. The location is unimportant. Whether it be Caracas or Chicago, Dakar or Duesseldorf, the setting is always the same, more or less. It includes a modernistic hotel or academic building, with the appropriate auditoria, seminar rooms, and refectories; book displays; a message center; the indispensable paraphernalia of recording and mimeographing, keeping a secretarial staff properly occupied. The participants are also more or less the same. Indeed, since the world of development experts is relatively small, most of them have met before, in all likelihood at the previous conference. So, upon arrival, there is much shoulder-clapping and (where culturally appropriate) Latin *abrazos*. And since most of the participants are engaged in many projects, there is much discussion, especially at the bar, of matters unrelated to the present meeting, such as agendas, deadlines (typically not met), job openings, and grants applications.

Most participants arrive and depart by plane, and the secretaries are kept busy with calls to the airlines, confirming reservations, changing itineraries. In consequence, regardless of the official program, there is an atmosphere of purposeful activity: Important people are here, doing important things.

The important people come from many different countries, yet

133

they seem very much alike, distinguishable more by function than by nationality. There are the bureaucrats from governments and international agencies—politely cautious, given to collecting as many documents as are made available, conservatively dressed (except for some Third World participants, who arrive and depart in conservative Western business suits, but change into colorful indigenous garb in between). There are the academics—less polite, less cautious, less interested in collecting documents, and prone to appearing in more informal clothing. On this particular occasion there are also some students. They mostly huddle together, easily spotted in their uniforms (beards, sweaters, jeans), and much of the time they try to look contemptuous of the establishmentarian proceedings. National differences? The Americans are the most polite (it is strenuous to represent the biggest imperialist power of them all, even if one is paying most of the costs). The Russians and their East European cohorts try hardest to present themselves as cosmopolitan *bons vivants*. Participants from Third World countries tend to be younger and to have higher expectations of the conference (many of them have been in this business for less time). There are (as yet) no Chinese, but a couple of Latin Americans have been in China recently. They are much in the forefront of attention, and are prepared to give "the Chinese point of view" whenever this seems relevant. The West Europeans, clearly, are the *busiest* (perhaps because they often speak several languages and, as a result, are one up on most of the others).

How does one speak about the poverty of the world in such a setting? Well, practice helps. In any case, important people are not usually addicted to a sense of irony. And it certainly helps that the poor are not in visible evidence. The "underlying populations" (as one speaker called them) are topics of the discussion, not participants in it. Yet, unnoticed by just about everyone, they were represented all along. After all, it is not possible to house and feed some two hundred people for several days without maids, kitchen workers, and so on. Inevitably, *they* constitute the only live specimens from the "underlying populations." (Again, the location of the conference is immaterial: In Caracas or Dakar they would be locals, in Chicago perhaps Puerto Ricans or Mexicans, in Duesseldorf Turks or other emphatically "underdeveloped" types.)

One can probably tell a lot about people by the way they treat those who clean their bathrooms or serve them their breakfasts. There are individual differences. But, on the whole, Americans are the most solicitous, individuals from Third World countries least so (they are used to servants). On this particular occasion, credit must go to the students for being the first to even notice this silent presence of the Third World in the midst of the important people. It was on the third day of the conference, at the opening of the morning plenary meeting. A young West German asked for the floor and, beard quivering and voice shakingly militant, pointed out the obvious: Here we were, talking about the poor peoples of the Third World, as if they were on another planet. But they were here all along, represented by the employees of the establishment where we were staying. They worked hard to keep us comfortable, and at exploitative wages. (He even knew, and told us, what their wages were.) The students had discussed the matter. They suggested that, as a sign of solidarity, two things be done: As of now the participants should make their own beds, and refrain from putting their shoes out to be shined overnight. This would show our awareness of the exploitative conditions under which these individuals were compelled to work, and would at least stop our connivance with two particularly degrading manifestations of this kind of "alienated labor" (as he put it).

Needless to say, there was a moment of acute embarrassment. The chairman that morning was an elderly Englishman, the sort that one could easily imagine in the heyday of the British *raj.* Who knows what fierce natives he had faced down in his younger years in what godforsaken corners of the empire; he certainly wasn't going to be flapped by a young German with a beard. "Thank you very much," he said, "is this a point of order?" Well, yes, it was. And, yes, there was discussion. One participant questioned whether the wages really could be called exploitative. Another opined that it wasn't our task at this conference to interfere in the economic policies of the host country. Several said that they would be happy to make their own beds, and a Russian drew laughter by saying that he much preferred leaving his bed unmade, especially after "certain delicate circumstances." And, yes, the young German was willing to put his "interesting suggestion" (thus the chairman) into the form of a motion. He did. The motion passed, with most of the participants abstaining, after which the proceedings resumed according to plan.

This was not the end of the matter. On the next morning the new chairman (a UN type of undefinable, quite possibly nonexistent, nationality) announced that there had been some unforeseen consequences to the motion of the preceding day. Word of the matter had gotten to the domestic staff at issue and had created a good deal of disturbance. It seemed that there had recently been some disputes about work rules between the management of the place where we were staying and the labor union representing the staff. Something about overtime. The shop steward had gone to the management and sharply protested what he suspected to be a trick to influence current negotiations in a manner unfavorable to the staff. The chairman suggested that we rescind the motion, since otherwise, who knows (thin smile), there could be a strike and we could end up not just having to make our beds and shine our shoes, but without food or heat. There was some laughter, some brief discussion, a rather complicated statement by the young German, and a unanimous vote to rescind the previous motion.

That *was* the end of the matter. At no point, as far as is known, was there direct conversation between any of the participants and the representatives of the "underlying populations." The fact that, on the remaining two days of the conference, there was no jam for breakfast and no dessert for supper is, in all probability, a mere coincidence.

Chapter V

ᛥᚬᛥᚬᛥᚬᛥ

POLICY AND THE
CALCULUS OF PAIN

THE HISTORY OF MANKIND is a history of pain. The pain inflicted by nature usually appears in the historical records only in its most spectacular manifestations, as in the most terrible famines, epidemics, or earthquakes. But the pain inflicted by men on each other is the indispensable raw material of the historian's reconstructions. Looking backward from the vantage point of the present, history appears as an endless series of massacres. The farther back these massacres lie in the past, the easier it is to overlook the human anguish they represent, especially if they are connected with what now appear to have been great turning points in history. Historians are very good at burying the trivia of individual suffering in the alleged magnalia (to borrow Cotton Mather's term) of the course of events. Philosophers of history have raised this trick of inattention to the level of an essential tool of their trade. When overlooking the pain becomes difficult, they provide its legitimations. The usual formula for the latter goes something like this: "Event X brought great suffering to many who had to live through it, but it was a good thing after all, because it led to event Y"—which event Y then usually turns out to be something from which the philosopher and his contemporaries now benefit. As Jacob Burckhardt pointed out (in his *Reflections on History*), this kind of philosophy of history has about the same logic as the farmer who sees proof of providence in the fact that a hailstorm destroyed his neighbor's field but not his own.

All men are vultures in that they live off the agonies of the past. At the foundations of every historical society there are vast piles of corpses, victims of the murderous acts that, directly or indirectly, led to the establishment of that society. There is no getting away from this fact, and there is nothing to be done about it. It is an inevitable burden of the human condition. But some men are vultures in a more active sense. They produce additional piles of corpses by their own actions. And they themselves, or more likely others in their service, produce the legitimations of the massacres even as the latter are taking place, and in some instances beforehand. It is this kind of thinking that is of interest here; it constitutes the ideological nexus between policy and pain.

Analysis of alternative policy options in terms of costs and benefits, of input and output, has become commonplace. Such analysis is typically very technical, and generally borrows its concepts and techniques from economics, even where noneconomic phenomena are involved. To say that such analysis is technical is ipso facto to say that it is value-free. As was pointed out earlier, it is not the intention here to question the validity of this kind of analysis, or, in principle, its utility. It is of great importance, however, to see its limitations. There should be no objection, on methodological grounds, to the technical and value-free analysis of policy problems. But it must be clear at the same time that policy invariably *also* implies problems of values. Sooner or later, avowedly or covertly, all policy considerations involve choices between values, and all policy decisions are value-charged. What is proposed here, therefore, is a *non*-value-free expansion of costs/benefits analysis.

More specifically, what is proposed is an input/output calculus of human suffering, aspects of which can be clarified in a technical way, without immediate value judgments. For example, it is possible to calculate quite objectively the relationship between a particular wage policy and the degree of deprivation it will entail for various groups. Or one may objectively describe the contribution of a compaign of terror to the attainment of particular political goals. But even if there is no moral intent in such analyses, any *application* of their results to policy making immediately and irrevocably takes place within a moral frame of reference. This is so even if, and perhaps especially if, the policy makers claim that

138

their actions should be understood in purely technical terms. Therefore, it is proper that the value presuppositions of the following argument be made explicit. They are very simple: *It is presupposed that policy should seek to avoid the infliction of pain. It is further presupposed that, in those cases where policy does involve either the active infliction or the passive acceptance of pain, this fact requires a justification in terms of moral rather than technical necessity.*

Every mode of analysis "slices up" reality in a particular way. Thus a map of the world drawn by someone interested in the distribution of rainfall will look different from a map designed to show the spread of American investments. The calculus proposed here suggests a different way of "slicing up" the sociopolitical realities of the contemporary world, a different way of "mapping" them. In the dichotomy of capitalist and socialist models of development, Brazil and China regularly appear as polar opposites. This allocation, of course, is highly defensible in certain respects: Brazil is today the largest and most dynamic case of capitalist development in the Third World, as China is the most important case of the socialist alternative. What is more, each model has been deemed a success *in its own terms.* The analysis proposed here, though, is precisely geared to question these terms. It suggests that, whatever the dissimilarities, the two cases belong in the *same* category in one crucially important aspect: *Both the Brazilian and the Chinese models assume the sacrifice of at least a generation for the achievement of their respective goals.* A comparison of these two cases will therefore be very useful in elaborating what is meant by the proposed moral amplification of policy analysis.

When the military seized power in Brazil in 1964, it proclaimed the beginning of what it called (and still calls) the Brazilian Revolution.[1] The immediate aims of the takeover were to prevent what the military perceived as the communist direction of the Goulart government then in office, to establish political order in the country, and to arrest the galloping rate of inflation. The long-range goal was the transformation of Brazil from a poor and backward into a rich and modern country. In 1971, as the military regime proclaimed its First National Development Plan, it stated as its first objective "to place Brazil, in a period of one generation, in the category of developed nations."[2] To attain this objective, the regime has formulated in considerable detail what is now widely called (by advocates as well as critics) the "Brazilian model of development."

What are the key features of the model, as defined by those in charge of it?

The model is explicitly and unabashedly capitalist. It presupposes that development is best achieved by a capitalist market economy, and both its economic and political policies are geared to providing a favorable environment for this type of development. Conversely, the model is not only explicitly antisocialist but is opposed to all forms of welfare policy deemed to hinder capitalist development. The model is defined as avoiding both "statism" and "denationalization." By "statism" is meant the control of central economic processes by the government; in the ideology of the regime, "statism" is identified with socialism, and is considered as equivalent to economic stagnation. By "denationalization" is meant the control of central economic processes by foreign interests. The ideology of the regime is emphatically nationalist, and in this respect if not in others it is fully in accord (at least on the level of rhetoric) with the current polemic against "dependency" in other Latin American countries. The capitalist development of Brazil is to be, in the long run, under the auspices of what is called "national enterprise"—that is, it is to be a Brazilian capitalism, controlled by Brazilians for Brazilian purposes. The opposition to "statism," however, by no means implies a laissez-faire role played by government. The Brazilian government intervenes very powerfully in all areas of economic activity. Its interventions, however, are understood to be for the protection and furtherance of a market economy. In addition, the opposition to "denationalization" does not imply a hostility to foreign capital. On the contrary, the regime has created unusually favorable conditions for foreign investments, which since 1964 have flowed into Brazil in what may accurately be described as an avalanche. But this foreign capital is understood by the regime as an indispensable aid to the furtherance of "national enterprise." Dependency on foreign economic interests is either denied by advocates of the model or presented as a temporary phase in the development process.

The key emphasis is on economic growth, as measured in terms of Gross National Product and per capita productivity. Indeed, the ideology of the Brazilian model is a textbook instance of what its critics call "developmentalism" or "growthmanship." For all practical purposes, in the rhetoric of the regime economic growth *is* development. Both economic and social policies are geared to "modernization," understood as the transformation of society in such a way as to facilitate rapid and enduring economic growth. For example, there is a massive government program of manpower training, PIPMO, which is viewed as the mobilization of "human resources" for economic growth. Even the educational programs of the government, such as MOBRAL, the vast literacy program, are defined in the same manner. The rationale of almost all government actions is explicitly economic, and the justifications are often stated in terms of technical economics. The "modernization" of the country is to be rapid and is to include the country as a whole. The latter goal is stated in terms of "national integration," meaning the overcoming of regional isolation and the economic rationalization of the continent-size expanse of Brazil. A potent symbol of "national integration" is the construction of the Transamazonic Highway, which, when completed, will link the impoverished Northeast with the pioneering areas of the Amazon Basin, and will link both with the more advanced regions of the south.

Conversely, there is a deemphasis of what may broadly be called the "distributionist" aspects of development. A less polite formulation would be that the model is "antiwelfare." One of the most-quoted dicta among advocates of the model is to the effect that "wealth must be created before it can be distributed." It is acknowledged that the short-term effects of the policies of the regime are increasing polarization of the population in terms of income distribution, and postponement in alleviation of the miseries of the most deprived groups. These effects are understood as being both necessary and temporary. In the long run, according to the ideology, all groups will benefit from the economic growth. An important aspect of this is the anti-inflation program of the government. Its economists concluded early that a rigorous policy of wage controls was essential to combat inflation, and this policy has been adhered to forcefully. The economic technicalities of the policy are complex (a key category is that of "monetary correction," which serves as a guideline to all government interventions in this area), but the practical consequences are quite simple: Severe limitations have been imposed on the economic advancement of large sectors of the population.

It is also acknowledged with considerable candor that such policies are difficult to pursue under conditions of representative democracy in the common Western sense. Brazil since 1964 has been a military dictatorship, only superficially adorned with some of the trappings of representative democracy. Apart from the actual practice of the government, even the new constitution formally gives near-dictatorial powers to the executive in all strategic areas of government. Apologists for the regime routinely deny its terroristic dimensions, but they generally admit its less than democratic character. The justification is the maintenance of political stability, which in turn is deemed essential for economic development. Democracy, like a more equitable distribution of economic benefits, will supposedly come later in the process of development.

The regime claims that it has gone a considerable way toward achievement of the goals set by the model. It has certainly succeeded in reversing the direction in which Brazil was moving under the Goulart administration (however one may wish to designate the same). It has also succeeded in imposing a condition that, in value-free terms, could be described as political stability. All organized opposition to the regime (with the possible exception of segments of the Catholic church) has either been suppressed or domesticated. All politically relevant media of communication are tightly controlled. Unlike the situation in some neighboring countries, there is virtually no guerrilla activity, rural or urban, in Brazil, and it is unlikely that any will develop. The country, in other words, continues to be firmly in the hands of the military government.

This political stability has indeed been utilized to provide a secure environment for the economic policies of the regime. The government claims that it has succeeded in bringing inflation down to a manageable rate. This claim is disputed by its critics (and, incidentally, it is only with regard to inflation that the critics charge that the government's statistics are fraudulent). Nobody disputes that in recent years Brazil has achieved remarkable economic growth. This achievement is what some enthusiastic commentators have called "the Brazilian miracle." In 1965, the year after the military took power, the GNP growth rate was 3.9 percent. The rate increased in an accelerated fashion from year to year. In 1972 it reached 11.3 percent. Between 1964 and 1970 (the year before the First National Development Plan was promulgated) the GNP increased by 52 percent; in the same period industrial production increased by 69 percent. To date there is no indication of a reversal in these trends. *In its own terms*, therefore, the model may be said to have succeeded in at least some of its short-run objectives, and to be well on the way to the long-run ones.

The terms of this assessment are put in question by asking about the costs of the model.[3] Even before such a critique gets to the matter of costs in human suffering, there are serious questions to be asked about the economic "distortions" of the model. The very first question will be: *What* is growing under the present policies? The answer is not clear in all details, but the general trend is clear enough: There has been a heavy expansion of capital-intensive (as against labor-intensive) industry, much of it producing durable consumer goods and much of it financed and/or controlled by foreign interests. The consumer goods produced (automobiles, television sets, refrigerators, and so on) remain unattainable luxuries for the bulk of Brazil's population. In other words, the priorities of production are geared to the consumption of a privileged minority. The role of foreign capital in this economic expansion has created a formidable national debt and has certainly promoted "dependency," at least in the economic sense. But the most important "distortions" have been brought about by the capital-intensive character of this type of industrialization.

If economic growth of such dimensions is tantamount to development, one may expect that its effects will be clearly noticeable in a decrease in unemployment. The opposite has been the case in Brazil. Unemployment has been growing, not decreasing. Thus between the censuses of 1960 and 1970 the percentage of the labor force in employment declined from 32.3 percent to 31.7 percent—not a dramatic decline, to be sure, but rather different from what one would expect during the unfolding of an economic "miracle." Even more ominously, the proportion of the labor force engaged in *industrial* employment also declined somewhat between the two census years. The import of these statistics may be captured by an image—that of, say, a Japanese-owned factory making sophisticated electronic equipment in the Northeast. Many such factories have been drawn there by a government policy of tax incentives to favor the poorer regions of the country. These incentives are unrelated to employment practices. Such a factory may even be fully automated— and it may import from Japan the few technicians needed to operate the automated plant. Quite apart from the question of whether Brazil really needs more sophisticated electronic equipment, and whether Japanese-owned factories should produce it, the impact of such a factory on its

143

immediate social environment may be exactly zero. The image is that of a gleaming modern plant, with a few foreign technicians watching over an automated production process, turning out goods for which nobody in the area has the slightest use—and all this, very likely, in a community in which there is massive unemployment and unrelieved human misery.

The polarization of the population also appears quite clearly in the government's own statistics. Thus between the 1960 and 1970 censuses there has been a decrease in the share of the lowest strata of the population in total national income. Again, the decrease has not been dramatic; but, again, the notion of a development "miracle" would make one expect a change for the better rather than for the worse. In 1970 one-third of the total national income was in the hands of 5 percent of the population; in the same year, the poorest 40 percent received 10 percent of the income. But this is not yet the worst of the tale told by these statistics. The economic condition of the poor has not only declined relative to that of the more privileged strata (declined, that is, in "distributionist" terms), but it has declined *absolutely*. This result is attributable to a combination of inflation and the wage policy designed to combat inflation. Thus, between 1960 and 1970 the real minimum salary is estimated to have *declined* by about 30 percent. These are national figures; in some regions the decline may have been even greater. To understand the significance of a 30 percent decline in wage income, one must be aware of what these wages actually are. Thus, in 1968, 50 percent of the population had an annual per capita income of one hundred and twenty dollars—or thirty-five cents a day! Put simply: In populations living very close to the subsistence margin, even a slight decline in income may spell disaster; a decline of 30 percent, although drawn out over a ten-year period, may spell the difference between survival and starvation. And even if one allows every argument put forth by advocates of the model in justification of these facts (such as the argument that more recent statistics are more reliable and therefore not strictly comparable with earlier ones, so that the deterioration may be less than it seems, or the argument that wage income figures have little significance in certain rural settings), a clear conclusion emerges: For a large portion of the Brazilian people the alleged economic "miracle" has meant not less but more misery.

The overall picture that emerges is that of two nations, one relatively affluent, the other in various degrees of misery. Such a state of affairs, of course, exists in many countries of the Third World. The sheer size of Brazil, however, with its enormous territory and its population of about one hundred million, makes for a particular situation. Using reasonable criteria of differentiation, one may divide this population into about fifteen million in the sector of affluence and eighty-five million in the sector of misery. To see the economic import of these figures, one must focus on the fact that fifteen million is a very large number of people—indeed, it is the population of quite a few important countries with advanced industrial economies. As one commentator put it, Brazil is a Sweden superimposed upon an Indonesia. This "Sweden," though, can generate an intensive economic dynamic of its own, by and for itself—without having any great effect on the "Indonesia." More specifically, the "Sweden" constitutes a sizable domestic market for consumer goods such as automobiles, television sets, or even air-conditioning units, thus permitting economically profitable production of these commodities. This is a feature of the Brazilian situation that is absent in most Third World countries, where the domestic market is simply too small for this type of industrialization to be profitable. In this way, the very size of Brazil contributes an additional dimension to the process of polarization. It also contributes a seeming plausibility to the rhetoric of the regime: With a little luck, a visitor may travel all over the country and see nothing but "Sweden," with some bits of "Indonesia" either being absorbed into the former or serving as a colorful backdrop for it.

This is the dry stuff of economics. Behind it lies a world of human pain. For a very large segment of the population, life continues to be a grim daily struggle for physical survival. There are, of course, regional differences, with conditions in the Northeast being the worst in the country.[4] Millions of people in Brazil are severely undernourished, and some are literally starving to death. Millions of people in Brazil are afflicted with diseases directly related to malnutrition and lack of elementary public hygiene, and are abandoned to these diseases with little or no medical care. As always, it is the children among whom these conditions take their greatest toll. There are areas in the Northeast where about a third of all children die before they reach the age of three and in which life expectancy at birth is in the thirties (it is now in the seventies in Western industrial countries). It is on *these* realities that one must focus in relation to the economic data on unemployment, income distribution, and so on. The crucial fact is: *These are realities that kill human beings.* The word "kill" here does not have the metaphorical sense it may have when people speak of underprivilege in the advanced societies—the sense of anomie, of wasted lives, of killing the spirit—but rather the most literal sense of *physical dying* and *physical death.* Needless to say, there is always the additional dimension of psychic suffering.

If only for reasons of comparison, it is tempting to try and arrive at a "body count" of all these victims. With some arithmetic on the demographic and economic data, it would be possible to arrive at a reasonable estimate. This is not the place for such an exercise. Suffice it to say that over, for example, a twenty-year period (as between the 1950 and 1970 Brazilian censuses) there would be a toll of several million human beings who, by the humane criteria of Western civilization, could be said to have died "prematurely" and "unnecessarily"—the first adverb referring to a comparison with even the poorest in an advanced industrial society, the second to a consideration of who could have been saved by various policies of public welfare. Put simply: Millions of human beings have died because Brazilian society is what it is. It is also useful to recall that a large percentage of these victims are children; the human costs of this situation are literally a "massacre of the innocent."

One point should be clarified in this connection: Opponents of the Brazilian model often couch their criticisms in terms of a comparison between the present situation and an ideal of egalitarian distribution. In other words, they criticize the status quo because of the large gap between the incomes of the higher and the lower strata. The question of just what is to be considered equity in income distribution is interesting, but it is *not* the burden of the present critique. It is not an abstract "lack of equality" that is at issue here, but the particular inequality between affluence and hunger. Put differently: The present critique of the Brazilian model is not that it is insufficiently egalitarian, but that it condones the starvation of children as an acceptable price for economic growth. The critique further assumes that a rejection of this price, through social policies that attack misery, is not necessarily tantamount to a program of radically egalitarian income redistribution.

When the Brazilian regime is discussed abroad, conversation usually centers on its terroristic character. There can be no question about the latter.[5] Since 1964, with varying periods of intensity, the Brazilian government has suppressed its opponents by terroristic means. The protection

146

of civil rights and liberties has been inoperative in cases involving "national security," which has become an area of arbitrary force by the police apparatus of the regime. The independence and jurisdiction of the courts has been systematically undermined in this area. Large numbers of people have been illegally arrested and imprisoned for political offenses (real or suspected). There have been assassinations of political opponents of the regime by its security organs and by vigilante groups tolerated if not directly organized by the same organs (such as the "commandos to hunt communists"). Most loathsome of all, there has been systematic use of torture throughout the country, both as a means to extract information and as an instrument of intimidation. The direct application of terror has been linked to a nation-wide network of domestic espionage and censorship of all media of communication. In all of this, a vast police apparatus has been built up, centralized in the security division of the military police. Most of this terror has been directed against middle-class opponents of the regime. On a different level of society, and mostly under the auspices of local rather than national police organs, there has been brutal violence against various elements of the "marginal population" (that is, real or suspected criminal elements in the lower classes). The so-called "death squads" are the most notorious example of this.

There is a connection between the terror and the economic policies of the regime. Execution of the latter, with its aforementioned price of suffering, has certainly been facilitated by the silencing of criticism and the intimidation of all potential rebels. Nor should there by any question about the repulsiveness of these realities. The facts about torture alone (a torture that has been continuous and "systemic," and which cannot therefore be excused as an occasional aberration) would suffice for a moral condemnation of the regime. Nevertheless, in the preceding critique of the Brazilian model the emphasis has been placed elsewhere—namely, on the human costs of the economic policies of the model rather than on its political "support structure." The reason for this is simple: Victims of the former have been vastly more numerous than victims of the latter. It is estimated that between 1964 and 1972 (when Amnesty International published its report on the matter) about two thousand individuals were tortured. During the same period the number of assassinations by police organs and vigilante groups was probably in the hundreds. In 1973 it was estimated that there were about twenty thousand political prisoners in

Brazil. These numbers in no way offer a moral justification of the terror, nor do they mitigate in the least the horror of any single instance. Nevertheless, in any assessment of the human costs of the Brazilian model it is the other realities of massive misery, involving millions of victims, that must take precedence.

How does the regime legitimate the human costs of its economic program? Needless to say, no advocate of the program would state its costs in the manner utilized here. However, unlike its position on the political terror (a position of simple denial), the regime's handling of the aforementioned economic realities has been remarkably candid. For a dictatorship, it has produced unusually honest economic statistics. Even the regime's critics have admitted this and indeed used official government statistics in their own arguments. Perhaps some of this can be explained by lack of efficiency in the censorship apparatus; the First National Development Plan proclaimed that its objectives were to be achieved "in accordance with the Brazilian natural character," and this at least potentially humanizing quality may have had certain influences even on the organs of oppression. All the same, the candor with which leading spokesmen and apologists of the regime have spoken about the inequities of the present situation is sometimes startling. Even the president, Emilio Médici, has been quoted as saying on one occasion that "the economy is doing very well; the people, not."

More than Latin insouciance or inefficiency lies behind this candor. There is a well-articulated legitimation, which essentially boils down to a single proposition: *The present inequities are a necessary and temporary stage in the process of development.* Both the necessity and the temporary character of the inequities are formulated in terms of economic theory. A term often heard in Brazil is that of "Gini's Coefficient," which refers to a measurement of income distribution produced decades ago by an Italian economist. Hardly heard outside technical discussions by economists in other countries, the term falls frequently from the lips of Brazilian bureaucrats and businessmen, who, one suspects, would not know a coefficient if they saw one. Whatever may have been Gini's own views, the way they are used in the ideology of the Brazilian regime is as follows: Economic growth inevitably produces sharp inequality in income distribution in the early stages. If this entails misery in the lower income groups, that too is inevitable. In the later stages of the process the misery will be alleviated and the distribution of economic benefits will also become more equitable. The important point is that all of this is understood to be the result of strictly economic mechanisms, functioning autonomously, without political interference. Indeed, any such interference with the strictly economic dynamic can only have deleterious results, inhibiting economic growth and thus postponing if not preventing the eventual alleviation of misery. The function of government in all of this is to facilitate economic growth, not to hinder it by misguided humanitarian interventions. European and North American economic history is supposed to illustrate the correctness of this view, but the stages of economic growth are assumed to be the same everywhere.

Delfim Neto, the economics professor who became minister of finance under the military regime and, for a while at least, virtual tsar of its economic policies, has taken this position frequently and forcefully. Assuming belief in this economic theory, a moral justification can be formulated quite readily: True, many people in Brazil today are suffering. True, the government is doing less than it could to alleviate this suffering. But the government policies are designed to elevate Brazil to the status of a fully developed society by the end of this century. When this goal has been achieved, there will be a sharp and general alleviation of misery. In other words, the suffering of this generation will contribute directly to the happiness of the next. In elementary human terms, parents are made to sacrifice themselves for the future of their children.

The Brazilian regime has had a bad press in the Western world. Thus there are few intellectuals who accept this line of reasoning, except perhaps some hard-nosed economics professors whose opinions were unscathed by the turmoil of the 1960s. But the regime has its "fellow-travelers" in other groups, notably in business and government circles in the United States. Both in Brazil and outside it one may meet Americans from these groups who reiterate the preceding legitimations with unrestrained enthusiasm. Some of them will react with irritation and aggressiveness to any expression of doubt about the intellectual presuppositions of this point of view. "Everyone in Brazil is very happy with the regime, except for a handful of leftist agitators and terrorists," said a State Department official in Washington (who also denied that there was any "repression" by the Brazilian government—except against people who, he opined, fully deserved it). "The Brazilians have nothing to apologize for," replied a colleague of his in Brasilia when asked about the legitimations of the model (he misunderstood the term "legitimations," but his own feelings about the matter were clear enough). Indeed, among some American businessmen there has emerged what could be called a Brazilian "zionism": Brazil is now the Promised Land of capitalist development and perhaps even the last best hope of the Free World. As to the "marginals" who are not immediately sharing in the bonanza of the "Brazilian miracle"—well, those people have never had it any better, they are not like us, and in any case their children will be grateful for what is happening now. Who knows—perhaps it feels different to be hungry in Recife than it would in New York. As another American admirer of Brazil put it: "One must remember that these people have a different attitude to suffering than we do. They have been used to it all their lives."

China, like Brazil, is a country of continental vastness. China, like Brazil, is going through a process of national transformation that has been held up as a model for other countries. Unlike Brazil, what is taking place in China comes after a decades-long convulsion of bloody war with outside forces and internal civil war. Unlike Brazil (which is ruled by a dictatorship but which cannot be called totalitarian), the present Chinese regime has established what is probably the most pervasive totalitarianism of the twentieth century and perhaps of human history. While the Brazilian regime has engaged in terror against selected opponents, the Chinese regime has imposed upon its subject population a terroristic system of apocalyptic dimensions.

Since 1949, when the Communists achieved victory in the civil war on the mainland, this terror has swept across China in a series of cataclysms. Periodically, one wave of terror was followed by a period of relative relaxation, which in turn would be followed by a new terroristic campaign. This flood and ebb can be explained in part by the changing exigencies faced by the regime, and in part by Mao Tse-tung's belief in the necessity of "protracted struggle," a consciously anti-Confucian view of historical progress through conflict and disharmony. While the intensity of terror varied greatly at different times since the "liberation" of 1949, its availability and constant threat has remained a permanent feature of the regime. As the terror went through its periods of high and low tide, the numbers of its victims went through similar variations. In terms of physical destruction of human lives, the worst period came shortly after the establishment of the regime, from about 1950 to 1955.[6]

At least partly out of accordance with Maoist ideology, major new policy steps of the regime have been introduced in campaigns given the appearance of "movements." Some of these campaigns sought to mobilize the population for positive policy goals, others to destroy opposition and instill terror. Usually the two aims have been conjoined.

The first of these great campaigns was the Land Reform Movement, 1950–1952. It was inaugurated to redistribute land ownership to the poorer peasants and to liquidate the "landlord" class. Teams of party agitators appeared in virtually every village throughout China, "classifying" the population and then whipping up those groups classified as properly proletarian against those designated as "landlords" and "rich peasants." The culmination of most of these visitations were so-called "struggle meetings," at which selected members of the enemy class were accused of various crimes before large assemblies, condemned by "the masses," and executed either on the spot or soon thereafter. Reliable estimates give the total of two million executions during this two-year campaign. It seems plausible that this first phase of the terror had widespread support among the bulk of the peasantry, who had strong interests in the land redistribution provided by the reform law. There is every reason to believe that the peasants thought this redistribution to be the culmination of the revolution; the Communists, of course, only saw it as the first step in the revolutionary process of collectivization. Following the example of the Soviet Union, the Chinese regime expropriated the new owners in the second step of the process, transferring the redistributed land from private ownership to collectivist "cooperatives." The main difference from the Soviet model was the speed with which the regime passed from step one to step two. The first redistribution was completed in 1952; "cooperativization" took place in 1955. At this second point the regime encountered much broader peasant opposition, as it did again in 1958, when it tried to force the new cooperatives into gigantic communes during the Great Leap Forward.

Different campaigns had different target groups and policy implications. The Suppression of Counter-Revolutionaries Movement, 1951, was directed against all possible sources of political opposition, including old supporters of the Kuomintang and other "bourgeois elements." The standard operating procedure of "struggle teams" and "struggle meetings" was again followed here, as indeed it was in most subsequent campaigns. Compared with the Land Reform Movement there were fewer executions (probably about five hundred thousand throughout China), but there was a vast wave of arrests. In this campaign was inaugurated the "Reform through Labor" program, which has remained a constant feature of the regime ever since and which (again in an adaptation of the Soviet precedent via the Maoist ideological tenet of "learning from the masses" by physical labor) has provided the regime with a large manpower pool of forced labor. It is estimated that between three and four million people were sent to "Reform through Labor" camps by the Suppression of Counter-Revolutionaries Movement, some of them remaining in these camps for many years. There are few data on mortality rates in these camps.

The Resist-America Aid-Korea Movement of 1951, launched after China's entry into the Korean war, was directed against all vestiges of Western cultural influence, especially against Western missionaries and Chinese Christians. The Thought Reform Movement, 1951–1952, was directed against intellectuals. The Three-Anti and Five-Anti Movements, 1952, were directed, respectively, against insufficiently zealous or corrupt cadres in government and party, and against businessmen. They resulted in virtually total destruction of remaining private businesses. The Judicial Reform Movement, 1952, dealt with the legal system and, among other things, abolished lawyers. The Fulfillment of the Marriage Law Movement, 1953, was directed against "reactionary" patterns of family life. It featured bitter "struggle meetings" at which wives and daughters were encouraged to denounce their husbands and fathers, and was marked by a wave of suicides both of men thus denounced and of women who either refused to play their assigned part or regretted it afterward. The Anti-Hu Feng Movement, 1955, began with an official attack on a literary figure by that name, who as far back as 1941 (!) had allowed himself some criticisms of a speech by Mao on literature and the arts. Again, it was directed against intellectuals guilty of inadequate "thought reform." The Elimination of Counter-Revolutionaries Movement, 1955, was once more a broad campaign against all possible opposition elements, opened by a directive by Mao himself ordering that 5 percent of every organization should be purged. The purge was mainly by imprisonment rather than by physical liquidation, though there was still a large number of executions.

The year 1955 marked a certain watershed in the history of the regime's terror campaigns. The largest physical massacres took place before that date. Subsequent campaigns were characterized by at least relatively milder forms of terror—psychological pressures, public humiliations, beatings and occasional torture, and, most important, imprisonment, forced labor, and forced migration. This does not mean that there was no more physical liquidation, but it became less important as an instrument of coercion. The sheer magnitude of the massacres that had already taken place, and the "prophylactic" memory of these in the population at large, were undoubtedly major factors in this shift of emphasis. The Anti-Rightists Movement, 1957–1958, was directed against intellectuals who had been imprudent enough to make use of the brief period of relatively free expression permitted in 1956 after Mao's injunction of "letting a hundred flowers bloom." It was followed by a broader All-Nation Rectification Movement. The Great Leap Forward of 1958 was accompanied by relatively little terror, mainly because resistance to it was general and massive.[7] The dismal collapse of this effort, which resulted in a sharp decline in Mao's own power and the irrational policies of the most zealous Maoists within the regime, led to several years of relaxation.

This was interrupted by the cataclysm of the Great Proletarian Cultural Revolution, 1966–1968, which was unleashed by Mao to break the power of those who "followed the capitalist line" (that is, advocates of pragmatic, rational policies) and to revitalize the revolutionary spirit.[8] Unlike all the previous campaigns, this was a *genuine* struggle during which Mao's Red Guards encountered vigorous and finally successful resistance—first by the entrenched government and party bureaucrats, then by a growing mass of industrial workers, finally and decisively by the regional commands of the People's Liberation Army. As a result, while there was terror by the Red Guards, it involved relatively little physical liquidation of opponents. Most of the victims of the Cultural Revolution (probably somewhat over one hundred thousand) resulted from skirmishes between different factions of Red Guards and their antagonists. In 1969, after the reestablishment of government authority with a very strong military component, there was a measure of terror against "extreme leftists" among the Red Guards themselves, including executions. The demise of the Cultural Revolution, however, was accompanied by a gigantic Transfer to the Countryside Movement, in which millions (one estimate goes as high as twenty million!) of people were deported from the cities to "learn from the peasants," many of them former Red Guards and other "troublemakers." The effects of this

153

continue to this day, as does the system of "May 7 Schools" for the "reeducation" of intellectuals and cadres. The peasant majority of the population was relatively untouched by these convulsions, and in the long run it probably benefited from them.

Western visitors reporting on China in the last few years have repeatedly commented on the differences in everyday social interactions as between today and the pre-1949 period. Whereas before the Communist takeover there was a tumultuous street life, with people pushing, fighting, and laughing, the scene today seems to be one of smooth, quiet cooperation. There is no dirt and there is no noise. Even Seymour Topping, one of the first American correspondents to enter China after the beginning of the current thaw, whose early reports were positively vibrating with awed admiration of everything he saw, remarked that street crowds in Canton seemed "strangely silent and ordered."[9] No wonder! After having lived through the holocausts outlined in the preceding paragraphs, any people would be inclined to cooperate quietly.

Anyone who looks at the record of the Communist regime since 1949 with even a modest intention of objectivity will be impressed by the enormous quantity of human pain directly traceable to the actions of the regime. It is a record of death, anguish, and fear, deliberately inflicted upon the must numerous people on earth. What is the actual number of victims? How many human beings were actually killed? There have been efforts to answer this question with numerical estimates.[10] This is a difficult undertaking, for both intrinsic and extrinsic reasons. It is intrinsically difficult because, in the nature of the case, only indirect evidence is available: The regime, obviously, does not publish yearly statistics on the number of people it killed. Estimates have to be put together by compiling information from the mainland press and from refugees' reports. The analyst of the Chinese terror is thus in the position of someone who tried to estimate the extent of Stalin's atrocities prior to the twentieth party congress or of the Nazis' persecution of the Jews prior to the end of World War II (in both instances, even the most anti-Stalinist and most anti-Nazi observers grossly underestimated the numbers of victims). The difficulty is compounded by the extrinsic fact of the pro-Chinese climate of opinion which, since President Nixon's visit to Peking, now stretches from Washington government circles, through the business community and the liberal news media, to the left-leaning intelligentsia. It appears that even a substantial number of China scholars have become very careful about making pejorative statements about the regime while they are waiting for their visas to the mainland. To ask about the number of Mao's victims in this atmosphere of Sinophile euphoria appears vulgar and inappropriate.

Morally significant questions have appeared vulgar since the days of the Hebrew prophets, and there is good moral reason for disturbing the current American mood about China (which, by the way, need not imply political opposition to the Nixon policy of detente between the two governments). All the same, as in the discussion of the human costs of the Brazilian model, this is not the place to attempt a "body count" of the Communist experiment in China. There can be no doubt, however, that the number of victims, even in the strictest sense of victims of physical liquidation, runs in the millions of human beings. One prominent American expert on China was asked recently to give his estimate of the number of outright executions during the worst period of terror, the years up to 1955. Assured that he would not be quoted by name, he replied: "No more than ten million, no less than five million." (It should be added that this individual is by no means identified as an enemy of the Communist regime and that, at any rate, his recent writing about China has been far from polemical.) Since 1955, there has been much less physical liquidation. But even leaving aside the monumental burden of psychic suffering—millionfold fear, anguish, and sorrow—there is the physical pain inflicted upon those who were hounded by the organized mobs of "enraged masses" in the various mobilization campaigns, and those who were imprisoned, sent to forced-labor camps and "May 7 Schools," or forcibly deported to the countryside. Millions of human beings were affected by these policies. There is no way of telling how many of them died in direct consequence. In this connection one should at least mention the policy of deliberate genocide carried out by the Chinese government in Tibet, after the suppression of the Tibetan revolt of 1959.[11]

Since the end of the Cultural Revolution, it appears that there has been a period of relaxation in China. There have been no mass campaigns of terror and executions. Western observers disagree on who is responsible for the moderations of the regime, even on who is presently in control, and what elements are likely to come to the fore in the future.[12] Yet there is no indication that the regime, despite its recent moderations, has dismantled its system of totalitarian controls (though it has given them

155

new names and, to a degree, new organizational forms). Terror still lurks behind every corner of the road, in vivid memory and as an effective threat, and no one can predict the political vicissitudes that might once more unleash it with full force. Perhaps the weight of human pain to be accounted to Chinese Communism can be summarized as follows: *This regime has succeeded in making one of the liveliest peoples in the world walk the streets without noise and without laughter.*

If these have been the costs, what have been the achievements of the regime? Among Marxists there has been endless discussion as to whether China does or does not represent the purest form of socialism to date. This discussion has little meaning for non-Marxists. Among the latter, the discussion of achievements has centered on economic matters, and there is now a widespread consensus that the economic condition of most Chinese has greatly improved as against the pre-1949 period.

Evaluation of the economic achievements of the regime is also beset with considerable difficulties.[13] Unlike the Brazilian government, the Chinese authorities issue only sparse economic statistics, and issued almost none at all between 1959 and 1969. Much economic information is still regarded as a state secret and anyone who divulges it is severely punished. Outside observers have to compile a picture through the limited data released by Peking (often this involves "reading between the lines"), data on trade with China released by other governments, and the necessarily selective reports of tourists and refugees. There is one generally accepted proposition: The regime has succeeded in eliminating starvation (the last widespread famine was probably in 1959, following the economic fiasco of the Great Leap Forward). All recent reports on China agree that food appears to be plentiful and cheap. To what extent this is due to the socialist policies of the regime is another question: A crucial factor is that the Communists were the first in many decades to establish a strong central government with authority over the entire country, permitting them to take measures against famine that had been impossible for a long time (beginning with such simple things as the operation of a nation-wide transportation system). Also, it is clear that a number of socialist policies, inspired by Maoist ideology, had severely detrimental economic effects, especially in the area of agricultural production. It could be logically argued that the economic gains were achieved by the immense diligence and productivity of the Chinese people *despite* the often surrealistic irrationalities of Maoist economic programs. Be this as it may, it is probably correct that most Chinese are better off today, in terms of nutrition and other basic necessities (housing and health are relevant categories), than they were before the Communist takeover. In aggregate amounts, these economic gains are modest. Once more, though, it is important to recall that in a population living close to the subsistence margin (this is so for a larger proportion of Chinese than of Brazilians) even small economic gains or losses can be of decisive importance.

It is virtually certain that the *distribution* of economic benefits is today much more egalitarian than it was before 1949. Except perhaps for the top political leadership secluded in the splendor of the Imperial City, there are few economically privileged groups, and the income gap between occupational categories is probably among the smallest in the world. Put differently, wage scales are highly egalitarian, despite the fact that the extreme egalitarian policies of the hard-line Maoists appear to have been quietly abandoned. Thus "material incentives," which were violently denounced during the Cultural Revolution, seem to have been restored in both industry and agriculture. Private plots, abolished in the communes in 1958, now seem to be generally tolerated and, according to some reports, account for an increasing proportion of agricultural production (in this way, quite possibly, reiterating the Soviet experience).

China is still a very poor country—as, indeed, its leaders keep saying in their desire to legitimate themselves as the vanguard of the Third World. By all conventional criteria China is still an underdeveloped society. Thus the *top* factory wage in 1971 was one hundred eight yuan (forty-two dollars) a month. While food and rents are very cheap, the limitations on consumption imposed by these wage levels become clear when one looks at some prices—for instance, of a wrist watch at one hundred twenty yuan, the cheapest transistor radio at thirty-one yuan, or a pair of leather shoes at seventeen yuan.[14] In view of this, the question of the likely future course of the Chinese economy is important. Again, there is widespread agreement that the future prospects are favorable if nondramatic. Economic growth rates since the early years of the regime have been very modest (since 1952, about 4 percent), but there seems to have been an acceleration since the end of the Cultural Revolution (1968–1971, 8.8 percent). The likelihood is that the Chinese economy will continue on a course of steady advance and that its benefits will be spread around fairly equitably, though no dramatic improvements are in prospect. In view of the fact that China is still overwhelmingly a country of peasants, it is especially important to look at the progress in agricultural production. This has been very modest indeed. It is thought-provoking that, in the period 1952–1967, the agricultural growth rate of China has been *precisely the same* as that of India, at 2.5 percent.[15] Need one recall that, during these years, there was no terror in India, no collectivization, and no "mobilization of the masses" in government-run campaigns? In 1973, at any rate, both China and India had to turn to foreign imports in order to feed their populations.

Whatever may have been the detrimental consequences of some Maoist economic policies, it seems plausible that (by contrast with the case of Brazil) the major human costs of this model must be accounted to the political rather than the economic policies of the Chinese regime, with the terror being the necessary focus of the accounting. How are these costs legitimated by advocates of the Maoist model? The most common response is a denial of the facts. Such denial is routine both with official representatives of the regime (in the now unlikely event that anyone raises the question with them) and with enthusiasts for Maoism (or what they perceive as such) outside China. The denial is commonly linked with a denunciation of all sources that affirm the facts being denied. This does not mean that all acts of official violence are denied, but the *dimensions* of the terror are enormously depreciated and contrary reports are invalidated as being the products of "imperialist propaganda." Whatever portion of the terror is admitted is then legitimated within the overall ideological frame of reference. Most basically: *The human costs exacted by the terror are interpreted as necessary and temporary aspects of the revolutionary process.*

The alleged necessity was continually reiterated during the Cultural Revolution in the following passage from the *Thought of Mao Tse-tung*, which Red Guards were in the habit of chanting in unison during acts of harassment or violence against "revisionists": "A revolution is not a dinner party, or writing an essay, or painting a picture, or doing embroidery; it cannot be so refined, so leisurely and gentle, so temperate, kind, courteous, restrained or magnanimous. A revolution is an insurrection, an act of violence by which one class overthrows another." In other words: To make an omelette, one must break eggs.

The alleged temporary character of these "not so refined" actions is legitimated by way of Marxist doctrine. The revolutionary process passes from establishment of the "dictatorship of the proletariat" through the "transition to socialism" to the millennial event of the "transition to communism." At the last the state will "wither away" and its coercive apparatus be dismantled. Different schools of Marxists disagree as to just where China is to be located on the road to the millennium. Except perhaps for the heady moment in 1958, when the Great Leap Forward was to be the beginning of the last "transition" (a claim, by the way, that impressed the Kremlin in about the same way as the Roman Curia would be impressed by the assertion that Jesus had just returned and was on his way to take over from the pope), even ardent Maoists have conceded that they were still operating this side of the coming of the kingdom. In this premillennial age, then, the coercive power of the state must continue to be used against counterrevolutionaries. The most prudent answer Maoists (as, indeed, other Marxists) can give, when asked when all this ugly business will come to an end, is the same answer given by the Revelation of St. John regarding the return of Jesus: "The Lord cometh *soon!*" So as not to confuse the moral issue, it should be pointed out that the earlier expectation legitimated martyrs while the more recent one legitimates the martyr makers. But in both cases an "adventist" propensity to fix precise dates in the near future has led to confusion and disappointments in the ranks of the faithful.

Unlike Brazil, China has had a very good press abroad, especially in recent years. As David Caute has shown, Western intellectuals have increasingly turned to China as they have become disillusioned with the Soviet Union.[16] These foreign sympathizers relate to the official legitimations of the regime in different ways. Some are self-consciously Maoist, imitating as best as they can, under unfavorable circumstances, the way of life enjoined by "the Great Helmsman" (Jean-Luc Godard has created a monument to this group in his film *La chinoise*). These people, of course, replicate the official legitimations *in toto*, as their will to believe is total. There are other Western Marxists who do not identify themselves as Maoists but who look to China as an important socialist alternative to what they consider to be the failure of the Soviet exemplar (the Italian group known by the name of its publication, *Il Manifesto*, is a good example). Their legitimations are more complicated than those of the outright Maoists; indeed, it sometimes sounds as if they feel they know better what is *really* going on in China than do the Chinese themselves. Both the first and second groups of sympathizers move within the universe of discourse of Marxist ideology, and thus their interpretations of Chinese events often have a doctrinaire character that has little significance to outsiders (the question of whether China is already poised to make the "transition to communism," or is still laboring over the "transition to socialism," is a case in point). In both groups the legitimation of the human costs of the Chinese experiment ranges between denial of the fact of these costs and assurance that the costs are "necessary and temporary."

The most interesting legitimations come from people who are neither Maoists nor Marxists, but liberals (and, of late, even a few conservatives) who profess appreciation of the regime's alleged accomplishments while disavowing credence in its ideology. Among them are individuals renowned for their political independence and intellectual nonconformity. The recurring phenomenon of the sudden collapse of all critical faculties into a veritable orgy of gullibility, typically on the occasion of a very brief and thoroughly regimented visit to China, merits detailed analysis that cannot be undertaken here. Comments made by James Reston to Eric Sevareid after a trip to China in 1971 may serve as an example. One should read these words very slowly, while keeping in mind the record of blood and tears that was outlined earlier: "I'm a Scotch Calvinist. I believe in redemption of the human spirit and the improvement of man. Maybe it's because I believe that or I want to believe it that I was struck by the tremendous effort to bring out what is best in men, what makes them good, what makes them cooperate with one another and be considerate and not beastly to one another. They are trying that."[17]

Once more, the degree of simple denial of the facts of the Chinese Communist holocaust varies in this third group. Recent American writing on the regime has displayed a deafening silence on the earlier, most bloodthirsty period. Where the "repressive" features of the regime are mentioned, they are typically legitimated in terms of the economic achievements: All this ugly business is, of course, deplorable, and not in accordance with our own values. But the Chinese people have been freed from the threat of starvation, they are increasingly better off, and it seems that most of them are reasonably happy with the situation. Or, in the word used by Kenneth Galbraith in writing about a visit to China, the present system "works."

Serious questions must be raised about this type of legitimation. As pointed out above, any assessment of the economic achievements of the regime is faced with formidable difficulties. Information is sparse and unreliable. It seems premature, to say the least, to maintain that the system "works," even in strictly economic terms. More weighty is the question of whether the extent to which it "works" can be attributed to the policies and ideology of the regime, or whether it is a case of the stupendous abilities of the Chinese people producing results as soon as they are given half a chance—as in the last few years, when the more grotesque follies of Maoism have been restrained in the economy. As to whether most Chinese are happy with the situation, there is no conceivable way of finding out, least of all by short-term visitors taken through selected places on guided tours. In terms of a *moral* assessment of the Chinese model, however, all the above considerations are off the mark: In order to provide even a rudimentary moral justification of the terror, it would be necessary to show that there is a direct causal relation between it and at least some of the alleged economic achievements. Put simply: Assuming that the Chinese people have more to eat today than they had before 1949, is this fact *in any way* due to the other fact that millions of their number were killed by the regime? Nowhere in the apologetic literature is the question posed in this way. The reason, no doubt, is because the answer is all too clear.

One more observation should be made on that aspect of the legitimation that emphasizes the difference between Western and Chinese values. Admittedly, this point is valid with regard to certain matters. For example, it is safe to say that the overwhelming majority of Chinese peasants have never had an interest in freedom of the press and that therefore they hardly feel deprived by its absence today. It is all the more important to understand the oppressiveness of the regime in terms of *their* values rather than those of Western intellectuals. In the center of the world of Chinese peasants were three values—the family as a social reality, the family as a religious reality (especially in connection with the ancestor cult), and the ownership (actual or aspired-to) of land. The Communists have, as far as they have been able, tried to smash the social reality of the traditional family; the most brutal aspects of this effort have been the alienation of children from their parents, deliberately fostered by agents of the regime, and the forcible separation of families in the policies of forced labor and "reeducation." The Communists have

161

done their best to destroy visible manifestations of the religious life, not only in the Buddhist and other formal organizations, but on the level most important to the peasant, that of the ancestor cult; one of the most cruel measures in this respect has been the destruction of tombs, traditionally placed in the midst of cultivated fields. The treachery of the Communists' policy on land ownership has already been mentioned. From the peasants' point of view, they were first lured into support of the revolution by the promise of land, which was then given to them and taken away again within a span of five years. If, therefore, one has some doubts about the happiness of Chinese peasants in the semimilitarized communes in which they now live, these doubts have nothing to do with Western prejudices or "bourgeois liberties."

The most contemptible aspect of the legitimation that "the Chinese are different from us" pertains to the taking of life. Supposedly, "the Chinese put a different value on human life." The thesis is debatable in terms of historical generalization. The Confucian ethic was preeminently pacific, and the history of Western civilization is not exactly easy to interpret as a record of the respect for human life. The thesis is not debatable at all on the level of individual pain. It hurts as much to die, or to see one's loved ones die, in China as it does in America. Indeed, it hurts as much to be hungry in both of these places as well as in Brazil. Perhaps one should expand the critique of this type of legitimation by pointing out its inconsistency—if human life really means so little in China, why should one *praise* the regime for eliminating hunger? Is it only death by execution, but not death by starvation, that the Chinese "feel differently" about? Perhaps, though, it is enough to express contempt for those who justify the suffering of others by their own allegedly superior sensitivity.

The purpose of this chapter has not been to engage in a detailed discussion of the recent histories of Brazil and China. Rather it has been to highlight the moral calculus that ought to be employed in the assessment of the human costs of different models of social change. Nor has it been the intention to equate the cases of the two countries. In terms of direct "repression" by organs of the state, Brazil compares to China as Switzerland to the empire of Genghis Khan. In terms of the equitable spread of economic gains, on the other hand, China is to Brazil as a kibbutz utopia is to medieval Europe in the heyday of feudalism. If China today can still be understood under the Maoist slogan "Politics takes command," then Brazil should get the slogan "Economics takes command." The difference between the two phrases points to the difference between the two models as well as between the kinds of human costs they exact.

It is all the more interesting to perceive the similarity between official legitimations of these costs. In both cases, what is crucially involved is an alleged certainty about the future course of events, and thus about the consequences of one's own policies. What the alleged course of "Gini's Coefficient" performs in one legitimation, the concept of the "transition to communism" performs in the other. It is true that there are harsh realities to the process under way, the legitimators declare, but these are necessary stages as the process moves toward its goal and will disappear when the goal has been reached: No more misery and no more crass polarization when Brazil will have become a "fully developed society"—no more coercive use of state power when China will have "attained communism." But what if these articles of faith are put in question? For articles of faith they are; there is no way of arriving at them by way of the available empirical evidence. What if they are wrong? Or even, what if one cannot be certain about them? It is at this point that the postulate of ignorance, as elaborated in the preceding chapter, becomes relevant morally. As the postulate is seen as pertinent to both cases, their respective legitimations collapse. What remains is a mass of human pain, willfully inflicted without any justification.

The value presupposition of this chapter has been the avoidance of human pain in the making of development policy. The calculus of pain must be applied to every model of development, as indeed to every model of deliberate social change. Neither the Brazilian nor the Chinese model can stand up under this application. As one looks at the available information in terms of the calculus of pain, *neither* model is morally acceptable. Conversely, *neither* case can be cited either in defense of or as a final argument against, respectively, capitalism or socialism. Brazil does not exhaust the possibilities of capitalism, and there are socialist possibilities beyond Maoist China. It is the quest of such other possibilities that should preoccupy anyone concerned with the mitigation of human suffering in the course of social change.

163

NOTES

1. For an account of these events by an opponent, see Miguel Arraes, *Brazil—The People and the Power* (Harmondsworth, Middlesex: Penguin, 1972). For the events leading up to the military takeover, see Joseph Page, *The Revolution that Never Was* (New York: Grossman, 1972). For a more personal report of one who lived through the takeover, see Marcio Moreira Alves, *A Grain of Mustard Seed* (Garden City, N.Y.: Anchor, 1973).

2. *First National Development Plan, 1972/74*, published in English by the Brazilian government (Brasilia: 1971). The economic data on Brazil are taken from a variety of mostly periodical sources and are all based on Brazilian government statistics. It was not possible to refer to an overview in book form in English.

3. The most trenchant economic critique of the model is by the Brazilian economist Celso Furtado. His major book on this is not available to date in English; it was published in Spanish as *Análisis del modelo brasileño* (Buenos Aires: Centro Editor de América Latina, 1972). Furtado, while not a Marxist, is politically on the left. This type of critique, however, has now spread to some surprising quarters. Even Robert McNamara, in an official address as president of the World Bank, has recently associated himself with important aspects of the critique (notably the criticism of the anti-"distributionist" orientation of the Brazilian model).

4. For a graphic account, see Paul Gallet, *Freedom to Starve* (Harmondsworth, Middlesex: Penguin, 1972).

5. See Report on *Allegations of Torture in Brazil* (London: Amnesty International, 1972).

6. See Chow Ching-Wen, *Ten Years of Storm* (New York: Holt, Rinehart and Winston, 1960); Doak Barnett, *Communist China—The Early Years* (New York: Praeger, 1964). For a detailed account of these years in one area, see Ezra Vogel, *Canton under Communism* (New York: Harper Torchbooks, 1971), cc. 2–4.

7. For a brief but excellent report, see Stanley Karnow, *Mao and China* (New York: Viking, 1972), c. 5.

8. See Robert Elegant, *Mao's Great Revolution* (New York: World, 1971); Edward Rice, *Mao's Way* (Berkeley: University of California Press, 1972).

9. Tillman Durdin, James Reston, and Seymour Topping, *The New York Times Report from Red China* (New York: Quadrangle, 1971), p. 141.

10. The most comprehensive attempt is to be found in a report prepared by Richard Walker for a subcommittee of the U.S. Senate Committee on the Judiciary, *The Human Cost of Communism in China* (Washington, D.C.: U.S. Government Printing Office, 1971). The report is unimpressive in its use of sources and seems motivated by the bias to set the number of victims as high as possible. For an eyewitness account of conditions in Chinese prison camps ("Reform through Labor" camps, in which people are permanently confined, as against "Education through Labor" camps, in which confinement is for

limited periods of time), see Bao Ruo-Wang and Rudolph Chelminski, *Prisoner of Mao* (New York: Coward, McCann & Geoghegan, 1973). The authors estimate a figure of sixteen million as reasonable for the inmates of these camps.

11. The term "genocide" is used deliberately. The charge of genocide was made in a careful report on the events in Tibet by the International Commission of Jurists, Geneva 1960. For a moving account of the same events, see the Dalai Lama's book, *My Land and My People* (New York: McGraw-Hill, 1962). The Tibetan record is particularly relevant to Peking's claim to lead the "anti-imperialist" forces of the Third World (as is China's more recent policy with regard to Bangladesh). Pro-Peking advocates have observed that Tibet was, after all, an integral part of China when these events took place. The statement is open to question juridically (in another report, Geneva 1959, the International Commission of Jurists concluded that Tibet was in fact and in law a sovereign state). More importantly, the moral persuasiveness of the observation is about that of, say, an assertion that the Nazis were justified in killing those Jews who were German citizens.

12. See, for example, Ching Ping and Dennis Bloodworth, *Heirs Apparent* (New York: Farrar, Straus and Giroux, 1973).

13. See the compendium prepared for the Joint Economic Committee of the U.S. Congress, *People's Republic of China—An Economic Assessment* (Washington, D.C.: U.S. Government Printing Office, 1972).

14. Data from Durdin et al., *The New York Times Report*.

15. Kuan-I Chen and J. S. Uppal, eds., *Comparative Development of India and China* (New York: Free Press, 1971), p. 46.

16. David Caute, *The Fellow-Travellers* (New York: Macmillan, 1973). For a comparison of earlier accounts of the Soviet Union with recent ones by visitors to China, see Paul Hollander, "The Ideological Pilgrim," *Encounter*, November 1973.

17. Durdin et al., *The New York Times Report*, pp. 354 f.

Chapter VI

᠖᠗᠖᠗᠖᠗

POLICY AND THE
CALCULUS OF MEANING

ONCE AGAIN it is appropriate that the considerations of this chapter be prefaced by a statement of the underlying value presupposition. Once again it is a simple one: *Human beings have the right to live in a meaningful world. Respect for this right is a moral imperative for policy.*

The need for meaning is almost certainly grounded in the constitution of man.[1] Man is the animal that projects meaning into the universe. Man names things, attaches values to them, and constructs vast orders of significance (languages, symbol systems, institutions) that serve as the indispensable guideposts for his existence. This human propensity for giving meaning, although it is represented by every individual and may sometimes be exercised in solitude, is fundamentally a collective activity. That is, human beings together, in groups of varying magnitude, engage in the enterprise of ascribing meaning to reality. Indeed, every human group, from the family to a national society, is at its center a meaning-giving enterprise. Meaning, in other words, is not something added to social life, that one may or may not want to look into, depending on one's particular interests. Rather, meaning is *the* central phenomenon of social life, and no aspect of the latter can be understood without looking into the question of what it means to those who participate in it.

The need for meaning has both cognitive and normative dimensions. Put differently, human beings must know both what *is* and what *ought to be*. Every society thus provides for its members both a "cognitive map" of reality and an applicable morality. The former tells people "where they are," the latter gives them directions on what to do in that particular "location." No morality makes sense without the accompanying "cognitive map." For example, a particular society may prohibit marriage to second cousins but allow it to third cousins. Before the individual can obey this moral injunction (or, for that matter, disobey it), he must be able to distinguish between these two types of relatives. It is a safe guess that most contemporary Americans would be incapable of passing this test, so this particular bit of morality would be meaningless for them cognitively as well as normatively. If one contends, therefore, that people have a right to their own meanings, it is not enough to understand this in terms of moral norms or values—that is, to see it as everyone's right to act "in accordance with his conscience." Every "conscience" presupposes a particular cognitive world view, a particular understanding of reality. The right to meaning thus necessarily extends to "philosophy" as well as morality—people have a right to live in a world "as they see it to be." Respect for the "conscience" of others necessarily implies respect for their "definitions of reality."

Neither collective nor individual life is possible without a framework of meaning (in both the cognitive and normative sense). A society cannot hold together without a comprehensive set of meanings shared by its members. An individual cannot make sense of his own life without such a set of meanings (be it in comformity with or deviating from the societal one). Ever since Emile Durkheim sociologists have had a term for the condition in which groups or individuals are deprived of such a framework of meaning: Such groups or individuals are said to be in a state of anomie. It is an almost intolerable condition, and it is indicative that Durkheim first studied it, and gave it its name, in an inquiry into the causes of suicide. To deny an individual, or a group, the meanings by which life is organized is to deny, often literally, the very possibility of living. Thus the aforementioned right to meaning can be aptly reformulated as a right to be protected against anomie. It is based on the recognition, discussed earlier in this book, that "men do not live by bread alone." The same recognition is implied by contemporary widespread protests against "materialism," both in the Third World and in the advanced industrial societies. In the end, it is widely seen today, all material advances are pointless unless they preserve the meanings by which men live, or provide satisfactory substitutes for the old meanings.

167

The human need for meaning is a historical and cross-cultural universal; it may safely be assumed to have existed throughout history and in all societies. It is important to understand, though, that to speak of a right in this area has quite different implications in modern as against premodern societies, because of a fundamental difference between these two societal types. In premodern societies most meanings are *given* to the individual by tradition, which is rarely if ever questioned by him. In modern societies an increasing sector of the spectrum of meanings is *chosen* by the individual. Put differently: In premodern societies most meanings are presented to the individual as taken-for-granted, typically sacred facts about which he has as little choice as about facts of nature— the values that govern family life, for example, are *there* in very much the same way as a rock, a tree, and the color of one's hair are *there*. By contrast, in modern societies a growing number of important meanings are offered to the individual in a sort of meaning-market in which he moves around as a consumer with a wide variety of options—as, for example, between different family values, life styles, or even sexual preferences. Consequently, a "right to meaning" has almost opposite implications within the two societal types: *In a modern society it implies the right of the individual to choose his own meanings. In premodern societies it implies his right to abide by tradition.*

Much of the discussion of "human rights," when applied to the Third World, is plagued by an incomprehension of this difference. The dominant assumptions and categories in this matter are of Western provenance. They always refer to this or that right of an individual freely to choose his own meaningful world without outside interference (notably on the part of the state). Such free choice, however, is neither desired nor even real to large numbers of people who continue to live within traditional frameworks of meaning. The Marxist denigration of the Western ideology of rights as "bourgeois liberties" only obfuscates the matter even further. The previous discussion of contemporary China may be recalled here: The Chinese peasant has little use for such "bourgeois liberties" (read more accurately: *modern* rights) as freedom to vote for the political party of his choice and to read its (uncensored) newspaper, freedom to select a religious preference from many available ones, or freedom to opt for a particular style of private consumption. But he is very much concerned with his right to maintain the uninterrupted worship of his ancestors, to live his own life in the protective proximity of their tombs, and to raise his children in accordance with traditional precepts. The Communist regime in China, therefore, is not to be reproached primarily for violating the "bourgeois liberties"; within the meaningful world of most Chinese people, it is the regime's assault on "peasant liberties" that is the primary issue (the Communists' physical terror is, of course, a different question).

The matter is further complicated by the fact that, in most of the world today, traditional frameworks of meaning are under severe stress and are in the process of changing their fundamental character. In other words, the matter is complicated by the global fact of *modernization*. There are many facets to this process, but a crucial facet may be expressed precisely as follows: *Modernization is a shift from givenness to choice on the level of meaning.* Tradition is undermined to exactly the degree in which what previously was taken for granted as a "fact of life" becomes something for which an individual may or may not opt. Consequently, in any situation undergoing modernization, it is often unclear which of the two versions of the "right to meaning" should pertain—the right to choose freely or the right to be left alone in the old givenness. This unclarity is not just in the mind of an outside observer; it marks the minds of those who are in the modernizing situation. It has often been remarked that individuals in the throes of modernization are torn, divided within themselves. A decisive aspect of this division is the ambivalence between givenness and choice. It is not difficult to see that anomie is a powerful threat under such conditions.

The nature of the shift may be illustrated by an episode. A visitor was talking with an elder of an Ujamaa village (collective agricultural settlement) in Tanzania. This particular village was inhabited by members of different tribes. The visitor asked whether traditional tribal ceremonies and dances were still being performed in the village. Yes, replied the elder. Once or twice a year there was a special occasion when members of the village got together and the different tribal groups performed their traditional dances. He added that this was a very good thing, since it helped the people in the village to understand each other better. The episode contains all the important ingredients of the shift: While tribal dances were previously performed at times designated by tradition, they were now staged for occasions chosen by the village council. Previously the performance was given as inevitable, now it was decided upon in an act of choice—and, by definition, the choice could be *not* to hold the event on a particular date. Furthermore, the dances were now performed for an audience of outsiders, while probably the most accurate description of the previous situation would be to say that the dances were held to be seen by the gods. Finally, a rationale was now attached to the enterprise: Previously the people danced because it was necessary to do so— they probably reflected about it as little as they did about eating or breathing. Now they danced because, supposedly, this was a good thing for the morale of the village. In sum, even if the motions of the dances remained unaltered in every detail, they would now no longer be the same dances; dancing then and dancing now are two drastically different activities.

Barring catastrophic events that would make people literally forget what has happened, the modernizing shift from givenness to choice appears irreversible. Once an individual is conscious of a choice, it is difficult for him to pretend that his options are a matter of necessity. This becomes quite clear in all movements to preserve or revive traditional ways to which the prefix "neo" may be attached. Thus a "nativistic" movement may violently reaffirm the superiority of the old ways, but the very violence of the affirmation reveals its inherent precariousness. The precariousness is rooted in the knowledge that the old ways are no longer inevitable, that there are people who have chosen to abandon them, and indeed that one could, in principle, make the same choice oneself. The traditionalist untouched by modernization will reject the new in an attitude of self-assured superiority. The "neo"-traditionalist will perform the act of rejection in a very different attitude of anger and defensiveness —because the new is, for him, a *temptation*. And there is, it seems, no way back to the old assurance.[2]

Is this shift for the better? The answer will obviously depend on the value one attaches to the freedom and autonomy of the individual. Anyone who identifies with Western cultural history will give a positive answer. To do so is not necessarily an expression of "ethnocentrism": It is possible to have a strong allegiance to certain values while, at the same time, understanding and respecting the values of others. But the way in which the right to a meaningful world was started here deliberately seeks to bracket the question of the superiority, or lack of same, of modern libertarianism and individualism. Such bracketing becomes possible if one reapplies the previously stated principle of "cognitive participation": It is not for the outsider (be he scientific observer or policy maker) to impose his own conception of rights and value priorities. His first task is to listen, as carefully as he can, to the manner in which these matters are defined by the insiders. The fact that this is not always easy, especially because of the ambiguities brought into play by modernization, provides no alibi for ad hoc impositions. Minimally, what is urgently required in the area of development policy is respect for the varieties and the inner genius of traditional ways of looking at reality.

It is valid and useful to understand modernization as an institutional process. However, one must also understand it as a process on the levels of meanings and consciousness. At its very heart, modernization is a transformation of the meanings by which men live, a revolution of the structures of consciousness.[3]

Since modernity is generally taken to be a good thing in the common-sense view in Western societies, while "backward" and "old-fashioned" are pejorative terms, it may be useful to look at it for a moment from the opposite point of view. From the viewpoint of a traditional conscious-ness, modernity is a sort of disease, a deeply abnormal and destructive deviation from the way men are intended (by nature, by the gods) to live. The etiology of the disease can be traced. There is no question about the original source of infection: It is Western civilization. Modernity, for whatever historical reasons, originated in one place, in Europe, and spread outward from there. Although today the disease has been diffused through-out the world and is now transmitted further by many non-Westerners who have been successfully infected, modernization and Westernization were historically concomitant processes. Modernity is a complex of insti-tutions and structures of meaning that originated in the West under historically unique circumstances, and it was the world-wide expansion of Western influence that diffused modernity to other cultures. It is doubtful whether any sizable territory today is immune to this influence. Modernity, however, is not an either/or matter. There is no totally modernized society. But modern institutions and structures of conscious-ness are unequally distributed in different societies as well as societal sectors, which may then be described as *more* or *less* modernized. If modernity is perceived as a pathological condition, then some societies are still healthier than others—to wit, those taken to be the most "backward" in the Western common-sense view.

It is not the purpose here to advocate such an epidemiological per- spective on modernization. It is only suggested as a corrective to the unexamined prejudice that modernization is necessarily a progress from lower to higher forms of social life. But whether one views modernity as a disease or as a desideratum, or whether (more wisely) one takes a differentiated attitude toward it, the mechanisms of its transmission are empirically available. It is possible to analyze in detail the "carriers" of modernity. These are economic, political, and cultural processes, many of them in complex interrelations with each other. Primary causes of modernity in the West were the technological transformation of the economy and the rise of the bureaucratic state. Consequently, primary carriers of modernization have been all the extensions into other parts of the world of the Western technologized economy and Western bureaucracy. Economic and political "imperialism" has been a major, but by no means the only, mechanism of transmission. The immense power of Western culture over the last few centuries has radiated outward through a variety of cultural influences that cannot all be subsumed under the heading of "imperialism." Thus there are various processes that may be designated as secondary carriers of modernization—notably the processes of urbanization, social mobility, mass education, and mass communications. Very often these secondary processes have been closely related to the penetration of non-Western societies by Western economic and political power, but they are also capable of acting independently. Thus, the glittering imagery of modernity has been diffused to areas in which there has been only minimal impact by modern economic or political forces.

Modern consciousness has many facets, and this cannot be the place for a detailed description. Only two key facets can be indicated here: *Functional rationality* and *plurality*. It has long been a truism that mod- ernity is the "age of reason," but the quality of this "reason" must be specified. It is not necessarily the "reason" of philosophers and scientists; that antedated the modern period and is today, at best, the property of a small minority. The rationality of a modern society is "functional" rather than theoretical; that is, it is a way of describing the everyday operation of numerous processes in ordinary social life. The original locations of this rationality are in technology, in the economy as it has been transformed by capitalism and by the industrial revolution, and in the institutions of bureaucracy (originally these were mainly agencies of the state). Rationality here implies not great sweeps of theoretical reflection, but a certain attitude of calculation, classification, and manipulation of reality. Such rationality is not "carried" by philosophers or scientists, but by engineers, businessmen, and bureaucrats. And it is this type of rationality that has invaded ever-wider areas of life in the course of modernization. One of its most important characteristics is what might be called "makeability": Reality is to be approached in a problem-solving mood, and once any given problem is correctly understood, then reality, at least in principle, can be "made over." While this is essentially an engineering mentality, it has now spilled over into areas of life that have no direct relation to technology.

Functional rationality is easily traceable to the primary carriers of modernization. Plurality is due more to what have been called the secondary carriers. Urbanization, social mobility, and the "knowledge explosion" have critically eroded all self-enclosed and thus self-assured worlds of meaning. The individual living in a modern city, oriented toward mobility and subjected to the onslaught of modern communications, must come to terms with a wide variety of people who have drastically different values and definitions of reality from himself—and with whom, nevertheless, he must coexist. This plurality has undermined the taken-for-granted adherence to traditional world views, and has been a major cause of the aforementioned shift from givenness to choice. The same plurality has especially tended to relativize and weaken religious and moral certainties; it lies at the root of the modern crisis in these two areas. In other words, the pluralization of the worlds of meaning by modern society has made certainty hard to come by—not only religiously and morally, but finally even with regard to the individual's own identity. Put simply: Modern men must continuously ask what they can believe, what they ought to do—and, finally, who they are.

Both functional rationality and plurality are difficult to live with. There are human needs and aspirations that cannot be satisfied by an engineering attitude. And there is a deeply grounded need for certainty. Modern society has generated a sort of solution to this problem in the emergence of the private sphere. The large public institutions—notably the economy, the state, and other large bureaucratized complexes—have fallen under the sway of functional rationality. Public life, especially under

173

urban conditions, has become highly pluralized. To compensate for this, as it were, there has developed what is now called private life—a social sector in which the individual can pursue his "irrational" needs and in which he is given considerable leeway to construct "little worlds" for the cultivation of a modicum of certainty. The dichotomization of the individual's social existence between the public and private spheres is one of the most important institutional manifestations of modernity. It has equally important consequences on the levels of meaning and consciousness. Thus an individual may be "alienated" at work, but find deep personal satisfactions in his family life. The larger society may provide the individual few certainties "to live by," but he is left free to seek out such certainties in religious groups, therapeutic programs, or other voluntary social relationships. While this has shown itself to be a viable solution for large numbers of people, it is inherently tenuous—precisely, once again, because the private sphere is based on choice rather than on givenness. Nevertheless, private life is for most modern individuals the principal focus of their striving, although of course any particular "life project" always takes place within the coordinates set by public institutions: The individual may want to construct a certain style of family life, but he must be able to afford it, which will depend on his occupational career and ultimately on the course of the economy.[4]

While modern consciousness has features that are the same all over the world, there are many different worlds of tradition. Thus the collision between modernity and tradition takes different forms. Some traditional worlds are more open to modernization than others. Nevertheless, almost everywhere the onset of modernization is experienced as a severe trauma, a collapse of the old certainties, and, for better or worse, the beginning of a journey into new worlds of meaning. The experience is eloquently expressed in the following passage, in the words of a man interviewed in the former Belgian Congo:

"I learned to feel close to the ancestors, and to know that we were one with them, although I still did not know where they lived or how. But when I put on the skin of the leopard and painted my body and became as a leopard, the ancestors talked to me, and I felt them all around me, I was never frightened at such times, but felt good. This is what we have lost, what we had taken away from us. Now it is forbidden for us to talk to our ancestors . . . so we can no longer learn

174

their will or call on them for help. We no longer have any reason for living, because we have been forced away from the ways of our ancestors, and *we lead other men's lives, not the lives of our fathers.*"[5]

Yet it is important to understand that modernity does not appear on the traditionalist's horizon *only* as a threat. It *also* appears as a great promise—of a longer and better life, of a plenitude of material goods (the "cargo"), but also of individual liberation and fulfillment. The reaction to modernization is frequently quite ambivalent, a psychologically complex mixture of revulsion and attraction. Occasionally there is direct and violent rejection, the attempt to stave off the threatening new world through determined resistance. On other occasions there is an enthusiastic embrace, with the "carriers" of modernization hailed as harbingers of redemption. More commonly (and more interestingly) the reaction is between these poles. Tradition and modernity then relate to each other through a variety of compromises and mutual adjustments, with the outcome varying greatly from one place to another. The compromises are institutional, but inevitably they also involve adjustments on the level of meaning (a process that may be called "cognitive bargaining"). Thus there are regimes whose purpose is to modernize their countries, making use of highly traditional institutions to promote this purpose—as the regime of Léopold Senghor in Senegal has done with the traditional Muslim leadership.[6] Apart from politics, traditional institutions have taken on very new functions and, in the process, have been forced to modify their self-conception—as in the case of caste associations in India, despite their foundation in the most traditional structures of Hinduism, operating to assist the social mobility of their members in the rational world of modern bureaucracy.[7] Traditional customs can actually be converted to become vehicles of modernity—as in Indonesia, where the traditional folk theater has been used to dramatize the conflicts of modernization and to indoctrinate the audience in modern attitudes.[8] Examples could be multiplied at will from the relevant literature.

Because modernization everywhere entails a rupture in the order of meanings, it calls forth resistance. Any meaningful world provides for its "inhabitants" a shelter against anomie, a place of security—a sort of home in reality. Conversely, modernization poses the potent threat of *homelessness,* and often the threat is realized in the experience of numerous individuals similar to the African quoted above. The loss of opportunity

175

to live "the lives of our fathers," with its profound religious and social implications, brings forth frustrations and anger of potentially violent intensity. Thus, from the beginning, modernization and countermodernizing reactions go hand in hand. This was so in Europe, the original center of the "epidemic." Reactionary rebellions, such as the Fronde in France, were a recurring phenomenon during the centuries of initial modernization. Similarly violent reactions, coupled with hatred of the foreigners involved, can be observed again and again in the non-Western countries subjected to the onslaught of modernity. The extermination of Christianity and almost all Western influence in seventeenth-century Japan is probably the most successful case on record of such resistance (it retarded the modernization of Japan by two full centuries—a remarkable success, in historical terms). But there are many others, such as the Boxer Rebellion in China, the Indian Mutiny, the rebellion of the Mahdi in the Sudan, and the Ghost Dance in America.

As modernization succeeds in transforming the institutions and meanings of a society, the more direct and violent expressions of countermodernization become rarer. This does not imply that the discontents have disappeared. In the Third World today there continue to be strong movements and ideologies (usually in the form of nationalism) that seek to control some of the less desirable features of modernity and to preserve at least some aspects of premodern tradition. The continuing influence of Mahatma Gandhi in the political thought of India, pan-Islamism (as in the ideology of the Qaddafi regime in Lybia), and the various versions of *négritude* (from the thought of Senghor, who gave the term political currency, to the "African socialism" of Julius Nyerere) may be cited as examples. In each instance there is a strong antimodern and anti-Western animus, and a desire to preserve some inner kernel of indigenous culture. At the same time most of these movements and ideologies do not reject modernity out of hand. They still desire the "cargo" of good things that modernity promises, from better agricultural techniques to a longer life. But the goal is to have these good things *without* the anomic features, the homelessness, of Western societies.

It is noteworthy that similar aspirations can be found in the advanced industrial societies. Recently they have been expressed powerfully by youth culture and counterculture movements. Here too there is deep discontent with the functional rationality ("dehumanization") and plurality ("alienation") of modern society. The more radical wing of these movements reject modernity outright and attempt to return to simpler, presumably healthier ways of life (as in some rural communes). More importantly, though, there is the desire to control rather than abolish modern institutions, to modify them in such a way that the benefits of modernity will be preserved but freed from their "dehumanizing" and "alienating" side effects. It is also noteworthy that in such counter-cultural milieus, in Europe and North America, there exists today a strong identification with the Third World. It may be argued that this identification is more than romantic sentimentality, that it is based on a sound instinct. What is sound is, quite simply, the recognition that intact traditional cultures provide meanings for their members that are lacking in fully modernized societies. This sense of lack may often be expressed in absurd ways, but it is nonetheless very real.

To say that modernity produces discontents is not in itself a value judgment. Thus it is quite possible to maintain that the achievements of modernity are well worth these discontents, indeed that "alienation" is the necessary price of individual freedom.[9] In that case, the desire to have *both* individual freedom *and* the security of "being at home" in society (not to mention the cosmos) is doomed to disappointment. Be this as it may, whatever one's values, it is important to understand the costs of modernity. "There are no free lunches," and modernization, even if one welcomes its basic thrust, is not free either. To what extent can the costs be reduced?

The answer to this question hinges on how one understands some key features of modernization. There is one view that conceives of modernity as a single, inextricable, inevitable entity—a kind of seamless robe, a whole that cannot be taken apart. In such a view, the idea of keeping some elements of modernity (such as technological innovations in the economy, or a well-functioning state apparatus), while abandoning others (such as the domination of much of life by an engineering mentality, or the isolation of people in a modern city), is a Quixotic fantasy. If one wants better nutrition, say, or a government that can effectively control floods or famine, then one will have to settle for the demise of poetry in social life and just get used to anomie. The opposite view holds that the several elements of modernity can be assembled or disassembled freely. Nothing is inextricably linked together, everything can be rearranged. Thus one might combine modern agricultural techniques with traditional rain dances, chattel slavery with a modern communications system, and polygamy with electric stoves.

The available evidence suggests that neither of these opposite views can be maintained. Modernization is not the irresistible juggernaut pictured in the first view—there are too many modifications, compromises, and even reversals of the process to make this view tenable. But on the other hand, neither is modernization a completely haphazard game, with rules and combinations to be changed at will—if nothing else, there is too much evidence of the powerful and highly consistent effects of the primary carriers, so much alike in their impact in different parts of the world. The matter is both more complicated and more interesting: It is not a question of having to submit to modernity as an inexorable fate, nor of being able to play with its components as if they were the infinitely variable pieces of an erector set. The question is this: *Which* components of modernity may be tinkered with, and *which* must be taken (or left) as a "package deal"? In other words, the question is one of *limits*. What are the limits of modernization? And what are the limits of all efforts to modify or control modernity?

If one sees the institutions and meaning structures of modernity being diffused by the primary carriers, and from the areas of social life most directly affected by the latter, one can attempt to measure the degree of such diffusion. For example, an engineering mentality is presumably unavoidable in the course of engineering activities. The "package" of this activity and that mentality is, therefore, *not* one that could be much tinkered with. But even the most devoted engineers are engaged in activities other than engineering, and carry their engineering mentality with them as they engage in these other activities. Indeed, many critics of contemporary culture have pointed out the sway of this mentality over such activities as sexuality, marriage, child rearing, or even religion. Is this unavoidable, too? If not, by what cognitive and social mechanisms can these other areas of life be shielded from the influence of the engineer's mind? Is it perhaps even possible to be an engineer on the job and a poet in the bedroom?

Put differently: Technology (especially in its application to economics) and bureaucracy have engendered inextricably "packaged" combinations of meanings and social patterns. Without these "packages" neither could exist—and, therefore, modern society and its "cargo" of benefits could not exist without them. This intrinsic and inevitable linkage pertains only to these areas of social life, yet the meanings and social patterns originally appropriate to technology and bureaucracy have been carried over into other areas, sometimes with great force. The question of possible modifications of modernity may, then, be formulated as follows: What are the processes of *carryover* between those areas in which modernity is indeed a seamless robe and other areas in which this only seems to be the case? Conversely, what are the possibilities of *stoppage* of this diffusion?

In terms of what may be called the classical solution to the discontents of modernity, the question of stoppage pertains to the dichotomy of public and private spheres. This is mostly a question of the *protection* of private life against the logic and the mental habits of the large public institutions. How can the individual, for instance, be calculating, controlled, and emotionally detached at work, and then come home and be generous, spontaneous, and warmly human? How can a good bureaucrat have a satisfactory sex life? Can an upwardly mobile executive be a good father? Can a successful professional continue to exhibit the classical virtues of femininity? There is also the question of whether there can be stoppage of the technological and bureaucratic mentalities as between different institutions of the public sphere itself. What elements of technological production can be "humanized" in the sense of nontechnological values? What are the respective limits of efficiency and civility in a bureaucratic organization? Can mass education be anything but a vast machine of "alienated" bureaucracy? How can the home-like warmth of homogeneous urban neighborhoods be reconciled with the technical demands of efficient city government? Very generally: How can there be reconcilation among various "particularistic" solidarities and the "universalistic" ethos of mass organizations? This second set of questions is more interesting than the question of the protection of private life because it involves possibilities of *institutional innovation*. And, despite the enormous differences between the two types of societies, it is possible that in this search for innovative options some of the experiments in Third World countries could turn out to be, at the least, very suggestive for the advanced industrial societies as well.

On the basis of a sociological understanding of modernization, a hypothesis may be ventured: The possibilities of stoppage with regard to modern consciousness will increase with distance from the primary areas

179

of technology, the technologized economy, and the bureaucratic state.[10] Thus, in all likelihood, it is futile to try to apply non-Western cognitive or normative principles to technological production, to try to run a factory as if it were a *Gemeinschaft*, or to try to apply "participatory democracy" to the bureaucratic structures of the national state. By the same token, however, it may be possible to create innovative institutional arrangements by which non-Western cultural patterns are preserved in sectors of education or in local government, or by which family life or religious activities are deliberately governed by countermodern values. In other words, the clearer a notion one has of the limits of countermodernization, the greater (and, one may add, more exciting) will be the possibilities of innovative experiments within these limits.

A term is widely used, especially in the ambience of the United Nations, that illustrates the policy problem very aptly: "Resistances to development." This refers to all the negative reactions that people have toward the development programs designed for their benefit. The term is usually employed in a pejorative sense. "Resistances to development" are, almost by definition, the actions of ignorant or superstitious people, who do not properly understand their own interests. Sometimes anthropologists and other experts in irrationality are hired to study the motives behind the "resistances." The solution to the problem (if coercion is eschewed) will finally be education: As the "resisters" are educated to understand the superior wisdom of the development program at issue, they will naturally start to cooperate.

The basic purpose of this chapter is to subvert the thinking that lies behind the term "resistances to development." An awareness of the costs of modernity, and therefore of the validity of the countermodernizing impulse, is an intellectual presupposition for such subversion. An episode may make the policy implications clearer.

In a number of African countries it is government policy (out of necessity rather than principle, in all probability) to enlist local participation in the construction of new schools. This is so in the country in which the episode took place. The national education ministry sends out so-called "persuasion teams" into villages for which new schools have been targeted. There is a meeting of the village community. If, as expected, the villagers agree with the project, they themselves construct the building for the school and another building to house the teacher. The ministry then supplies the teacher and the necessary equipment, including books. Since the desirability of schools is now widely believed in even in the remote hinterlands, the "persuasion" is usually a fairly easy affair. In this particular instance it was not. There was strong and unanticipated opposition to the new school. The main opponent was an old man, a village elder. His argument went something like this:

"We don't want your school. What good will it do our children? If they stay in the village, they will learn nothing useful. All they will learn is to despise the ways of their fathers and to have desires that cannot be fulfilled. But if, to satisfy these new desires, they leave the village, where will they go? Like so many before them, they will go away to the city. We know what the city is like. Many from the village have been there and have told us about it. The city is a bad place. People there are unhappy and violent. There is not enough work for everyone. We don't want our children to go to the city. And we don't want them to be dissatisfied here. Therefore, we don't want your school."

African meetings tend to be wordy affairs, so the discussion went on all night. The young men from the education ministry did their best to convince the villagers, but in the end the decision went against them. After many hours, in the first dawn, they climbed into their landrover and drove off, defeated. As they left the village, the old man, who had become greatly exercised by the long discussion, followed them out and stood in the road, shaking his fist at them.

An American who had gone along on this expedition took some photographs, including one of the old man shaking his fist. He showed these pictures in a seminar in this country. The members of the seminar divided into two groups quite neatly—those who identified with the old man, and those on the side of the earnest young men from the education ministry. This division has both emotional and ideological undertones (for example, in terms of sympathy or lack of sympathy for the counter-culture). But there is also the matter of insight involved—namely, the capacity to appreciate the *logic*, indeed, the *rationality*, of the old man's argument.

Quite apart from emotional or ideological identifications, the policy position recommended here is that so-called "resistances to development" should be taken with the utmost seriousness; they should *not* be hastily explained as ignorance or superstition. There are important intellectual considerations behind this position; they were explicated previously in terms of the postulate that all worlds of consciousness are, in principle, equal, and that therefore no one is capable of "raising" anyone else's consciousness. This is a theoretical as well as a moral position. But there are also pragmatic reasons for this position: *Policies that ignore the indigenous definitions of a situation are prone to fail.*

This is hardly a novel insight. To a surprising degree, for example, it influenced British colonial policy in the past. It is furthermore an attitude that has long been popular among ethnologists and anthropologists, who have frequently warned that institutions and meanings cannot be easily transplanted from one culture to another. Yet in the discussion of development since World War II there has only recently been a spreading awareness of all this. In the original heyday of "developmentalism," into the mid-1960s, the alleged experts were far too sure of themselves to be susceptible to such lines of thinking. The recent change is probably due to two principal factors—first, the sharpening of Third World nationalisms, and second, the practical failures of many development programs (nothing opens the mind more than a good fiasco). Thus the recent literature and public discussion of development policy increasingly emphasizes the importance of indigenous perceptions and values, and the desirability of looking for alternatives to the mechanical transplantation of Western institutional models.[11]

All "resistances to development" entail *counter-* definitions of the situation. These may be normative or cognitive, or both. If they are normative, what is involved is the defense of traditional values against the values of the modernizers. If they are cognitive, it is traditional views of reality that are being defended against the *Weltanschauung* of modernity.

With regard to the normative aspect, the policy implications are relatively straightforward. The problem is essentially *political*: To what extent will those who are in charge politically allow any countervalues to stand in the way of government programs? Sometimes this question can be put in terms of democratic controls or participation. In the end it is likely to resolve itself into a question of force: How much coercion is deemed possible, necessary, or acceptable by those who are politically in charge? In other words, it may not be feasible to ride roughshod over indigenous objections. Or it may be judged unnecessary (in the sense, perhaps, of uneconomical) to do so. Finally, it may even go against the moral scruples of the political elite. The case of Vietnam provides a grisly illustration, especially for Americans, of what may happen when policy in a Third World country systematically ignores the indigenous norms in the definition of the situation.[12] But the cognitive aspect of the matter is probably the more interesting. What it involves is, finally, the necessity of "learning from the peasants" (though hopefully in a sense diametrically opposed to the Maoist one). While this is less obvious than respect for indigenous norms and values, it is probably more important for development policy in the long run.

Agricultural development is a good area for illustrations of the necessity for policy makers to adjust to local knowledge, and conversely of the price of ignoring indigenous definitions of the situation.[13] Thus policy makers have misperceived the economics of particular areas because they looked at measurements of yield in terms of land rather than labor, mistakenly considering the latter rather than the former as the scarce resource. They have failed to understand that the peasant's time budget must give priority to his food rather than his cash crops. They have failed to take seriously the peasant's view on what is good or bad for the soil. After enumerating these and other policy failures, two British agricultural experts recently insisted on the urgent need to create procedures for *listening* to the peasants:

> "This may not seem at all remarkable, indeed obvious and commonsensical as an approach. But the hard and sad fact is that government servants and some researchers are not inclined to spend many hours listening and learning: *they think they know already*. Moreover, they often rush out and back from their offices or homes or headquarters always in a hurry and never with time to spend a day listening. The cost is great in the potential benefits foregone."[14]

Mutatis mutandis, the same observation may be made with regard to any other area of development policy.

The transplantation of institutions and processes from one culture to another is often highly "dysfunctional." This is nothing new. For example, in the eighteenth century all things Chinese had high prestige in Europe. In 1750 a Swedish diplomat in the Ottoman Empire paid for a Bulgarian farmer to travel to Sweden for the purpose of demonstrating the use of threshing equipment derived from China. This equipment had come to be widely adopted in Mediterranean countries. Since it involved threshing on an open platform, it was very usable in warm climates, but very impractical in Northern Europe. Nevertheless, through government pressure, it was widely adopted in Sweden.[15]

When the German colonial government in Tanganyika sought to bring the blessings of European civilization to the natives, they introduced the modern plow there and urged the African farmers to us it. Parts of Tanganyika had long observed the practice of preventing soil erosion by the construction of terraces around the fields. The German plows destroyed these terraces. This was promptly understood by the African farmers, who pointed it out to the German experts. The latter, in the calm assurance of their superior knowledge, dismissed the farmers' protests as typical native ignorance and superstitious fear of all innovations. (It may be added that the German colonial officials did not even have the excuse of not understanding the Africans' language—all government officials in German East Africa had to learn Swahili. But the purpose of this, no doubt, was not to facilitate listening to the Africans, but rather to give them orders.) The government continued to push the plow— with the result that large areas of agricultural land were severely damaged. The story does not end there. When the British took over from the Germans after World War I they repeated exactly the same mistake, with exactly the same results. After World War II American plows were exported in large numbers to Greece and India, again with the same results. And in Burma it was the Soviets who repeated the performance. A few years ago visitors reported that large quantities of Soviet tractors were rusting in a lot near the Rangoon airport, where they had been discarded after it was discovered that their effect on the land was devastating.[16]

It might seem that agricultural technology would be one area in which such mistakes could not be made. After all, the practical consequences are immediate and obvious. If in fact such mistakes are made there, it is easy to see how they would be made in other areas, where the practical penalties for ignoring local knowledge are less immediate

or obvious. Again, it should be stressed that the "dysfunctional" trans-
ference of practices and institutions from one culture to another is nothing
new in history. What is new in recent years is that such irrationalities
can now be massively imposed through the powerful agencies of modern
government.

One of the most instructive examples from recent development
literature concerns a birth control program in India.[17] It is worth elaborating in some detail. During 1956–1960 the Harvard School of Public
Health, with funds of the Rockefeller Foundation and the Indian government, carried out a birth control experiment in a group of villages in
the Punjab. There was then a follow-up study in 1969. The experiment
consisted of the propagation of contraceptive foam tablets in some of the
villages, while another group of villages was left alone, in order to serve
as a control group. The whole operation was accompanied by an
impressive research apparatus. The results of the experiment were very
depressing. Between the inception of the program and the follow-up
study there was indeed a decline of the birth rate, apparently due to a
rise in the age of marriage rather than to use of the contraceptive tablets,
and (more important) the decline was the *same* in both the experimental
and the control populations. It may be added that the total cost of the
experiment was around one million dollars. What had gone wrong?

The answer is quite simple: Almost all those connected with the
experiment (Indians *no less* than Americans) refused to listen to the
initial objections of the villagers. The presupposition of the experiment
was the conventional Western wisdom on birth control: The more
children a family had, the less was its chance for economic betterment.
Therefore, birth control was in the rational self-interest of the villagers.
The villagers denied this. They claimed that, on the contrary, they were
better off economically precisely the more children they had. This assertion was classified by the experimenters as a typical case of irrational
"resistance to development." Indeed, an anthropologist was hired to
study the perceptions of the villagers, grounded as they undoubtedly
were in traditional religious values and superstitions. And efforts were
made to "Indianize" the staff as much as possible.

What happened subsequently is very funny. When the villagers saw
that the experimenters would not listen, they told them what they wanted
to hear—and they threw the contraceptive tablets away. Thus an early

report stated that 90 percent of the villagers were in favor of contraception; the report assumed (falsely, it turned out) that a similar percentage was using the tablets. Here is how one villager explained his "acceptance" of the tablets (needless to say, he never used them): "But they [the staff] were so nice, you know. And they even came from distant lands to be with us. Couldn't we even do this much for them? Just take a few tablets? Ah! even the gods would have been angry with us. They wanted no money for the tablets. All they wanted was that we accept the tablets. I lost nothing and probably received their prayers. And they, they must have gotten some promotion."[18]

The villagers' assertion was a perfectly rational one based on the agricultural labor market. For each family the cost of an additional child is negligible, but the potential increase in income is quite large. Children permit increased productivity on the family's land, as well as saving on hired labor. Also, family income increases as a result of wages earned by its members. As there are more brothers, some work to finance the schooling of others, whose higher income after graduation then pays for the education of the brothers who saw them through school. In simple fact: For the villagers, children are a highly rational economic investment. Here is what one villager told a member of the experimental staff: "You were trying to convince me in 1960 that I shouldn't have any more sons. Now, you see, I have six sons and two daughters and I sit at home in leisure. They are grown up and they bring me money. One even works outside the village as a laborer. You told me I was a poor man and couldn't support a large family. You see, because of my large family, I am a rich man."[19]

This rationale will hold as long as agricultural production is based on very simple technology, so that the size of the working family will determine income. If the staff of the project had listened to the villagers, instead of having an anthropologist study their alleged superstitions, they would have had no difficulty understanding this. They would incidentally have saved a million dollars. The moral of the story is simple, too.[20]

The plea in the preceding chapter was for a *humane* approach to development policy. The plea in this chapter could be described as for a *humanistic* approach, not in the sense of humanitarianism but of the humanities in the classical Western sense. Humanism, from the Renaissance on, has meant a respect for the place of values and meanings in the affairs of men. The humanities have been the disciplines that have studied human events from within, as it were—from within the subjective perceptions of reality that animate actors on the historical scene and that make their actions intelligible to an outside observer. Humanism in this sense has been widely dismissed as unscientific in the ambience of the social sciences, particularly in Anglo-Saxon countries. The discussion of this chapter indicates that this dismissal may have unfortunate consequences. A humanistic approach to development policy (and just as much to the other areas of politically controlled social change) will be based on the insight that no social process can succeed unless it is illuminated with meaning from within.

NOTES

1. For a detailed discussion of the implications of this for an understanding of society, see Peter Berger and Thomas Luckmann, *The Social Construction of Reality* (Garden City, N.Y.: Doubleday, 1966).

2. Attempts to deny the shift from givenness to choice may still be found in the most modernized societies, typically in subcultures committed to premodern traditions. Traditional Judaism in America is an interesting example. One may come across spokesmen for Orthodoxy telling American Jewish students that their Jewishness is ontologically given and that this imposes inevitable obligations upon them—while the students' own experience tells them that their "Jewish identity" is *a project* for which they may or may not opt. Paradoxically the Orthodox spokesman's activity itself presupposes the empirical fact that Jewishness is far from being ontologically given: It makes no sense to exhort someone *to be* something, unless that being is in some way a matter of decision rather than destiny. By contrast, Jews in a traditional *shtetl* might require exhortation to meet their religious and moral duties—but their "identity" was given, for better or for worse, and no one would have thought of making it a topic for exhortation.

3. For a detailed analysis of this, see Peter Berger, Brigitte Berger, and Hansfried Kellner, *The Homeless Mind—Modernization and Consciousness* (New York: Random House, 1973). For the religious component, see Peter Berger, *The Sacred Canopy* (Garden City, N.Y.: Doubleday, 1967), p. II.

4. On the level of individual experience, a crucial characteristic of modern consciousness is "life planning." See Berger, Berger, and Kellner, *The Homeless Mind*, pp. 72 ff. This, in turn, is related to the specifically modern experience of time. One of the grossly neglected aspects of modernization has been its transformation of human temporality. A recent effort to fill this gap is Rudolf Rezohazy, *Temps social et développement* (Brussels: La Renaissance du Livre, 1970).

5. Colin Turnbull, *The Lonely African* (Garden City, N.Y.: Anchor, 1963), p. 178. Emphasis added.

6. Lucy Behrman, *Muslim Brotherhoods and Politics in Senegal* (Cambridge, Mass.: Harvard University Press, 1970).

7. R. S. Khare, *The Changing Brahmans* (Chicago: University of Chicago Press, 1970).

8. James Peacock, *Rites of Modernization* (Chicago: University of Chicago Press, 1968).

9. The connection between freedom and "alienation" has been pointed out by the contemporary German sociologist Arnold Gehlen, in his essay "On the Birth of Freedom from Alienation," in *Studien zur Anthropologie und Soziologie* (Neuwied/Rhein: Luchterhand, 1963), pp. 232 ff. Gehlen, however, is a conservative thinker with severe doubts about the worth of this bargain.

10. The thinking behind this hypothesis is explicated in detail in Berger, Berger, and Kellner, *The Homeless Mind*.

11. Not surprisingly, in view of the historical antecedents, this viewpoint has been strongly represented in Britain. See, for instance, Guy Hunter, *Modernizing Peasant Societies* (New York: Oxford University Press, 1969). Perhaps the demise of the highly "ethnocentric" French colonial empire has facilitated the reception of similar ideas in France—as in Jacques Austruy, *Le scandale du développement* (Paris: Marcel Rivière, 1968). In this country, the influence of Karl Polanyi has stimulated similar lines of thinking, particularly among anthropologists and economists. See George Dalton, *Economic Anthropology and Development* (New York: Basic Books, 1971). The influence of Ivan Illich has more recently been in the same direction. See his latest work, *Tools for Conviviality* (New York: Harper & Row, 1973).

12. See Frances FitzGerald, *Fire in the Lake* (Boston: Little, Brown, 1972).

13. For an overview, see Raanan Weitz, ed., *Rural Development in a Changing World* (Cambridge, Mass.: M.I.T. Press, 1971).

14. Robert Chambers and Deryke Belshaw, "Managing Rural Development," mimeographed (Brighton: Institute of Development Studies, University of Sussex, 1973), p. 5.27. Emphasis added.

15. See article by Paul Leser in Anthony Wallace, ed., *Selected Papers of the Fifth International Congress of Anthropology and Ethnological Sciences* (Philadelphia: University of Pennsylvania Press, 1960), pp. 294 f.

16. I am indebted to Paul Leser for these examples.

17. See Mahmood Mamdani, *The Myth of Population Control* (New York: Monthly Review Press, 1972).

18. Ibid., p. 23.

19. Ibid., p. 109.

20. The moral is *not* that uncontrolled population growth is a good thing for India. It clearly is *not* a good thing. But the error was to confuse the national interest with the individual self-interest of the villagers. It may be doubted whether appeals to the national interest can induce people to have fewer children. There is no doubt that this result cannot be achieved by telling people that they are being harmed by the very thing they know to be of benefit to themselves.

INTERLUDE

A TALE OF
TWO MORALITIES

M ANUELA keeps dreaming about the village.[1] She does
not think about it very much in the daytime. Even when she thinks
about Mexico, it is not usually about the village. In any case, during
the day it is the brash, gleaming reality of California that dominates,
its loud demand for full attention pushing into the background the
old images and feelings. It is at night that the village comes back,
reclaiming its power over Manuela. It is then as if she had never
left it—or, worse, as if she must inevitably return to it.

It is often very hot in the village, though at night one may
freeze. The earth is dry. Time moves very slowly, as the white
clouds move through the brightly blue sky over the brown and arid
hills. Times moves slowly in the faces of the people, too, and the
faces too are brown and arid. Even the faces of the very young
seem to hold old memories. The children do not smile easily. The
day is measured by the halting motion of shadows over houses and
trees. The years are mostly measured by calamities. The past is
powerfully present, although there are few words for it. No one in
the village speaks an Indian language, though everyone has Indian
blood. Can the blood speak, without words? Do the dead speak
from the earth? Somewhere in this blue sky and in these brown
hills there are very old presences, more threatening than consoling.

190

Some years ago the schoolteacher dug up some Indian artifacts and wanted to take them to the city, to sell them to a museum. Calamity struck at once, all over the village. The dead do not want to be disturbed, and they are dangerous.

The village is distant. Distant from what? Distant from everything, but most importantly distant from the places where time moves quickly and purposefully. There is no paved road, no telephone, no electricity. Even the schoolteacher only comes on two days of the week. He has two other villages to take care of, and he lives somewhere else. To get to the nearest bus station one rides on a donkey for three hours over footpaths of trampled dirt. Time and distance determine the world of the village, in fact and in Manuela's dreams. If she were to put it in one sentence, this world, she would have to say: It is very far away, and life there moves very slowly. On the maps the village is in the state of Guerrero, in a very specific location between Mexico City and the Pacific Ocean. In Manuela's dreams the village is located in the center of her self, deep down inside rather than out there somewhere.

Manuela was born in the village twenty-two years ago. Her mother died shortly afterward. Her father, already married to another woman with seven legitimate children, never acknowledged Manuela. Indeed, he has never spoken with her. She was raised by one of her mother's brothers, a man without land and much of the time without work, with a large family of his own that he barely managed to support. There was never any question about the family obligation to take care of Manuela; the only question at the time, lengthily discussed by her grandfather and the three uncles still living in the area, was which of the three would take the baby in. But this obligation did not greatly exceed supplying the bare necessities of life. There was never the slightest doubt about Manuela's status in her uncle's household as the unwanted bastard who took the food out of the mouths of her more deserving cousins—and she was told so in no uncertain terms on many occasions. If there was little food, she would be the hungriest. If there was hard work, she would be the one to do it. This does not mean that she received no affection. She was a very pretty, winsome child, and often people were kind to her. But she always knew that affection and kindness were not her right, were given to her gratuitously—and, by the same token, could be gratuitously taken away again. As a child Manuela wished for someone who would love her all the time, reliably, "officially." However, she was only dimly unhappy in her uncle's household, since she knew nothing else. She was often hungry, sometimes beaten. She did not have shoes until her tenth birthday, when her grandfather made her a present of a pair. This was also the first occasion when she went outside the village, accompanying her grandfather on a visit to the doctor in the nearest town.

Her grandfather and one of her uncles in the village were *ejidatários*, belonging to the minority that owned parcels of land under the village *ejido* (agricultural cooperative). Most of the time the uncle with whom she stayed worked on this land, too, though he would hire himself out for work elsewhere when there was an opportunity. When she was not working in the house or taking care of her little cousins, Manuela also worked in the fields or with the animals belonging to her family. After her tenth birthday she sometimes worked for outsiders, but she was expected to turn over the money she received for this. Sometimes she succeeded in keeping a few coins for herself, though she knew that she would be beaten if found out. She was allowed to go to school and, being very bright, she learned to read and write well. It was her brightness that attracted her grandfather, who was amused by her and took a liking to her (much to the annoyance of her cousins).

"Bad blood will show." "You will come to no good end, like your mother." Manuela must have heard this hundreds of times during her childhood. The prophecy was fulfilled when she was fifteen and made pregnant by the secretary of the *ejido*, one of the most affluent farmers in the village. When her condition could no longer be concealed, there was a terrible scene and her uncle threw her out of the house. Her grandfather, after slapping her a couple of times rather mildly, gave her the address of an aunt in Acapulco and enough money to pay her busfare there. It was thus that she left the village.

Manuela marveled at Acapulco and its astonishing sights, but, needless to say, she lived there in a world far removed from that experienced by the tourists. Her aunt, a gentle widow with two children and a maid's job in one of the big hotels, took Manuela in very warmly (at least in part because she could use some help in the house). Manuela's baby was born there, a healthy boy whom she named Roberto. Not much later Manuela also started to work outside the house.

A Mexican *campesino*, when he migrates, normally follows an itinerary taken before him by relatives and *compadres*. When he arrives, the latter provide an often intricate network of contacts that are indispensable for his adjustment to the new situation. They will often provide initial housing, they can give information and advice, and, perhaps most important, they serve as an informal labor exchange. Such a network awaited Manuela in Acapulco. In addition to the aunt she was staying with, there were two more aunts and an uncle with their respective families, including some twelve cousins of all ages. This family system, of course, was transposed to the city from the village, but it took on a quite different character in the new context. Freed from the oppressive constraints of village life, the system, on the whole, was more benign. Manuela experienced it as such. Several of her cousins took turns taking care of little Roberto when Manuela started to work. Her aunt's "fiancé" (a somewhat euphemistic term), who was head clerk in the linen supply department of the hotel, found Manuela a job in his department. The uncle, through a *compadre* who was head waiter in another hotel, helped her get a job there as a waitress. It was this uncle, incidentally, who had gone further than any other member of the Acapulco clan, at least for a brief time. An intelligent and aggressive man, he worked himself up in the municipal sanitation department to the rank of inspector. Through a coup, the details of which were shrouded in mystery but which were safely assumed by everyone to involve illegality of heroic proportions, Uncle Pepe amassed the equivalent of about one thousand U.S. dollars in a few months' time, a staggering sum in this ambience. With this money he set out for Mexico City, ostensibly to look into a business proposition. In fact he checked into one of the capital's finest hotels, made the rounds of nightclubs and luxury brothels, and returned penniless but not overly unhappy a month later. The clan has viewed him with considerable awe ever since.

Manuela now had a fairly steady cash income, modest to be sure, but enough to keep going. This does not mean, however, that she could keep all of it for herself and her child. The family system operated as a social insurance agency as well as a labor exchange, and there was never a shortage of claimants. An aunt required an operation. An older cousin set up business as a mechanic and needed some capital to start off. Another cousin was arrested and a substantial *mordida* was required to bribe his way out of jail. And then there were always new calamities back in the village, requiring emergency transfers of money back there. Not least among them was the chronic calamity of grandfather's kidney ailment, which consumed large quantities of family funds in expensive and generally futile medical treatments.

Sometimes, at the hotel, Manuela did baby-sitting for tourists with children. It was thus that she met the couple from California. They stayed in Acapulco for a whole month, and soon Manuela took care of their little girl almost daily. When they left the woman asked Manuela whether she wanted a job as a maid in the States. "Yes," replied Manuela at once, without thinking. The arrangements were made quickly. Roberto was put up with a cousin. Uncle Pepe, through two trusted intermediaries, arranged for Manuela to cross the border illegally. Within a month she arrived at the couple's address in California.

And now she has been here for over a year. California was even more astonishing than Acapulco had been when she first left the village, but now she had more time to explore this new world. She learned English in a short time and, in the company of a Cuban girl who worked for a neighbor, she started forays into the American universe, in ever-wider circles from her employers' house. She even took bus trips to Hollywood and San Francisco. For the first time in her life she slept in a room all by herself. And, despite her regular payments for Roberto's keep, she started to save money and put it in a bank account. Most important, she started to think about her life in a new way, systematically. "What will become of you when you go back?" asked the American woman one day. Manuela did not know then, but she started to think. Carmelita, the Cuban girl, discussed the matter with her many times—in exchange for equal attention paid to her own planning exercises. Eventually, one project won out over all the alternatives: Manuela would return to go to commercial school, to become a bilingual secretary. She even started a typing course in California. But she would not return to Acapulco. She knew that, to succeed, she would have to remove herself from the family there. She would go to Mexico City, first alone, and then she would send for Roberto.

This last decision was made gradually. It was the letters that did it. Manuela, some months before, had mentioned the amount of money she had saved (a very large amount, by her standards, and enough to keep her and Roberto afloat for the duration of the commercial course). Then the letters started coming from just about everyone in the Acapulco clan. Most of the contents were family gossip, inquiries about Manuela's life in the States, and long expressions of affectionate feelings. There were frequent reminders not to forget her relatives, who took such good care of Roberto. Only gradually did the economic infrastructure emerge from all this: There was to be a *fiesta* at the wedding of a cousin, and could Manuela make a small contribution. The cousin who had been in jail was still to be tried, and there were lawyer's expenses. Uncle Pepe was onto the most promising business opportunity of his "long and distinguished career in financial activities" (his own words), and just three hundred American dollars would make it possible for him to avail himself of this never-to-recur opportunity—needless to say, Manuela would be a full partner upon her return. Finally, there was even a very formal letter from grandfather, all the way from the village, containing an appeal for funds to pay for a trip to the capital so as to take advantage of a new treatment that a famous doctor had developed there. It took a while for Manuela to grasp that every dollar of her savings had already been mentally spent by her relatives.

The choice before Manuela now is sharp and crystal-clear: She must return to Mexico—because she wants to, because of Roberto, and because the American authorities would send her back there sooner or later anyway. She can then return to the welcoming bosom of the family system, surrender her savings, and return to her previous way of life. Or she can carry through her plan in the face of family opposition. The choice is not only between two courses of action, but between two moralities. The first course is dictated by the morality of collective solidarity, the second by the morality of personal autonomy and advancement. Each morality condemns the other—as uncaring selfishness in the former case, as irresponsible disregard of her own potential and the welfare of her son in the latter. Poor Manuela's conscience is divided; by now she is capable of feeling its pangs either way.

She is in America, not in Mexico, and the new morality gets more support from her immedate surroundings. Carmelita is all for the plan, and so are most of the Spanish-speaking girls with whom Manuela has been going out. Only one, another Mexican, expressed doubt: "I don't know. Your grandfather is ill, and your uncle helped you a lot in the past. Can you just forget them? I think that one must always help one's relatives." Manuela once talked about the matter with the American woman. "Nonsense," said the latter, "you should go ahead with your plan. You owe it to yourself and to your son." So this is what Manuela intends to do, very soon now. But she is not at ease with the decision. Every time another letter arrives from Mexico, she hesitates before opening it, and she fortifies herself against the appeals she knows to be there.

Each decision, as dictated by the respective morality, has predictable consequences: If Manuela follows the old morality, she will, in all likelihood, never raise herself or her son above the level she achieved in Acapulco—not quite at the bottom of the social scale, but not very far above it. If, on the other hand, she decides in accordance with the new morality (new for her, that is), she has at least a chance of making it up one important step on that scale. Her son will benefit from this, but probably no other of her relatives will. To take that step she must, literally, hack off all those hands that would hold her back. It is a grim choice indeed.

What will Manuela do? She will probably at least start out on her plan. Perhaps she will succeed. But once she is back in Mexico, the tentacles of the old solidarity will be more powerful. They will pull more strongly. It will be harder to escape that other village, the village of the mind within herself. The outcome of the struggle will decide whether the village will be Manuela's past or also her future. Outside observers should think very carefully indeed before they take sides in this contest.

NOTE

1. Manuela's story is fiction, made up as a composite from several true stories. Manuela does not exist. But many Manuelas do exist, not only in Mexico but all over the Third World. Their moral dilemma must be understood if one is to understand "development."

Chapter VII

❧❧❧❧❧❧❧

THE CASE OF AMERICA—
IN QUEST OF A STANCE

IN RECENT YEARS it has become fashionable once more (by no means for the first time) to question the possibility of detached observation and analysis. This questioning has been useful up to a point, in that it has served to show up a variety of prejudices and vested interests masquerading under the guise of objectivity. Thus Latin American critics have been able to demonstrate the degree to which some of their Northern colleagues have been peddling capitalist ideology under the banner of allegedly value-free social science. A useful consequence of this has been that social scientists from the United States, in dealing with Third World problems, have become much more "ideology conscious," and thus more self-critical. Not so useful has been the further consequence that some of them have either despaired of even the possibility of their studying such problems at all, or have overtly placed their work under the aegis of an ideological commitment. In the first case there has been the assertion that only Third World social scientists can adequately study Third World problems (an assertion paralleled, of course, in other areas, such as the study of the problems of racial minorities or of women). In the second case there has developed the approach of "advocacy research," which means that the work of the social scientist is infused from beginning to end with a political purpose. The former position leads to a stance of intellectual and moral self-denigration which seems to be particularly congenial to liberals with a propensity for near-limitless guilt. The latter position is more appealing to those on the political left, leading to a stance of self-assertive militancy that is typically associated with both moral and intellectual arrogance.

If this book were only an undertaking in social science, it would suffice to characterize both these positions as a self-liquidation of the scientific ideal and to reaffirm the continuing validity, and urgent importance, of the scientist's efforts toward objectivity and detachment. The intention of this book, however, is political and ethical, over and beyond any social-scientific elucidations. This intention dictates a different response to the question about the "existential location" of the observer or analyst. The question can be put quite simply: "Where do you stand, as a morally responsible person?" If the only purpose at issue is a social-scientific undertaking, it is permissible to reply: "None of your damned business—read my book and argue with it on its own terms." Such a reply is not enough in the present case. An American social scientist can, in my view, deal with Third World problems in an objective manner and, as long as he stays within the framework of social science, make no apology for this. In other words, he is perfectly entitled to "bracket" the fact that he is an American—and, indeed, such "bracketing" is the first requirement of any effort toward objectivity. But as soon as he ventures out to speak politically and ethically, he must ask himself (even if others don't) what it means to do *as an American*.

There are many places in the Third World where an American is first of all perceived as an enemy. There was the young man in Kenya who approached me with a broad smile and who, when I was introduced as an American professor, turned around and walked away without a word. There was the student in Brazil who told me that the reason she trusted me with her political views was that she had read some of my books and therefore knew that I was not a "typical American." There are the worse instances when one is perceived as a friend and ally by the people representing what one considers to be humanly repulsive forces and policies, again simply on the basis of one's American identification. I recall the Brazilian government official who began his conversation with me (the rest of the conversation consisted of his vigorous defense of the status quo in Brazil) by making a florid little speech, thanking me for the sacrifices made by the United States on behalf of the "Free World" in Vietnam. The concrete human context will have to determine the manner in which an individual may want to disclaim such misidentifications. The general requirement will have to be to think through "the case of America" in connection with Third World development, not just analytically, but in an attempt to find an ethically acceptable political stance.

There has been a historic nexus between America and the myth of growth. In all likelihood no major society has been dominated as much as this one by the ethos of "onward and upward" and "bigger and better." The myth is embodied in key assumptions of what Gunnar Myrdal has called the "American creed," it has colored outsiders' perceptions of American at least since de Tocqueville, and it has probably been an important formative force for the American national character. The same myth has been potent in America's relations with what today is called the Third World. Everywhere America presented itself as the embodiment of modernity and progress—in the wonders of its technology and economy, but no less in the social, political, and cultural institutions allegedly linked to these wonders. This self-presentation has met with very wide acceptance: Others came to perceive this society in much the way Americans perceived it themselves, and this perception has spurred imitation, though not always of those things that Americans were most anxious to have imitated. In the nineteenth century American missionaries failed in their campaign to convert China to Christianity, but their activities were successful in implanting American ideas of progress through technological productivity and social engineering. More recently, the imitations of American political institutions in Asia and Africa are hardly a success story, but there can be no question about the continuing pull of American culture, from American fashions in clothing and popular music to such classically American ideas as equality between the sexes or the right of the individual to marry freely on the basis of love. It is important to keep in mind that the "cargo cult" of the myth of growth has always held out these cultural values along with its promises of economic affluence.

Within American society itself, the "American creed" has long succeeded in "coopting" the emotional appeal of the other myth, that of revolution. Perhaps this began all the way back, with the designation "revolution" applied to the events that led to the establishment of an independent American republic—events that, in cool historical perspective, were anything but revolutionary except in a narrow political sense. The notion that this country originated in a "revolution" allowed Americans to feel that they had already achieved what others were still struggling for, and at least until the onset of the Cold War this notion served to legitimate American popular sympathies with revolutionary movements elsewhere, especially if the latter were directed against European colonial powers. One may observe this ideological stance from the identification of the United States with Latin American independence movements in the nineteenth century (at least on the level of rhetoric it is still operative in the "inter-American system") to American attitudes to the dismemberment of the European colonial empires after World War II. Some years ago *Fortune* magazine could successfully apply the description "permanent revolution" to American society, and similar ideas are again being voiced by some as the bicentennial of 1976 approaches. The underlying emotional context of all this was characterized by optimism, self-confidence, and the typically missionary conviction that one's good fortune should be shared with others.

A measure of the change that has recently taken place is afforded by looking back to the curious blend of arrogance and benevolence (again a typically missionary mixture) with which the United States sought to impose its political and social patterns upon the defeated Axis nations. The policies of the American occupation in Japan are probably most instructive in this regard, though (contrary to currently fashionable visions of "racist" America) there was a comparable evangelistic effort in Germany. It is quite difficult today to recapture the national mood in which policies like these appeared morally and politically plausible. Even more recently, John Kennedy's inaugural address of 1960 expressed an ideological stance that requires a considerable empathetic effort by today's reader. Americans who have grown to maturity in the last decade feel in the presence of ancient history when reading or listening to accounts of this, after all, very recent past, when almost anywhere to be an American meant to represent the most widely held aspirations of men for a better future.

The 1960s subjected this ideological and psychological constellation to severe shocks. Much more time will have to elapse before the causes for this can be fully grasped. There is little doubt about the proximate causes, notably the fiasco of American policy in Indochina and the continuing crisis of the domestic racial situation. It would seem premature to speculate whether these events really played the crucial role they seemed to at the time, or whether they were simply the occasions for much more deeply rooted tensions to come to the fore. Be this as it may, the self-image of America as the vanguard of progress was attacked with unprecedented vigor from within the most vocal groups in the society. A substantial portion of the intelligentsia moved abruptly to the left ideologically and politically. As a result, in academia, in important segments of the literary and publishing worlds, and not least in the mass media, a highly critical view of America and its role in the world became respectable—and, in some circles, taken for granted. A kind of malignant transformation took place. The more extreme version of the new image, represented by the New Left, displaced the America of progress, democracy, and a better life for all with an *Amerika* of repression, exploitation, and global imperialism, with all these evils perceived as endemic to the very nature of the society. The more moderate version, as stated by a large body of liberal opinion makers, did not quite equate America with Hitler's Third Reich, but continuously stressed its character as a "sick society."

The political critique of America's self-image was reinforced by a succession of social and cultural movements which emphasized different alleged malignancies of the society. Black nationalism and the militant movements of other racial minorities portrayed "racism," or even "genocide," as being at the heart of the national character. Culture prophets, often inspired by the youth culture and its adult hangers-on in the so-called counterculture, depicted America as pathologically violent, pestilent with sexual inhibitions, and dehumanizing in its basic values. The more radical wing of the ecology movement presented America as the major despoiler of the earth, a sort of technocratic cancer, and radical feminists saw the country as one great bastion of predatory "male chauvinism." Whatever these different attacks may have lacked in ideological unity, they shared a fairly unanimously negative vision of American society. In many instances the attacks expressed a passionate hatred of America such as has only rarely been directed against a society by some of its own most privileged and intellectually articulate members.

At the time of writing, the most turbulent phase of this assault on the "American creed" from within the country appears to have passed (though only an imprudent observer would venture to diagnose its demise). It is also important to recall that large segments of the population remained relatively unshaken by all this turbulence, continuing to believe in the old virtues and holding fast to all kinds of views that the opinion makers (*sic*) were declaring to be "obsolete" or "discredited." Even so, it is safe to assume that the old optimism and self-confidence have been disturbed even among large groups who never felt that the country was in desperate crisis. At the very least, their perspectives on America and the world are no longer taken for granted in the old way— and that, in itself, is a major transformation. What it spells is, precisely, the "loss of innocence." Even in these groups one may speak of a crisis of the "American creed." In other groups, especially in a large portion of the college-educated upper middle class and probably among the majority of American blacks, varying degrees of a negative "definition" of America have become quite firmly established.

To reiterate: The future course of all this cannot be predicted with any assurance. Especially unpredictable are the political implications. Thus it is not at all impossible that the ideological and psychological frustrations of this time of crisis may lead to what Freudians call a "reaction formation"—a violent reaffirmation of everything that has been attacked. What is of interest in the present context is the way in which (to remain a moment longer with Freudian metaphors) the Third World is utilized to "abreact" American ideological agonies. Put differently: As Americans struggle with their self-image, the Third World is made to serve as a mirror. To be sure, it is not the only mirror. There is always Europe. There is Israel, for American Jews. And for some on the left the Soviet Union may still provide a mirror effect (not necessarily positive). Nevertheless, as Americans seek to "define" themselves anew, the Third World serves for many as an important point of reference with regard to this aspiration.

The aforementioned historical antecedents make this plausible. From the beginnings of the American republic its citizens have tended to understand themselves in terms of a global mission. As American Christianity saw its scope as extending "from Greenland's icy mountains to India's coral strand," so American political evangelism reached "from the halls of Montezuma to the shores of Tripoli." For better or for worse, Americans have always had the propensity to link their national aspirations with a "manifest destiny" transcending the borders of the republic. Since World War II this ideological utilization of the Third World has had expressions ranging from one end to the other of the political spectrum. In the liberal center there continued the image of America as the harbinger of economic progress, democracy, and human uplift in the Third World. (A good account of this may be found in the recent book by Robert Packenham—*Liberal America and the Third World*, 1973.) One may think here of the rhetoric that legitimated Point Four, or the Alliance for Progress, or the establishment of the Peace Corps. The same rhetoric still goes on today, even if somewhat muted, in much public discussion of development assistance. On the political right there has been the self-image of America as the bastion, indeed the last best hope, of the "Free World," in terms not only of military might but of its allegedly superior moral values and social institutions. The rhetoric of the old China Lobby may serve as the perfect example of this stance. And if such notions have been "discredited" among academics, or among editorial writers for *The New York Times*, it would be rash to assume the same for Rotary Club members in the Middle West, military officers, or even some important executives of corporations with Third World interests.

It is particularly intriguing to see the survival of this missionary impulse even in the American left. In the late 1960s, when there were many people of this political persuasion who really believed that a revolution in America was possible or even imminent, there was the widespread assumption that such a revolution would be a particular blessing to the Third World. This assumption was logical within a particular interpretation: If America was indeed the foremost imperialist power, and if American imperialism was the foremost reason for the miseries of the Third World, then revolutionary overthrow of this "system" would naturally benefit all those who were its victims in Third World countries. It is only in these terms that one can understand a perspective that linked campus riots in California with peasant insurrections in Southeast Asia in a comprehensive global "strategy." What is even more intriguing is that the same perspective was shared by people in the Third World. I recall a discussion with Latin American students in Mexico in the late 1960s. They were all stridently anti-American and almost all convinced that violent revolution was the only solution of the problems of Latin America. What impressed me at the time, though, was that their expectations seemed to be directed not to what was going on in the guerrilla activities of their own continent, but to what I thought were rather trivial events in places like Columbia University. In a strangely inverted way, it seemed, there was here a continuation of the old image of America as mankind's last best hope—even if now a putatively revolutionary America was to embody this hope.

In the American left, among American blacks, and in the counter-culture there continues to be strong identification with the Third World. It has different ideological and psychological components in these three groups. In the counterculture it is based, at least in part, on an essentially correct instinct that grasps the commonalities between the discontents of modernity in America and the resistances to modernization in tradi-tional societies. It is an oversimplification to dismiss this perception as nothing but romantic illusion. Among American blacks there is the understandable desire to look for allies abroad, especially in Africa, not only politically (where this desire has little if any empirical foundation) but in their quest for a cultural identity. As to the political left, wide-spread disillusionment with regard to the Soviet Union has naturally redirected attention to the socialist experiments in the Third World. Whatever else may be involved in these identifications, in each case the Third World serves as a foil for the self-definitions, and indeed self-constructions, of Americans. And whatever sympathies one may have with the motives (my own sympathies are unequally distributed among the three groups), it is necessary to reject all these "uses" of the Third World.

The rejection can be stated very simply: *It is not the purpose of Third World countries to solve the "identity problems" of Americans*—be they Peace Corps volunteers, dispirited Christians, or would-be revolu-tionaries. If there is one lesson to be learned from this last decade, it is that it is high time for Americans to surrender their grandiose self-definitions, whether in the positive vision of their society as "God's own country," or in the masochistic inversion of this vision in which America becomes the Beast from the Abyss. It is neither. Renunciation of these self-important visions is not only morally but politically indicated. The relationship between America and the Third World must be thought through in terms of realities, not on the basis of psychological needs—least of all the psychological needs of Americans.

The realities at issue are, above all, realities of power. Large parts of the world today hold the image of America as the paramount embodiment of imperialism. To many intellectuals this image is linked with the Marxist-Leninist theory of imperialism, and to a substantial number this theory explains everything done by the United States in the Third World. We have discussed the theory of imperialism earlier, and there is no need to repeat the discussion. The theory has serious defects in general and, in consequence, its application to the case of America has uneven plausibility. In some areas of the world interpretations based on it are considerably plausible, at least on the surface; this is notably the case in Latin America. In other areas only the most tortuous argumentation can squeeze the empirically available facts into the strait jacket of the theory. The most important instance of this is undoubtedly Vietnam, where none of the economic dynamics alleged in the theory appear to have been operative. Insofar as the Vietnamese adventure is held up as the most crass expression of American imperialism of the post-World War II period, failure of the theory to explain this instance is significant.

If, therefore, we speak here of realities of power, this does not imply their interpretation in Marxist-Leninist terms. For this reason it might be advisable to refrain from using the word "imperialism," unless one wishes to refer to the phenomenon as intended by the theory. Be this as it may, America is certainly an *imperial* power, using the word in its pre-Marxist and not necessarily pejorative sense. America today is not just a national society but an imperial system with tentacles of power reaching across the oceans. It constitutes the center of a network of alliances with a large number of states ranging in status from independent partners to satellites. There are countries (and not only in Latin America) where the political representatives of the United States, whatever their formal titles, function as imperial proconsuls vis-a-vis the indigenous authorities. Needless to say, this political power has at its disposal a gigantic machinery of military power—indeed, the most destructive such machinery in the history of mankind. Like the political power, the military power is transoceanic in scope, with bases scattered all over the globe. If such a combination of political and military power constitutes an "empire," then there are only two true imperial powers in the world today, the United States and the Soviet Union—a fact not to be lost sight of amid the current talk of realignment.

There can be no doubt that American political and military power relates to American economic power, and in some places it may well do so in the manner depicted in the theory of imperialism. Thus American intervention in Guatemala in 1954 followed a script that could have been plagiarized from a Marxist textbook. In general, however, relations between these two power complexes are less direct. As already mentioned, no visible American economic interests were involved in the country's imbroglio in Indochina, a failure of policy with political and ideological rather than economic roots. Indeed, an argument could be made that *imperial* interests, in the sense of political and military empire, often serve to restrain the exploitative interests of economic *imperialism*: The proconsuls must often be concerned to keep the traders in check— with the intriguing implication that, in some instances, disappearance of the proconsuls could actually strengthen the predatory power of the traders. However, whatever its relations with American government, American business is in itself a global power. It has its own network of partners and satellites in an international corporate system spanning the oceans. With the coming of the so-called multinational corporations it has become hard in many cases to disentangle the American interests from those of others (notably the West Europeans and the Japanese), but it remains true that American economic decision makers exercise vast power far beyond the borders of the United States. In some areas of the Third World that power is overwhelming if pitted against the indigenous political or economic structures.

The facts just recited are, of course, well known. The recital was made in order to stress that rejection of the notion of American imperialism as propagated by Marxists is in no way to deny the palpable reality of American power, in the Third World or elsewhere. These facts should now be put together with the events discussed earlier: *America is an imperial power. It is also an imperial power that has become uncertain in its sense of mission.* The aforementioned crisis of the "American creed" has affected the exercise of American imperial power throughout the world. This is probably more important in the case of government than of the corporations, for two reasons: Government is more subject to democratic controls, and thus more vulnerable to shifts in public opinion, and government generally requires a greater measure of ideological legitimation (after all, for most practical purposes the profit figures suffice to legitimate corporate activities). As far as American political and military power is concerned, there is good reason to think that it has become more hesitant in the last few years. It is too early to say to what extent this new "mood" in America will redound to the advantage of the other superpower and significantly change the international balance of power. The recent coincidence of the fourth

Arab-Israeli war and the deepening Watergate crisis opens the possibility of chilling scenarios (even if one posits that the former event was not directly caused by the latter). The uncertainty regarding American power in the world is fertile ground for efforts to construct new legitimations of whatever power continues to exist. Put differently: *An imperial power in decline is prone to ideological repair jobs.*

To some extent, at least, this is a healthy reaction. People always start thinking when they are in trouble, as individuals or collectivities. Nothing said here, therefore, is intended to denigrate reflection about "what America is about" in these troubled times. The present concern is with the way in which the Third World is being introduced anew into the discussion of America's "national purpose." It is an old habit creeping back in, and it is a bad habit. With the "Free World" ideology of the right having taken a bad beating in Indochina, it is the liberal and left versions of this old dream of America's mission to the poor that are more likely to come to the fore: The United States is no longer to be the world's policeman, but its social worker. This may be a more attractive role in some ways, but it remains ethically questionable and it is, if anything, even less realistic politically than the role it is to replace. The root difficulty with the proposition is that the Third World does not want us in *either* role.

Relations between America and the Third World involve a large number of political and economic problems. It is not the intention of this chapter to make specific policy recommendations, but a general, *negative* emphasis emerges from the preceding considerations. It is probably more urgent to reflect on what America should *not* do in the Third World than on what it should do in a positive way. Put differently: I am not at all sure what America can do *for* the Third World, but I am convinced that there are a number of things that America has been doing *to* the Third World that it should stop doing. Vietnam is a paradigm of this proposition. As far as American government policy is concerned, this means above all a shift to much greater restraint in the exercise of political and military power. This shift will have to be accompanied by a deescalation of ideological rhetoric and evangelistic fervor, *not* by a quest for new proving grounds for our "national purpose" in the Third World. The same negative emphasis applies to economic policy, both governmental and private. The basic problems in this area have to do with trade—problems of great complexity that cannot even be touched upon here. I see no way in which these problems can be solved by a new fervor about aid (however desirable such aid may be in specific instances). There are the further problems of political controls over the actions of private business, especially the multinational corporations. Again, I cannot see how these problems will be solved by an appeal to America's "national purpose."

I am not presenting a brief for *Realpolitik*. Everything said so far in this book has been based on the assumption that policy should be judged, and if possible modified, by moral considerations. This is a very different thing, though, from seeking to infuse the policy makers with some new ideological definition of their purpose. The much more promising course is to begin with the assumption that both American government and American business will continue to act from motives of pragmatic self-interest—and *then* to reflect about the realistic possibilities of imposing moral limits or morally indicated modifications upon the policies at issue. Needless to say, this is a much more complicated and painstaking task than the construction of a new national ideology. It is most salutary to recollect what, it seems to me, is a major lesson of the past decade: American involvement in Vietnam was motivated by ideology far more than by *Realpolitik*. Indeed, it was *disinterested* in the most terrible way imaginable. As far as the question of "national purpose" is concerned, I would say this: *Whatever America is about, it is not about the Third World.* There may be individual Americans and American voluntary associations with a sense of mission in this area, and in some cases this may be a good thing. Their actions, however, fall under a different logic from that of governmental and business policies. To confuse the two logics is an invitation to disaster for the former as well as the latter. This distinction, needless to add, is well grounded in the traditions of American society.

It is a recurring process of history that empires succeed each other. Just as power is acquired by a nation, so it is lost again, for a variety of reasons. But power is just about never given up voluntarily, as the result of an ideological decision. Even in the unlikely case that a power elite made such a decision (gripped, perhaps, by some state of collective religious hysteria), actual translation of the decision into practice would turn out to be very difficult. Thus it would be no easy task to dismantle

American imperial power. Almost immediately there would be near-chaos in many parts of the world, and pressures on American leadership to stop the dismantling process would quickly become irresistible. What is more, such a decision would be morally irresponsible to an extreme degree. But there is no reason to pursue these considerations, which have nothing to do with the realities of the situation; perhaps they only come to mind at all to the extent that comparable fantasies of the recent "peace movement" in America have not entirely faded from memory. It is necessary to assume, then, that America will not voluntarily surrender its imperial power—and that it should not. By the same token, American imperial power will continue to be an important political and economic reality for the Third World, even if its military presence will diminish in a "lower profile." But does this mean that America's significance for the Third World is limited to these facts of power?

I think there is a lesson to be drawn from the aforementioned cultural influences of America. A curious fact about this influence is its apparently high degree of independence from America's imperial power. To be sure, there are cultural concomitants to American economic and political penetration. One only has to watch Latin American television to grasp this point. But the relation of cultural and economic-political influence is by no means simple. There are countries very much dominated by American power, economically and politically, which evince few signs of American cultural influence. Conversely, countries that are in no way dependent on American power are highly susceptible to the cultural impact. Everywhere one finds individuals and entire strata who, while vigorously anti-American ideologically and in their political activity, are just as vigorously imitating indubitably American cultural patterns. Thus vociferous advocates of pro-American "Free World" policies may detest American influences in the area of women's rights or popular music, while these same influences may be enthusiastically endorsed by vociferous antiimperialists. Right-wing colonels may abhor miniskirts, and left-wing guerrillas may be jazz enthusiasts. What does this mean? I believe it means at least one (perhaps cheering) thing: *America is imitated culturally not because of its power but because of its image of modernity.* More than any other society, America continues to be perceived as the vanguard of modernity—even by those who would radically revolutionize its political, economic, and social institutions. It is this perception, rather than awe of American power, which accounts for the enormous pull of

American culture. If this is so, a further proposition suggests itself: *America can be most significant for the Third World by being itself.* In saying this, I do *not* mean some Wilsonian utopianism of America as the harbinger of democracy or the fount of other sociopolitical virtues. I mean an acceptance of the challenge posed by the image of modernity. To a considerable degree this challenge is independent of the challenges posed by American imperial power, and it may even survive the latter.

Talcott Parsons has recently characterized America as the "lead society," precisely in the sense of this image. He has been sharply criticized for the alleged ethnocentrism if not chauvinism implied by this phrase. The allegation may or may not apply to Parsons, but it misses the essential point. "Lead society" may be an unfortunate term, but the fact remains that America is indeed, by any number of criteria, the society in which the transformations brought on by modernization have gone farthest on the largest scale. America is the most modern of any large society. To say this is *not* to say that everyone else must follow the "lead," *nor* that all or even any of these modern transformations are a good thing. Rather, it is to say that *America constitutes a gigantic laboratory for the experiment of modernization.* It seems to me that *this* is its foremost significance for others—and, if you will, its "mission" or "national purpose." America will meet the challenge by carrying on the experiment with imagination and moral sensitivity, not for others but for itself—and precisely because of this it will provide lessons, both positive and negative, to others embarked on similar experiments. These lessons may well be reciprocal. Only with an abandonment of the messianic delusions of "manifest destiny," in any of its ideological incarnations, will Americans be free themselves to learn from others. What happens in Kansas may well carry lessons for Indonesia—*mutatis mutandis*, the reverse may also be true.

The current contest between the attitude of social engineering and the utopian imagination in this country may be cited as an important example of America's continuing experimentation. It is a truism to point out that America is the country *par excellence* of the social engineering mentality. Americans have always been pragmatic, experimental, inclined toward technical solutions, and prone to translate theoretical dilemmas into practical programs. This deeply grounded "methodism" of the American mind has come to be challenged seriously by various eruptions of utopianism from within the society. It is interesting to note how many utopian movements, now world-wide in scope, have either originated in America or received an unmistakably American stamp here—from the "student revolution" of the 1960s to Women's Liberation. The clichés of anti-Americanism seem to have been coined first by Americans, and Parisian Maoists exhibit a "life style" of unmistakably Californian provenance.

As has been contended earlier in this book, at least some of these utopian movements can best be understood as reactions against the discontents of modernity—in which case it should hardly be surprising that they have a particular American affinity. It has also been contended that one of the foremost challenges of modernization is to find solutions to the discontents it produces, or, in other words, to seek out the acceptable limits of modernity and its counterformations. It seems to be that American society, because of both its past history and its present character, is a particularly promising laboratory for this quest. The challenge is above all one of finding syntheses between the innovative skills of the social engineer and the innovative imagination of the utopian critic. In this quest, America and the Third World can usefully provide mirror-like images to each other. America shows the Third World one particularly potent image of what modernity can be in a highly developed form; the Third World shows America a kaleidoscope of societies thrusting themselves toward modernity. The advantage is mutual: If we can show them what they might become, they can show us alternatives to our own course. I suspect that, in both cases, the parties will find as much to imitate as to avoid.

A notable example of what I have in mind here is the problem of pluralism. As modernization proceeds, a paradoxical institutional process sets in. On the one hand, modernization pluralizes social life. Where people previously lived in unified, relatively simple, and highly integrated social structures, they now come to live in structures that are enormously variegated, organized in extremely complex ways, and constantly threatened with the anomie that results from an absence of integrative meanings. This pluralization of social life has far-reaching consequences in all institutional areas—from the plausibility of religion to the stability of family relations. It also produces severe discontents and, ipso facto, hunger for alleviation of the threat of anomie and for meaningful reintegrations. The paradox lies in the fact (masterfully analyzed by Emile Durkheim in the period of classical sociology) that the modern state has come to represent the only credible candidate for such reintegration; all other likely candidates have either been swept away (such as the institutions of village, guild, or extended family) or are unsuitable for the task of comprehensive reintegration (such as modern economic institutions or voluntary associations with very limited scope). At least since the French Revolution a variety of political movements have sought to construct a state in which there will be true "fraternity"—in which, that is, the political community will protect the individual from anomie and provide him with a meaningful order in which to live. The psychological roots of modern totalitarianism are to be found in precisely this aspiration. The modern state, however, is by its very nature incapable of fulfilling this redemptive promise. Invariably, therefore, the political structures set up by the successful among those movements (regardless of whether they be designated "right" of "left") betray the original promise and aggravate the anomie from which they were to provide relief. The paramount task, as Durkheim saw, is the quest for *intermediate structures* as solutions to this dilemma of modern society—structures which will be intermediate between the atomized individual and the order of the state. American pluralism, even in its failures, provides a unique object lesson to anyone concerned with this problem. Conversely, the variety of institutional experiments and compromises now going on in the Third World offer highly suggestive lessons toward the same end.

Gilbert Murray's phrase "failure of nerve" fits with particular aptness an imperial power that has become uncertain of itself, including its basic political values. If such a state of affairs continues over a period of time, an even nastier term that suggests itself is "decadence." Has America become decadent? The possibility cannot be excluded, least of all by a repetition of the delusive notion that this is still a "young country"— hardly plausible as the republic approaches its two hundredth anniversary. Whatever may be the verdict on America's putative decadence, only a limited number of overall scenarios lead on from the present moment of uncertainty and decline. One: The decline may continue, with others taking over abroad and the domestic scene going through ever-deepening political, social, and economic crises. Two: The decline may be arrested by the rise of a new power elite, reintegrating the society by force and legitimating itself by an ideology with, at best, only surface connections with the American democratic tradition. Three: The decline may be arrested through a revitalization of the "American creed," and by the successful solution of the society's problems by democratic and pluralistic means.

I find myself unable to rank these three scenarios in any order of probabilities. I only know that the third scenario is the only one that promises a tolerable political and moral situation. America's relations with the Third World are unlikely to be a major factor in deciding which of these possible futures will in fact be our fate. But everything that has been said in the last pages on these relations hinges on the assumption that the third scenario is more than a forlorn hope. Only an America that has regained its self-confidence will have anything to offer to others, and only such an America will have the capacity to learn from others.

Chapter VIII

❦❦❦❦❦❦❦

POLITICAL ETHICS—
IN QUEST OF A METHOD

BOTH ENGAGEMENT AND DETACHMENT can be dehumanizing if carried to excess. The *enragé* fanatic is no less a repulsive figure than the theoretician to whom human anguish is nothing but an occasion for intellectual exercises. Reason imposes moral obligations no less than compassion, and to be fully human surely requires reflection as well as action. It is foolish, therefore, to absolutize either engagement or detachment. Rather, one ought to ask about the appropriateness of either attitude to specific human activities.

In recent years, at least in the social sciences, the idea has become fashionable that detachment on the part of a scientific observer of human events is impossible and/or morally reprehensible. Instead, at all times and in all places, the scientist, just like any other individual, is enjoined to live out to the full his values and commitments. This idea can be expressed in sophisticated methodological theories, yet behind it lies a remarkable vulgarity of the imagination—namely, the notion that an individual can be only one thing. The notion is a kind of *machismo* of the mind, an endless strutting that is finally comical. Don Juan cannot meet any woman without trying to seduce her, just as the fanatically engaged intellectual cannot encounter any problem without embracing it (in fantasy if not in fact) by political action. And just as Don Juan never really perceives a woman, so is the latter type incapable of seeing a social phenomenon as it really is. In both cases there is the immaturity of being unable to exercise restraint. By contrast, maturity is the capacity to endure distance from the object of one's passion.

I'm quite willing to concede that there are situations in which even the limited detachment of the scientific observer is difficult to sustain, situations in which active participation appears as the one overriding human imperative. As the same time, I'm not prepared to condemn in principle the attitude of some who remain permanently in a stance of disengagement from the struggles of their time. It is quite possible for different individuals to have different vocations. I must, however, confess that I have rarely been able to sustain an attitude of permanent disengagement, even though I find it important that such an attitude be assumed temporarily for purposes of scientific understanding. In other words, I deem it both feasible and desirable to view the social and political realities of our time *sine ira et studio*; but for myself, at any rate, it seems to be neither feasible nor desirable to persist in this posture of detachment. Over and over again I find myself propelled out of detachment by the moral urgencies of the historical situation. I suppose this means that, at heart, I am a moralist. The long struggle of the American mind with its Puritan heritage has given that term a pejorative connotation in American English, so perhaps it will sound better if I plead guilty to the charge in French: I admit to being *moraliste*. I admit so specifically with regard to the subject matter of this book. And while, in principle, I will defend the right of a social scientist to deal with questions of development in an attitude of permanent disengagement, I must also confess that I find it somewhat difficult to sympathize.

Scientific detachment implies at least a temporary escape from one's "location" in history. Engagement is always in terms of and out of such a specific "location." For this reason, to speak out of engagement must imply sensitivity to the particular audience. This point has been discussed in the preceding chapter with regard to an American social scientist encountering the Third World and the imagery of Americans established there. Sensitivity must also extend to different topics on which one may speak. Whether an American social scientist speaks to fellow Americans or to others, he can do so in quite different tones when speaking about the policies of his own society than when speaking about policies of other societies. Thus, with regard to the questions raised in the preceding chapter, I was dealing with my own society and its options—with "what we should do." A quite different tone is indicated when an American social scientist deals with the policy options of Third World countries —with "what you should do." First, it must be clear that no outsider is in a moral position to prescribe policies for these countries, least of all an outsider from one of the large imperial powers. Didacticism must be ruled out of order from the beginning. At the same time it seems to me that this does not impose a rule of silence. Is it possible for an American social scientist to speak to the policy options of Third World countries without *either* didacticism *or* self-denigration? I think it is, though in all likelihood the tonality that this calls for can only be made credible in the face-to-face situation and is hard to convey in cold print. Be this as it may, it seems necessary to me that, close to the conclusion of this book, I state some tentative propositions on the policy options faced by Third World countries. In the soil of face-to-face encounter just mentioned, the other party has the right to expect candor (and I need hardly add that, in saying this, I have specific individuals in mind). The following propositions, then, appear to me to be plausible as a result of the various analyses undertaken in this book.

If there is *one* proposition that today dominates in the Third World, at least among its politicians and intellectuals, it is that there is little hope for Third World countries to emerge from poverty unless they free themselves from their present state of dependency on the rich countries. I think one must begin any discussion of policy options for the Third World by assenting to this proposition. It is, in its essence, a correct and crucially important definition of the situation. This need not imply that one assents to the proposition in all its forms, especially the form given to it in the Marxist-Leninist theory of imperialism. Thus I would not assent to the view that the poverty of the Third World was historically caused by its penetration by Western imperialism, nor that the affluence of the West continues to be based on Third World exploitation, nor that socialist revolutions in the Third World are the only way to remedy the condition of dependency. It is plausible, however, that much of economic relations between Third World countries and the affluent Northern Hemisphere are detrimental to the former. Put simply, in most bargains between the poor and the rich, the latter get richer and the former, at best, don't gain very much. It is also clear, in that case, that development, if it means anything at all, must mean a change in this relationship.

The currently fashionable notion of dependency is further correct in that it perceives the clue to the situation to be political. There are, to be sure, various economic policies that poor countries may undertake to improve their bargaining position, or perhaps to get into a position where they don't have to strike such unequal bargains. But the presupposition of any such policies is that the economic destiny of a country is in the hands of its own government, and not of governments or (possibly worse) nongovernmental economic structures promoting interests that have nothing to do with or are downright detrimental to the development of the country. Put simply, in a situation in which the rich are continuously stepping on the poor, there is little hope for improvement if the actions of the latter are ongoingly controlled by the former—including the actions taken to stop being stepped on. In other words, the presupposition of development is political sovereignty in the formulation and execution of economic policy. The objection to this proposition, to the effect that no country in the world today can be fully sovereign politically or fully independent economically, has little merit. The issue is not total sovereignty or total independence. Only the nuclear superpowers come close to the former politically, and very few countries in the world can even fantasize about the latter economically. The issue, of course, is relative sovereignty and relative independence. But in these relativities lies the difference between some hope and no hope at all. Thus if Indonesia, say, aspires to the economic independence of France, or Guatemala to the political sovereignty of Belgium, these are aspirations that can realistically take into account the inevitable interdependencies of the modern world.

I don't see how any doctrinaire statements can be made about the steps necessary for a country that seeks to achieve this political aim. Everything will depend upon the particular circumstances of the country in question. The doctrinaire view that only violent revolution can lead to the desired result is just as distortive as the opposite doctrine that revolution is never a necessary condition for development. I will contend that only fanatics will prefer a violent course of action for its own sake, and I will take the moral position that such a course should always be the last rather than the first resort. At the same time, I believe that there are situations in the Third World in which, with however much reluctance, one must conclude that the revolutionary option is the only plausible one. The chances for success of revolutionary movements directed against the power structures set up by "metropolitan" interests will again, of course, vary greatly in different situations, with regard to both domestic and international factors.

I also don't see how a general doctrine can be formulated on the economic policy to be followed once political sovereignty is a fact. The circumstances of Third World countries are far too variegated, so that every "development model" has only limited exportability. If the external economic relations of the Third World add up to one big bad bargain, there are two general options theoretically: To get a better bargain, or to withdraw from bargaining altogether. Individual countries differ enormously in their capacity to take either course. I believe that Third World governments will be better off, the more their decisions in this area are determined by pragmatic rather than ideological considerations (and I would certainly include the liberal ideology of "free trade" in this injunction against doctrinaire decisions).

As has been discussed extensively in earlier chapters of this book, such a pragmatic attitude will cut across the capitalist/socialist dichotomy. It seems amply clear to me that the big bad bargain can take all possible forms: A poor country can be exploited by a rich country, no matter whether the latter is capitalist or socialist, and no matter whether the former's inner economy is organized along capitalist or socialist lines. The mechanisms and the rhetoric may be different in these various cases, but the underlying facts may be very similar. Once more, then, I believe that decisions on the economic organization of a Third World country will be far better made in pragmatic rather than ideological terms. Very likely there are countries whose circumstances are such that socialism offers the best chance of marshaling their resources for development; very likely there are others where this option would be detrimental to development. I lack the economic competence to specify the respective sets of circumstances. I should add that one of the major reproaches to be made against the economists is their lack of helpfulness for such specification. It seems plausible that both economic and noneconomic factors will have to be taken into account in this alternative—such as available natural resources or the possibility of regional cooperation on the economic side, and the historical and cultural background of a country on the noneconomic side. Thus large countries rich in natural resources, or countries that might integrate their economies in regional groupings with their neighbors, probably have a better chance with the capitalist option than countries lacking these circumstances. On the other hand, even given these circumstances, there may be a historical trend toward socialism that makes the capitalist option implausible, or there may be cultural traits that inhibit emergence of capitalist enterprise.

The condition *sine qua non* of development, it is proposed, is that the economic policy of Third World countries be in the hands of their own governments. Obviously, not any kind of government will meet this condition. Governments can be corrupt or honest, incompetent or reasonably efficient, tottering on the brink of rebellion or reasonably in control of the country. Gunnar Myrdal, in one of the more felicitous neologisms in the field, has characterized the "soft state" as one of the major impediments to development—the term applies precisely to weak, incompetent, and corrupt governments. One may agree with Myrdal, but still emphasize that strength alone does not fulfill the condition. The uses to which such strength is put are equally important, and very strong governments may (for ideological reasons, for instance) engage in policies of economic folly. The main point to stress is that political sovereignty will mean little if anything for development, unless it is undergirded by a viable political structure. And viability means primarily two things— that the government is interested in the development of the country in the first place (as against lining its own pockets), and that the government carries on policies that are in fact conducive to development. Put differently, removal of the "soft state" is a necessary but not sufficient condition of development. This is important to stress in view of the tendency, especially among intellectuals, to be overawed by the exercise of political strength: A strong government may, after all, be a bad government. In practical terms, the building of a viable political structure is crucially linked to the formation of viable "cadres," and one of the major questions facing Third World countries involves the manner in which administrative staffs are selected and trained. This question will have to include the ideological "inspiration" available for the formation of dedicated and able government personnel.

Many problems regarding the inner economic and political organization of Third World countries cannot even be touched here. There is the crucial economic problem of the place of agriculture in development policy. There is the crucial political question of the degree to which development policy can be carried out through decentralized governmental agencies and by means of "intermediate structures" independent of government. I do not have ready-made answers to these questions—and I very much doubt that anyone has. What concerns me here is rather the attitude in which such problems are tackled. In this connection I would reiterate strongly the main point made in the previous discussion of the "calculus of meaning": All material development is, in the end, futile unless it serves to enhance the meanings by which human beings live. This is why it is so important to be careful about riding roughshod over traditional values and institutions. To be sure, starvation is a worse threat than anomie, but once the immediate threat of starvation is removed, problems of meaning will inevitably come to the fore. This means that the "calculus of meaning" becomes important for development policies in precisely the measure that one gives them any chance of success. The one factor in the Third World today that allows some optimism in this regard is that of nationalism. Both liberal and politically left Westerners are too prone to view nationalism as a simply negative factor (an understandable tendency, perhaps, in view of what nationalism can be blamed for in the West). The situation in the Third World is much more complex. Whatever else may be said about Third World nationalisms, they *also* stimulate a respect for indigenous tradition, a bias against mindless transplantation of Western institutions, and a desire to find innovative solutions to societal problems. These are healthy propensities indeed.

Formulation of public policy in a Third World country clearly faces practical as well as theoretical problems very different from those faced in America. Yet there is one general proposition which, I think, applies to both universes of discourse: The making of policy ought to steer a course somewhere between *enragé* ideology and "merely technical" pragmatism. In other words, both situations need "cadres" that are capable of combining a commitment to human values with cool intelligence, moral engagement, openness of mind, compassion, and competence. I'm not at all sure which situation is more auspicious for their emergence.

From the beginning there has been an interest in this book broader than the discussion of some problems of Third World development. This interest has been in a method by which ethical considerations can

221

systematically be brought to bear on public policy options. I have a strong bias in favor of a case approach analogous to that of Anglo-Saxon common law. I'm very suspicious of abstract ethical principles in general, and doubly so when these principles are to be applied to policy options. Such principles tend either to be so general that they are of no practical use, or to produce blindness to any alternatives to the one course prescribed "on principle." This book, then, has been as much a quest for a method in political ethics as it has been a discussion of development problems. The latter, in other words, has been "a case" for purposes of the former. It so happens that, both morally and empirically, it is one of the most important cases in the world today. Thus the last thing in my mind has been to "use" the development problematic for a cold-blooded exercise in ethical theorizing; on the contrary, I'm very much engaged with this problematic for its own sake, and for pressing human reasons. This does not change the fact that some general lessons for political ethics may be drawn from this particular case.

The term "method," in the present chapter heading, is used advisedly. It denotes a quest for something much less elegant than a comprehensive doctrine or a summa of universally applicable principles. A method is an avenue of approaching problems, a *modus operandi*, a "kit" of rules-of-thumb—if one prefers, it is an overall bias. As such, almost by definition, it is open-ended, always subject to revision, operative "until further notice." These qualities in no way detract from its importance. They only provide safeguards against rigidity in thought or in practice.

Indications have been given through the preceding chapters as to the kind of method I envisage: It should be a method that seeks new approaches to situations of political relevance, approaches that will cut across the ideological dividing lines. Such a method will not ignore the contradictions among different ideological interpretations, nor will it remain neutral at all times with regard to these interpretations. But its inclination will be irenic rather than polemical. If one's principal goal is the elaboration of a method of evaluation of policy options that is to have practical political applicability, the object will be to arrive at new perspectives that have a chance of winning assent from people with quite divergent ideological presuppositions. It is precisely the widespread inability of intellectuals to do this which so often exasperates those with practical political responsibilities. Insofar as the method envisaged has a *moraliste* ambition, it will particularly stress what I have called the calculi of pain and of meaning. There can be no social change without costs. The questions to be asked with intense seriousness are just what the particular costs are, who is being asked to pay them, and whether the putative gains make these costs acceptable. There can also be no social change without disturbances in the order of meaning. Again, it is necessary to ask the same questions concerning the relation of costs and hoped-for gains. It seems to me that a method containing these components is applicable to a wide variety of cases. Indeed, such a method can only be developed further by testing it against policy problems quite different from those discussed in this book.

The method envisaged presupposes a stance of soberness, an intellectual if not personal modesty. I would reiterate here what I have called the postulate of ignorance. All political action takes place in a context of inadequate information and inability to foresee the future. Not only does this fact make it all the more important to engage in the above-mentioned calculi, but it should produce a particular awareness of the overwhelming probability that one's own acts will have unforeseen consequences. Even though one cannot know what these will be, the knowledge that no project for social change is likely to be realized in accordance with its design should make one anxious to imagine the nondesigned consequences that are possible. This, too, it seems to me, is a component of the method that could be systematized to a degree in applying it to different cases of policy relevance.

I suppose that the method also implies a sense of the irony of history and of the burdens of power. Indeed, one could make a good argument to the effect that both the fanatic and the technician avoid the *sentimiento trágico* that comes from honest confrontation with the realities of the human condition. The fanatic avoids it by convincing himself that he possesses all the right answers, the technician by denying that there are any deeper questions. The psychological gain may be similar in both instances. One of the burdens that must be confronted comes from a paradox previously alluded to, that of wishing to let others decide and of having to decide for others. Those in power may have a genuine desire to allow the subjects of policy to participate in the decisions that have to be made, through whatever modalities of political participation. This desire may well extend to what I have called "cognitive respect"— a recognition that no outsider, including the outsider who possesses power, is in a position to "know better" when it comes to the finalities of other people's lives. *Nevertheless*, the exercise of power means to make choices—and, inevitably, these choices will supersede the wishes and definitions of reality of others whose power is less. This paradox can be moderated, but it cannot be dissolved. Its burden is the inescapable consequence of political action in any group that is too large for ongoing face-to-face interaction, and in which, therefore, there cannot exist a sort of continuous plebiscite by which, at least optimally, all decisions are based on consensus.

In all of this there continues to be a surprising relevance to Max Weber's views both on the methodology of the social sciences and on political ethics—surprising because these views were stated shortly after World War I, more than half a century ago. Weber's position is expressed most eloquently in the two essays "Science as a Vocation" and "Politics as a Vocation," which originally were lectures delivered before students of the University of Munich in 1919. Despite the calm tone of Weber's exposition one can sense even today the climate of political desperation of Germany at this moment—in the wake of catastrophic military defeat, gripped by deepening economic crisis, threatened by violent revolutionary movements of both left and right. In this situation Weber, in short succession, stated his positions on the "value-freeness" of the social scientist and on the moral responsibility of the political actor. The two positions make the best sense when looked at together. For the social scientist Weber insisted on one overriding obligation— that of looking at social reality with objectivity, without injecting his own values or taking into account his personal hopes or fears. For the political actor Weber insisted on the most painstaking moral responsibility, and especially the knowledge of being responsible for the consequences, intended and unintended, of his own actions. The two positions are stated with equal passion. It is in this double passion that Weber's greatness lies. Both in his thought and in his life he tried to bear without flinching the enormous tension between detachment and engagement. And he had contempt for those who sought relief from this tension, be it by denying that moral options are real or by absolutely espousing one single option—the psychological escape routes of, respectively, the positivist and the doctrinaire ideologist.

It seems to me that these views are timely today, as are Weber's specific discussions of political ethics. He distinguished between two

224

types of politically relevant ethics—the "ethics of attitude" (*Gesinnungs-ethik*, also translated into English as "ethics of absolute ends") and "ethics of responsibility" (*Verantwortungsethik*). The former insists that nothing is ethically valid except adherence to absolute values that permit no modification by empirical circumstances. In this type of ethics the moral attitude of the actor is all that matters: If he is morally pure, the consequences of his actions are strictly irrelevant. Weber had respect for this, as in the case of Tolstoy, whom he discussed as a representative of the pacifist version of the "ethics of attitude." Nonviolence is here taken as an absolute end, and moral purity implies a sovereign disregard of the consequences of the results of one's refraining from violent means. Despite his respect for at least the greater representatives of this ethics, Weber left no doubt as to where he himself stood passionately. It was on the ground of an "ethics of responsibility," by which the political actor does not seek some inner purity in adherence to absolute norms, but, often with anguished anxiety, tries to act in such a way as to effect the most humane consequences possible. Weber knew very well that such a course necessarily involves getting "dirty hands" and that the choice between available alternatives may sometimes be tragic. In the most moving passage in the essay on politics, Weber approvingly cites Machiavelli praising the man who esteems the welfare of his city higher than the salvation of his own soul.

It is almost superfluous to draw out the contemporary relevances of Weber's views. During the late 1960s an exceptionally arrogant "ethics of attitude" took center stage in American politics. While the immediately political aspects of this have receded recently, there continues to be a widespread belief that questions of ethics are essentially questions of the inner purity of individuals. The notion of "authenticity" is closely related to this belief. The final ethical goal for an individual is to become and remain "authentic"; calculation of consequences and the ethical compromises it invariably entails are ipso facto manifestations of "inauthenticity." Such an ethics is, almost by definition, politically inapplicable; in the few cases where a measure of application succeeds, the consequences are likely to be disastrous. Politics is always the practice of the possible, not the search for absolute moral purity. Put differently, the political actor and the saint are mutually exclusive human figures.

As to the social sciences, the situation today is marked by a dichotomy between technicians and utopians. In America, at any rate, the technicians still constitute the great majority. These are people who pretend to (and sometimes do) describe existing social reality with pedantic precision. They disclaim interest in any proposals for changing existing reality, and specifically refuse participation in any efforts to draw out the moral implications of their own analyses. This would not be bad, and indeed might be welcomed from a Weberian standpoint, if the disclaimer and the refusal were motivated simply by a desire to keep clear lines between value-free scientific analysis and value-laden political engagement. But in practice these lines are not just marked off—they are only rarely crossed. Robert Packenham (in his recent book *Liberal America and the Third World*) observed that even most American social scientists studying "political development" in the Third World had little interest in the policy implications of what they were doing—they were interested in perfecting their theories, not in linking them up with such unscientific areas as politics and morality. This had two equally unfortunate consequences: "Merely technical" social science was vulnerable to morally dubious uses (the field of "counterinsurgency" is an important case in point). And the political and moral explications of social-scientific work were left to those who lacked the intellectual discipline and respect for data that characterize the social scientist at his best.

Put differently: If a social scientist scrupulously signals when he is speaking qua social scientist, and when as a morally concerned and politically engaged individual, this is to be welcomed. The trouble begins when most social scientists exhibit little moral concern or political engagement at all. It is one thing to be value-free in scientific work, quite another to have no value commitments at all. An old German cabaret joke is to the point here. A government official is expressing his moral philosophy: "When I am on duty, I am a swine. I am always on duty."

Against this majority of technicians stands a much smaller group of utopians, less noisy now than they were a few years ago, but still influential out of proportion to their actual number. These are people who can, at the drop of a hat, produce glittering visions of a better society. But not only are these visions prefaced by grossly distortive analyses of the status quo; even more seriously, from the utopians' own point of view, there are usually only the most implausible prescriptions on how to get from the deplored status quo to the hoped-for utopia. Intellectual acumen is mostly exhibited in efforts to demolish the positions of ideological adversaries. In these efforts there is indeed a "critical" attitude which unfortunately rarely extends to one's own intellectual constructions, and even less to the political programs of one's ideological coreligionists. The disdain for scientific canons of argumentation in much of what passes today as "advocacy research" may be cited here. Occam's Razor gives way to Marcuse's Shovel. The most *uneconomical* explanations of social reality are quite acceptable, as long as they fit the ideological bias of the theoretician in question.

It seems important to me, both politically and for the social sciences in America today, that this dichotomy of pedantry and utopianism be transcended. We cannot do without the intellectual self-discipline enjoined so passionately by Weber. We also cannot do without the utopian imagination. While these are two distinct movements of the human mind, they are by no means contradictory and can be undertaken, albeit with tensions, by the same individual. I think we badly need individuals who are capable of both movements and who can bear the tension this entails. We need "pedantic utopians," and we need exercises in "pedantic utopianism" in every important area of policy. One of my own utopian fantasies is that there may emerge places or "schools" in which such an approach is carefully cultivated in research and teaching. Such places or "schools" would be equidistant from the antiseptic amorality of "counter-insurgency research" and the moral hysteria of the New Left.

It is possible to spend much time and energy on working out one's own system of ethics. This will mean different things to different people. In my case it means a rather complicated correlation of a Christian understanding of man, an unavoidably conservative view of history, and the radically debunking perspective of sociological theory. There is also, however, the difficult and politically motivated task of arriving at ethical propositions that might also be acceptable to those who cannot agree with one's own system. I think that such an enterprise will most profitably begin with negative starting points. That is, it will not begin by seeking assent to some common denominator between conflicting ethical systems (say, between Christians and Marxists, or between conservatives and liberals), but rather by looking at specific situations in which there will be a common *no*. The preceding discussions of Third World situations have provided ample occasion for such nay-saying: No to children living in garbage, *no* to exploitation and hunger, *no* to terror and totalitarianism, *no* to anomie and the mindless destruction of human meanings. I think it is such concrete cases, in which individuals with very different ideological presuppositions will together say *no*, that hold most hope for new approaches of political action. From these concrete instances of saying *no* one may then move ahead to the painstaking task of finding alternatives which will not only be morally acceptable, but which will work.

POSTLUDE

IN THE VALLEY OF
THE FALLEN

ONE may travel from Madrid in an air-conditioned bus, in the company of West German tourists with the latest photographic equipment and the protein-richest picnic provisions carried in gaily colored plastic bags. With its reasonably efficient and (still) relatively inexpensive tourist accommodations, Spain attracts millions of tourists per year.

The landscape of New Castille appears to be what it has always been. A monotheistic landscape. Wide, barren, grey. A landscape for men of single will. El Cid riding against the infidels and Don Quixote against the windmills. For those with a penchant for ancient history (the guidebooks for German tourists make no mention of this) there are roadsigns that evoke the great battles of the Civil War. The Guadarrama Valley. Irún. The Alcázar of Toledo. When the Republicans besieged the fortress of the Alcázar, held for months by a small contingent of Nationalist cadets, they let the captured son of the commander of the fortress speak to his father on the telephone. The son would be shot unless the fortress surrendered. "Die bravely, my son," replied the commander. We don't know whether he died bravely; we do know that he was shot.

Reprinted, in slightly revised form, from *Worldview*, September 1972. Permission to reprint is gratefully acknowledged.

The Spanish Civil War still captures the imagination of many, usually for all the wrong reasons of partisan myopia. It was anything but the last clear-cut conflict between good and evil, as which many still have a vested interest in seeing it. It was a conflict full of moral ambiguities, with unspeakable brutality on both sides. It was also, at least as seen by the Nationalists, a passionate effort to hold at bay the forces of modernity, to turn Spain back to the virtues of an earlier age. Hovering over the banners of the Falange was the vision of that Siglo de Oro, when men were still men, and when there was honor in Spain. And arrayed against these banners were all the ideals of modern democracy and revolutionary salvation, enlisted in the cause of the Republic. It is hard to estimate which side bore the greater burden of illusion.

There is disagreement as to the precise number of people killed in the defense of Madrid. The fighting went on a very long time, and neither side kept reliable records. Every square mile of this territory was fought over with ferocity. How did that slogan go? "They shall not pass!"

They did pass. They marched into Madrid in triumph. The monument to their triumph can be reached by a good road, though not too many tourists are interested. It is just a few kilometers from the Escorial, the Valle de los Caídos—Valley of the Fallen. Most of it was built in the 1950s, one is told, by the labor of political prisoners.

A mountain, topped by a gigantic cross. Around the cross, heroic statuary. The approach is across a vast platform, built to hold many thousands gathered for patriotic rituals. A cathedral is hewn into the mountain. One enters through a grim double gate, walking for what seems a very long time into the inner depth of the mountain. Far inside is the altar, directly beneath the cross on the mountaintop. In front of the altar, flat in the pavement, is the tomb of José Antonio, founder of the Falange, who was executed by the Republicans. Back of the altar, one surmises, a place is reserved for Franco. Two wooden doors flank the altar, bearing the inscription MUERTOS PARA DIOS Y ESPAÑA and the dates of the Civil War. Behind those doors, going even more deeply into the mountainside, are the tombs of thousands who fell in that war. Originally all the

230

dead were Nationalist. Recently, in a gesture of reconciliation, some Republican dead were added.

One leaves the necropolis, back to Madrid through rush-hour traffic, back to an air-conditioned hotel. According to the best estimates one million people died in the Spanish Civil War. *And the Spain that is now emerging has nothing to do with what either side fought and died for.*

To be sure, there is much uncertainty about what happens after Franco. A new Spain is emerging. But insofar as one can be certain of anything in history, it will *not* be the Spain of fraternal liberty which, in images of magnetic power, drew the allegiance and (to a lesser degree) the self-sacrifice of the left from the corners of Europe. *Nor* will it be the Spain of restored grandeur, of faith, honor, and manhood, for which the other side marched into the holocaust. Most likely it will be a Spain gradually integrated into the bustling world of the Common Market, run not by visionaries but by technocrats, its eyes fixed not on glory but on the economic indicators. Not the worst fate, one might say. But what would *they* say now, all those entombed so splendidly behind the Escorial? Could it be that they did not pass after all? Who won?

Most "lessons of history" are fraudulent. But we do know that most victories are ephemeral. "Falange in the opposition!," proclaims a slogan frequently seen now on the walls of Madrid. Few visions survive a single generation. Few historical actions lead to the intended consequences. This insight need not be paralyzing. Political morality does not demand visions or certainties, only that we act as best we can. The best political morality is informed by the heavy knowledge of the past. Its fruits are humility and compassion.

Our time is full of visions of the future, loudly and arrogantly proclaimed. Moral self-righteousness is evenly distributed throughout the political spectrum. They all tell us so confidently where it's at today and where, if only they have their way, it will be tomorrow. Yet in fact they know so very little, all these self-confident prophets of doom and salvation. It is necessary to cultivate the quiet art of disbelief. It is necessary to act quietly and disbelievingly, out of that compassion which is the only credible motive for any actions to change the world.

231

History is a stream of blood, behind us, carrying us. Our age scoops up the blood in plastic bags and stores it, out of sight, for electronic retrieval. There is an obligation to remember, not in the memory cells of computers but in the heaviness of the heart. Over the memories of pain looms the solitary figure of the Virgin of Consolations, ever wiping the brows of the Quixotes of this world.

Index